PORTUGUESE VERBS EXPLAINED

an essential guide

by

Manuela Cook

Lusophone Publishing

PORTUGUESE VERBS EXPLAINED
an essential guide

Copyright © Manuela Cook 2004, 2009

ISBN: 978-0-9561220-0-1

British Library Cataloguing in Publication Data
A catalogue record for this book is available from the British Library.

First published 2004

Second edition 2009

Published by

Lusophone Publishing
PO Box 60
Greenhithe
DA10 9BE
UK

www.lusophonepublishing.com

Contact: enquiries@lusophonepublishing.com

Printed in Great Britain for Lusophone Publishing
by Witley Press Limited, Hunstanton, Norfolk

CONTENTS

Contents

Introduction

Portuguese Verbs Explained is for:

- both independent study and class-based learning;
- absolute beginners and those who want to brush up and advance their Portuguese;
- learners with no knowledge of grammatical terminology and those with some basic knowledge; and
- learners of the Portuguese language on both sides of the Atlantic and anywhere else where it may be spoken.

Verbs are words for an action, like 'to walk', and for a state of being, like 'to be'. They change, mainly according to person (*I walk* but *he walks*; *I am* but *you are*) and according to time (*I walk* or *walked*; *I am* or *was*). Verbs can also change according to the way in which the action or state is presented, for example, whether it is a mere statement of fact, as in '*I was* not in this country yesterday', or whether it is the expression of a wish, as in 'I wish *I were* a millionaire'.

This book explains how the Portuguese verb system works. You will learn how to use the Portuguese verbs and change their forms to communicate in a variety of situations. These changes are described in nineteen units, each one concentrating on a specific area, including the person, or people, to whom the action or state refers. There is an additional section on the second person, that is to say, the verb endings for 'you'.

Explanations are given in plain English. They are also illustrated with examples that have been translated into English, particularly having in mind the learner with no prior knowledge of Portuguese. There are sets of exercises for each unit with a key at the end of the book, catering in particular for the self-taught learner. The verb forms explained are of general use throughout the Portuguese-speaking world. Any relevant variations are highlighted.

The book also includes the following features to give you extra support and make your learning a more enjoyable and rewarding experience:

➤ systematic comparisons between English and Portuguese verbs pointing out the similarities and differences between the two;
➤ tables of regular, irregular and other special verbs for an overall view of verb endings and other changes;
➤ a Portuguese-English vocabulary list containing the verbs used in the examples and the exercises;
➤ complementary notes and 'learning aid' paragraphs giving tips and avoiding pitfalls;
➤ a glossary of grammatical terms providing clear definitions in simple English;
➤ puzzles and quizzes for exercises; and
➤ a cross-reference index at the end of the book.

How to use this book

You can use this book as a course of study and as a reference tool.

Using **Portuguese Verbs Explained** as a course book

Open the book on page 1 and simply work your way through the units, following the explanations and instructions you come across. Take your time, do only a few pages a day and give what you learn time to sink in.

Grammatical terms are explained as they appear in the units. You can also find further assistance in the Glossary of grammatical terms at the end of the book.

Always do the exercises after each unit, to put into practice what you have learned and test yourself. Check your results against the Key. Go again through any points you haven't mastered yet before moving on to the next unit.

In the tasks you are given, sentences are translated into English, but you may want extra help. In the Verbs Vocabulary List you will find the meaning of the verbs you have to modify in your exercises.

Using **Portuguese Verbs Explained** as a reference book

There is an easy-to-use Cross-reference Index at the back of the book. This provides a practical and quick route to locate any specific points about the verbs.

The index takes both a grammar-led and a usage-led approach. If you are unsure of the appropriate grammatical term, you can look up a verb form according to what you want to say in entries such as *future (talking about)* and *like (I would/should)*. You may be directed to one page — as is the case for *old (... years old)* — or you may be directed to several pages — as for *road directions* — showing what you have selected as it appears in different units.

For an overview of verb endings, you have the Verb Tables after the main body of the book. These tables cover both regular and irregular verbs. They also include summary lists and charts of other special verb features studied in the units.

Verbs in today's Portuguese-speaking world

Portuguese is spoken by over 200 million people and is the third most spoken European language in the world, after English and Spanish. It is the official language of Angola, Brazil, Cape Verde, Guinea-Bissau, Mozambique, Portugal, including the Azores and the Madeira Islands, and Saint Thome and Principe; and it is co-official with other languages in East Timor, Equatorial Guinea and Macau. There are also significant Portuguese-speaking communities in the United States of America and Canada; in South American countries such as Paraguay, Argentina and Venezuela; in Luxembourg, Andorra, France, Spain, other countries and regions in continental Europe and in the British Isles; in South Africa, Namibia and other African countries; and in Australia.[*]

Portuguese speakers across the continents share a common language but inevitably there are variations. The verb forms you will learn in this course are of universal application within the Portuguese-speaking world, but, following the same practice as the distinction made between British and American English, any relevant alternative forms of expression are explained for Portuguese on both sides of the Atlantic.

European Portuguese preferred forms, from Portugal, are sign-posted 'Eur.', while Latin American Portuguese forms, from Brazil, are sign-posted 'Am.'. In general these different forms are not mutually exclusive. For example, for 'I am buying', 'eu estou comprando' and 'eu estou a comprar' (Eur.) means that the latter version is first choice in European Portuguese but the former can be used anywhere, including Portugal.

The Portuguese language you meet in **Portuguese Verbs Explained** is standard common ground which is applicable anywhere in the Portuguese-speaking world. Dialectical variants peculiar to a country or region have a limited usage and are therefore avoided. Finally, the Portuguese orthography you see in this new edition has been updated so as to comply with the recent spelling agreement for uniformity amongst the different Portuguese language countries. In 2005 Brazil adhered to the new requirements and in Portugal the changes were formally confirmed in 2008.

*****

I hope you will find this book pleasing to use and helpful. It seeks to anticipate and address difficulties frequently experienced by English speakers when learning Portuguese verbs. I hope my efforts are successful in your case and would be grateful to receive your comments. This book is for you and your views will be welcome. You can contact me directly at the following email address: mcook_portuguese@hotmail.com

Manuela Cook

* A web search on "Portuguese" will give you further information on the language and where it is spoken.

Infinitive and Conjugation

The **infinitive** is the name of the verb and the form under which a verb usually appears in a dictionary. A **conjugation** is how a verb changes its form according to a set of rules.

Infinitive

-ar -er -ir verbs

The infinitive is the basic form of the verb. In English, the infinitive is usually signalled with 'to' as a separate word (*to buy*). In Portuguese, the infinitive is signalled with the verb ending (comprar, *to buy*). This ending can be either -**ar**, -**er**, or -**ir**.

comprar	vender	partir
to buy	*to sell*	*to leave, depart*
chegar	saber	abrir
to arrive	*to know*	*to open*
caminhar	fazer	preferir
to walk	*to do*	*to prefer*

The odd one out

There is an exception to the Portuguese normal -**ar**/-**er**/-**ir** infinitive endings: pôr, *to put*. This is an irregular verb with an irregular infinitive.

Although being the odd one out, pôr is not entirely on its own. It has some compounds, for example, compor, *to compose, organize*, dispor, *to arrange*, impor, *to impose*. The graphic accent (^) is omitted in the compounds. You will learn these and other irregular verbs later in the book.

Conjugation

As doing and being words, verbs change form according to who does, or is, something (the person) and when this happens (time).

person:

For 'person', in English we rely mainly on the words *I*, *you*, etc. In Portuguese, equivalent words are used (**eu, você**, etc.) but in general the verb ending also changes.

eu compro, *I buy*; **você** compra, *you buy*; **eles** compram, *they buy*.

time:

For 'time', in English we often rely on a change inside the core part of the verb (*buy – bought*). In other cases, an ending is added on (*walked*). In Portuguese, endings are the first means of showing time.

eu compro – comprei, *I buy – bought*; você compra – comprou, *you buy – bought*; eles compram – compraram, *they buy – bought*; eu caminho – caminhei, *I walk – walked.*

To do these changes is called to 'conjugate' the verb. To conjugate a Portuguese verb, you have to give it endings for both person and time.

How can you tell what endings to use?

The different infinitives (in **-ar**, **-er**, or **-ir**) correspond to three different patterns of change. This is known as the three 'conjugations'.

Verbs ending in **-ar** belong to the first conjugation.
Verbs ending in **-er** belong to the second conjugation.
Verbs ending in **-ir** belong to the third conjugation.

Our model verbs for the three conjugations are

comprar   **vender**   **partir**

Verbs ending in **-ar** will take the same endings as model verb **comprar**; those ending in **-er** will take the same endings as **vender**; and those in **-ir** the same endings as **partir**. Most verbs belong to the first conjugation. The endings for the second and third conjugations are similar.

2

(Irregular verbs are exceptions that will also be explained to you)

In some of the units you will learn the three conjugation endings for different 'tenses'. These are also summarized in the Verb Tables on pages 210 and 211.

'Tense' is the name given to a set of verb forms for the different persons, either in the present, past or future. In addition to time, a tense also indicates whether it expresses a fact, a wish, a command, etc. This is known as 'mood'. Unless stated otherwise, the tenses you will learn are in the 'indicative' mood, that is, they are ordinary tenses that express a statement of fact. There are other moods, such as the 'subjunctive', which will be explained to you as we go along.

We will start with the present tense, in the next unit.

Exercises

1.1 Find the infinitive for an English verb by filling in the gap in this sentence with words from the box: I would like to _____ / _____ / _____ / _____.

eat	sleep	swim	travel

1.2 You have looked up a few English verbs in an English-Portuguese dictionary and you have made a note of their Portuguese translation.

This is your list:

speak	falar	**eat**	comer	**shut**	fechar
swim	nadar	**drink**	beber	**travel**	viajar
sleep	dormir	**replace**	repor	**allow**	permitir

Sort the Portuguese verbs you have found in the dictionary into four columns, by conjugation (whether -*ar*, -*er*, -*ir*, or any odd one out).

3

Present

In its basic meaning, the Portuguese present tense, or simple present, translates its English counterpart.

Eu compro pão todos os dias.   I buy bread every day.
Eles vendem apartamentos.   They sell apartments.

However, the Portuguese simple present is a very versatile tense. It has also other functions, including some that relate to the past and some that relate to the future, depending on the context.

FORM

To form the present, remove the infinitive final **-ar**, **-er**, or **-ir**, and add the endings shown in bold below.

When one person is being talked about or talked to:

eu	compro	vendo	parto
I	*buy*	*sell*	*leave*
você (*)	compra	vende	parte
you	*buy*	*sell*	*leave*
ele/ela	compra	vende	parte
he/she	*buys*	*sells*	*leaves*

When two or more people are being talked about or talked to:

nós	compramos	vendemos	partimos
we	*buy*	*sell*	*leave*
vocês (**)	compram	vendem	partem
you	*buy*	*sell*	*leave*
eles/elas	compram	vendem	partem
they	*buy*	*sell*	*leave*

(*) and (**) - Other 'you' forms are explained in Unit 3.

You may have noticed that some endings appear more than once in the verb forms above. It is the same for 'you' (singular) and 's/he'. It is also the same for 'you' (plural) and 'they'. This means that you have only four different endings to learn.

4

The table below sums up what you need to learn for regular verbs. On the left, 'subject' means whoever does the action or experiences the state (eu, *I*, você, *you*, etc.). The other three columns show the endings for the different persons in the three conjugations.

I buy / sell / leave   etc.
eu compro / vendo / parto   etc.

subject	1st conj.	2nd conj.	3rd conj.
eu	-o	-o	-o
você, ele/ela	-a	-e	-e
nós	-amos	-emos	-imos
vocês, eles/elas	-am	-em	-em

Note: There are also some irregular and other special verbs which are explained in detail later in this unit. Non-regular forms in the examples below, pages 5-7, are identified with (•).

USE

As in English, the Portuguese present is used:

(a) For a general statement where no particular time is thought of.

Nós falamos Português.	*We speak Portuguese (can speak...).*
Eu trabalho na cidade.	*I work in town.*
Ela gosta de música.	*She likes music.*
A Terra gira em torno do Sol.	*The Earth rotates around the Sun.*
Ele é(•) médico.	*He is a doctor.*
A casa é(•) grande.	*The house is large.*
Tenho(•) muito prazer.	*I am delighted* (to meet you).
	I have great pleasure in meeting you.

(b) For a habitual or repeated action or state (physical, mental or emotional).

Ele toma café todas as manhãs.	*He has coffee every morning.*
Geralmente eu vou(•) de carro para o trabalho.	*Usually I go to work by car.*
Ela está(•) doente muitas vezes.	*She is often ill.*

5

(c) For a timetabled, or firmly planned, future event.

O concerto começa às 21:30 h.	*The concert starts at 9.30 pm.*
Estou(•) de volta daqui a uma hora com o próximo noticiário.	*I am back in an hour with the next news update.*

(d) For a past event you want to present more vividly.

Pedro Álvares Cabral avista o Brasil no dia 22 de abril de 1500.	*Pedro Alvares Cabral sights Brazil on 22nd April 1500.*

(This use is sometimes known as the 'historic present')

Similar to English, the Portuguese present is used:

(e) For something relating to the time of speech, which may translate into an English simple present or present continuous (*(do)ing*).

Aqui está(•)	*Here it is!*
Hoje é(•) domingo.	*Today it is Sunday.*
Ele vai(•) bem.	*He is keeping well.*

(f) For an instruction or order given as a description of a course of action, which may translate into an English present or imperative (tense for commands).

Você pode entrar.	*You may come in.*
Você vira à direita na próxima esquina.	*You turn right at the next corner. / Turn right at the next corner.*
Você lava o carro antes do almoço.	*You wash the car before lunch. / Wash the car before lunch.*

Unlike English, the Portuguese present is used:

(g) With an expression indicating elapsed time – like **há**, *for* (literally *there is*), or **desde**, *since* – for a state or an action that began in the past and is continuing to the present (and possibly to the future), translating *have/has (been)* and *have/has (done/been doing)*.

Ela é(•) uma pessoa doente desde a morte do marido.	*She has been a sick person since her husband's death.*
Eu moro aqui há(•) dez anos.	*I have lived here for ten years.*
Nós aprendemos Português há(•) um ano.	*We have been learning Portuguese for one year.*

(h) For the future (with an expression of time indicating future where this is not clear from the context), translating an English -*ing* tense.

Ele chega este fim de semana.   *He is arriving this weekend.*
Eu falo com ela amanhã.   *I am talking to her tomorrow.*

(i) For the future to express intention and promise.

Depois nós conversamos.   *We will talk later.*

Verbs with spelling changes

A verb form consists of two parts, the 'root', or main core, and the ending.

root   ending

compr	ar
compr	o
vend	e
part	imos

comprar   *to buy*
(eu)   compro   *I buy*
(ele) vende   *he sells*
(nós) partimos   *we leave*

Some verb roots undergo spelling changes. This happens for two fundamental reasons:

(1) The end part of the root changes to adjust to different endings. These are purely 'orthographic', or spelling, changes.

(2) The central part of the root changes pronunciation when stressed and this is shown with a different spelling. These are known as 'radical', or root, changes.

Orthographic (spelling change only)

Second and third conjugation verbs (-**er** and -**ir** verbs) with root ending in **c**, **g** or **gu** change before **a** or **o**, for '*I*' forms, as follows:

c   changes to   ç
g   changes to   j
gu   changes to   g

conhe**cer** (*to know*)   eu conhe**ço** (*I know*)
des**cer** (*to climb down*)   eu des**ço** (*I climb down*)
prote**ger** (*to protect*)   eu prote**jo** (*I protect*)
diri**gir** (*to direct*)   eu diri**jo** (*I direct*)

7

fugir (*to flee*)   eu fujo (*I flee*)
erguer (*to lift*)   eu ergo (*I lift*)
distinguir (*to distinguish*)   eu distingo (*I distinguish*)

In general, compound verbs belonging to the family of any of the above share the same features.

reconhecer (*to recognize*) eu reconheço (*I recognize*)
(*like* conhecer)

Radical (spelling change as a result of core change)

Third conjugation verbs (**-ir** verbs) with **e**, **o** or **u** in the central part of the root change as follows:

e changes to **i**   for *'I'* forms
                           in verbs like **repetir**
e changes to **i**   for *'I'*, *'you'*, *'s/he'* and *'they'* forms
                           in verbs like **progredir**
o changes to **u**   for *'I'* forms
u changes to **o**   for *'you'*, *'s/he'* and *'they'* forms

repetir (*to repeat*)   eu repito (*I repeat*)
despir (*to undress*)   eu dispo (*I undress*)
vestir (*to dress*)   eu visto (*I dress*)
sentir (*to feel*)   eu sinto (*I feel*)
servir (*to serve*)   eu sirvo (*I serve*)
ferir (*to injure*)   eu firo (*I injure*)
mentir (*to lie, tell a lie*)   eu minto (*I lie, tell a lie*)
inserir (*to insert*)   eu insiro (*I insert*)

progredir (*to progress*)   vocês progridem (*you progress*)
prevenir (*to prevent*)   eles previnem (*they prevent*)

cobrir (*to cover*)   eu cubro (*I cover*)
dormir (*to sleep*)   eu durmo (*I sleep*)

subir (*to climb up*)   você sobe (*you climb up*)
acudir (*to go to help*)   elas acodem (*they go to help*)

In general, compound verbs belonging to the family of any of the above share the same features.

descobrir (*to discover*)   eu descubro (*I discover*)
(*like* cobrir)
preferir (*to prefer*)   eu prefiro (*I prefer*)
(*like* ferir)

Some verbs share features from both types.

fugir (*to flee*)   u → o and   g → j
eu fujo (*I flee*); você, ele/ela foge (*you flee, s/he flees*)

seguir (*to follow*)   e → i and   gu → g
eu sigo (*I follow*)

In general, compound verbs belonging to the family of any of the above share the same features.

conseguir (*to get, obtain*) eu consigo (*I get, obtain*)
(*like* seguir)

Note:
There are some small sound variations in the root which are not shown in spelling. This is sometimes the case when a sound is pronounced more open because it is in the stressed part of the word – e.g., the highlighted letter in 'falar' (*to speak*) corresponds to a sound resembling the highlighted letter in the English word *ago*, but in 'eu falo' it sounds more like the highlighted letter in the English word *arm*.

Other cases

There are also some other changes in a number of verbs.

❑ First conjugation verbs ending in **-ear** have **ei** before the ending except for the '*we*' form.
passear (*to stroll, take a walk*): eu passeio, você, ele/ela passeia,
     vocês, eles/elas passeiam; *but normal form in* nós passeamos
recear (*to fear*): eu receio, você, ele/ela receia, vocês, eles/elas
     receiam; *but normal form in* nós receamos

❑ First conjugation verbs in **-iar** are in general regular, like confiar (*to trust*), but a few follow the same pattern as the verbs ending in **-ear**.

9

---

incend**iar** (*to set on fire*): eu incend**eio**, você, ele/ela incend**eia**, vocês, eles/ elas incend**eiam**; *but normal form in* nós incendiamos.

The same applies to ans**iar** (*to long to*), med**iar** (*to mediate*), od**iar** (*to hate*) and remed**iar** (*to put right*).

☐ Second conjugation verbs in **-oer** end the '*you, s/he*' form in **-ói**.

m**oer** (*to grind*): você, ele/ela m**ói**; *but normal form in* eu moo, nós moemos, vocês, eles/elas moem

d**oer** (*to hurt*): d**ói**; *but normal form in* doem

Note: Verb **doer** is normally conjugated in two forms only, **dói**, *(it) hurts*, and **doem**, *(they) hurt*. See 'Defective verbs', in Unit 3.

☐ Third conjugation verbs in **-air** have an **i** throughout except in the '*you, they*' form. (Note that **a** → **ai** in the '*I*' form)

s**air** (*to go/come out*): eu s**aio**, você, ele/ela s**ai**, nós s**aímos**; *but normal form in* vocês, eles/elas saem

The same applies to other verbs such as contr**air** (*to contract*), distr**air** (*to distract*), retr**air** (*to withdraw*) and tr**air** (*to betray*).

☐ Third conjugation verbs in **-uir** are in general regular but end in **-i** in the '*you, s/he*' form.

incl**uir** (*to include*): você, ele/ela incl**ui**

The same applies to other verbs such as distrib**uir** (*to share out*), fl**uir** (*to flow*), infl**uir** (*to have an influence*).

The following two verbs are exceptions in the '*you, s/he*' form and respective plural.

constr**uir** (*to build*)	você, ele/ela constr**ói**, vocês, eles/ elas constr**oem**
destr**uir** (*to destroy*)	você, ele/ela destr**ói**, vocês, eles/ elas destr**oem**

Note: These two verbs also appear with normal forms:
constrói, constroem *or* construi, construem
destrói, destroem *or* destrui, destruem

❑ Third conjugation verbs ending in **-uzir** drop the final **e** in the '*you, s/he*' form.

cond**uzir** (*to lead*): você, ele/ela cond**uz**; *but normal form in* eu conduzo, nós conduzimos and vocês, eles/elas conduzem

The same applies to other verbs such as introd**uzir** (*to introduce, insert*), prod**uzir** (*to produce*), red**uzir** (*to reduce*), reprod**uzir** (*to reproduce*) and sed**uzir** (*to seduce*).

Graphic accents

In addition to the changes explained above, some verb forms take a graphic accent where there is a sequence of two or more vowels (**a, e, i, o, u**).

This shows which vowel is stressed in speech. This is the case with the form for '*we*' (nós) in **-air** and **-uir** verbs, which takes an acute accent (´).

sair (*to go/come out*): nós sa**í**mos

infl**uir** (*to have an influence*): nós influ**í**mos

(For a chart of root and spelling changes, see Verb Tables at the end of the book)

Irregular verbs

Some verbs are said to be irregular. They have anomalous forms and do not take the endings shown for the three conjugations earlier in the present unit, in all or some persons (*I, you*, etc.). As we saw in Unit 1, verb **pôr** is irregular even in the infinitive.

The most common verbs that are irregular in the present tense are listed below (for a full list of verb forms, see Verb Tables, at the end of the book).

caber, *to fit*
eu **caibo**, você, ele/ela **cabe**, nós **cabemos**, vocês, eles/elas **cabem**
crer, *to believe*
eu **creio**, você, ele/ela **crê**, nós **cremos**, vocês, eles/elas **creem**
dar, *to give*
eu **dou**, você, ele/ela **dá**, nós **damos**, vocês, eles/elas **dão**
dizer, *to say*
eu **digo**, você, ele/ela **diz**, nós **dizemos**, vocês, eles/elas **dizem**
estar, *to be*
eu **estou**, você, ele/ela **está**, nós **estamos**, vocês, eles/elas **estão**
fazer, *to do, to make*

eu **faço**, você, ele/ela **faz**, nós **fazemos**, vocês, eles/elas **fazem**
haver, *to exist, there to be, to have*
eu **hei**, você, ele/ela **há**, nós **havemos**, vocês, eles/elas **hão**
ir, *to go*
eu **vou**, você, ele/ela **vai**, nós **vamos**, vocês, eles/elas **vão**
ler, *to read*
eu **leio**, você, ele/ela **lê**, nós **lemos**, vocês, eles/elas **leem**
medir, *to measure*
eu **meço**, você, ele/ela **mede**, nós **medimos**, vocês, eles/elas **medem**
ouvir, *to hear*
eu **ouço**, você, ele/ela **ouve**, nós **ouvimos**, vocês, eles/elas **ouvem**
pedir, *to ask for*
eu **peço**, você, ele/ela **pede**, nós **pedimos**, vocês, eles/elas **pedem**
perder, *to lose*
eu **perco**, você, ele/ela **perde**, nós **perdemos**, vocês, eles/elas **perdem**
poder, *can, may, to be able*
eu **posso**, você, ele/ela **pode**, nós **podemos**, vocês, eles/elas **podem**
pôr, *to put*
eu **ponho**, você, ele/ela **põe**, nós **pomos**, vocês, eles/elas **põem**
querer, *to want*
eu **quero**, você, ele/ela **quer**, nós **queremos**, vocês, eles/elas **querem**
rir, *to laugh*
eu **rio**, você, ele/ela **ri**, nós **rimos**, vocês, eles/elas **riem**
saber, *to know*
eu **sei**, você, ele/ela **sabe**, nós **sabemos**, vocês, eles/elas **sabem**
ser, *to be*
eu **sou**, você, ele/ela **é**, nós **somos**, vocês, eles/elas **são**
ter, *to have*
eu **tenho**, você, ele/ela **tem**, nós **temos**, vocês, eles/elas **têm**
trazer, *to bring*
eu **trago**, você, ele/ela **traz**, nós **trazemos**, vocês, eles/elas **trazem**
valer, *to be worth*
eu **valho**, você, ele/ela **vale**, nós **valemos**, vocês, eles/elas **valem**
ver, *to see*
eu **vejo**, você, ele/ela **vê**, nós **vemos**, vocês, eles/elas **veem**
vir, *to come*
eu **venho**, você, ele/ela **vem**, nós **vimos**, vocês, eles/elas **vêm**

In general, compound verbs belonging to the family of any of the above share the same features. E.g., contenho (**conter**, *to contain*, like **ter**); satisfaço (**satisfazer**, *to satisfy*, like **fazer**); sorrio (**sorrir**, *to smile*, like **rir**); suponho (**supor**, *to suppose, assume*, like **pôr**).

Using verbs 'estar', 'ser' and 'ter'

(A) How to distinguish between **estar** and **ser**, the two Portuguese verbs 'to be':

Verb **estar** (*to be*) is for something that can change easily. In contrast, verb **ser** (*to be*) is used to characterize something or someone.

ser (inherent condition)

eles são ingleses	*they are English*
ela é de Portugal	*she is from Portugal*
eu sou casado	*I am married*
eu sou engenheiro	*I am an engineer*
eles são altos	*they are tall*
ela é doente	*she is ill* (chronic condition)

estar (transitory condition)

nós estamos de férias	*we are on holiday*
ela está doente	*she is ill* (temporary condition)
ele está contente hoje	*he is happy today*
eu estou com sede (*)	*I am thirsty* (*... with thirst*)
ela está com fome (*)	*she is hungry* (*... with hunger*)

(B) In its basic meaning verb **ter** corresponds to English 'to have' but in some cases translates verb 'to be'.

(i) as in English

ela tem olhos azuis	*she has blue eyes*
nós temos um filho e uma filha	*we have a son and a daughter*
essa cidade tem muitos parques	*that city has lots of parks*

(ii) unlike English

eu tenho trinta anos	*I am thirty years old*
	(I have (completed) 30 years)
eu tenho sede / fome / frio (*)	*I am thirsty / hungry / cold*
	(I have thirst / etc.)
a mesa tem um metro e meio	*the table is one and a half*
de comprimento	*metres long*
	(the table has a length of 1.5 m)

(*) these constructions are interchangeable: eu tenho sede = eu estou com sede.

Exercises

2.1

(A) The following sentences contain **-ar**, **-er** and **-ir** verbs that take regular endings. Rewrite these sentences starting each one with **nós** (*we*). The first one has been done for you.

1	Eu moro em Londres. *I live in London.*	**morar** *(to live)*	Nós moramos em Londres. *We live in London.*
2	Eu trabalho numa escola perto daqui. *I work in a school nearby.*	**trabalhar** (*to work*)	
3	Eu aprendo Português há dois meses. *I have been learning Portuguese for two months.*	**aprender** (*to learn*)	
4	Eu abro uma conta bancária amanhã. *I am opening a bank account tomorrow.*	**abrir** (*to open*)	

(B) For each one of the boxes below, find a word that can be shared by the different subjects on the left. Number 1 has been done for you.

	morar	**trabalhar**	**aprender**	**abrir**
	1	2	3	4
você ele/ela	mora			
	5	6	7	8
vocês eles/elas				

2.2

The words missing in the sentences below belong to verbs that are irregular or have spelling changes and were explained to you in this unit. Find the missing verb forms in the word search box and complete the sentences. Nr. 1 has been done for you.

1 Eu ___sou___ inglês. (**ser**)
 I am English.
2 Eu _____ de férias. (**estar**)
 I am on holiday.
3 Nós _____ americanos. (**ser**)
 We are American.
4 Eles _____ esse país. (**conhecer**)
 They know that country.
5 Ele _____ amanhã. (**vir**)
 He is coming tomorrow.
6 Ele _____ para o hotel agora. (**ir**)
 He is going to the hotel now.
7 Nós _____ com fome. (**estar**)
 We are hungry. (…with hunger)
8 Ela _____ dez anos. (**ter**)
 She is ten years old. (…has (completed) ten years)
9 Eu _____ ir lá este fim de semana. (**poder**)
 I can go there this weekend.
10 Eu _____ chá mas ele _____ café. (**preferir**)
 I prefer tea but he prefers coffee.

V	O	I	S	E	T	E	P
A	U	S	O	M	O	S	O
I	B	Z	U	B	J	T	S
P	R	E	F	I	R	O	S
D	L	V	E	M	X	U	O
E	S	T	A	M	O	S	T
G	P	R	E	F	E	R	E
C	O	N	H	E	C	E	M

Person and Subject

Speech naturally presupposes two persons: a person who speaks, known as the 'first person', and a person spoken to, the 'second person'. So in English *I* and *we* are pronouns of the first person, singular and plural respectively (one person speaking, or more than one). The pronoun for the second person is *you*. Beyond these two persons, there is the whole world of people and things that may be spoken about. For all these we use the pronouns of the 'third person', *he, she, it*, and plural *they*.

The Portuguese language equally has its own pronouns for the first, second and third person. You met them in Unit 2 as the subject of the action or state expressed by the verb.

Personal pronouns subject

	1st person	**eu**	*I*
Singular	2nd person	**você**	*you* (one individual)
	3rd person	**ele / ela**	*he / she / it*
	1st person	**nós**	*we*
Plural	2nd person	**vocês**	*you* (more than one)
	3rd person	**eles / elas**	*they*

When compared, two differences stand out between the Portuguese and the English personal pronouns subject.

For the second person, English uses one same form (*you*) for both singular and plural, while Portuguese distinguishes between singular (**você**) and plural (**vocês**) when referring to respectively one or more than one individual.
(See section '*You*' below)

For the third person singular, English distinguishes between *he, she* and *it*, that is, masculine, feminine and neuter, while Portuguese masculine and feminine pronouns (**ele / ela**) also cover neuter.
(See section '*It*' below)

16

You

For the Portuguese second person, you have learned **você-vocês**.

você compra   *you buy*   second person singular
vocês compram   *you buy*   second person plural

The Portuguese language has also an older set of pronouns for 'you': **tu-vós**. These subject pronouns take their own verb endings.

tu compras   *you buy*   second person singular
vós comprais   *you buy*   second person plural

In the older **tu-vós** system, **vós** has become archaic in most of the Portuguese-speaking world but is used in some special circumstances such as liturgical prayer. Its singular **tu** is still in wide circulation, but there are variations in practice.

In European Portuguese the **tu** format is a more familiar alternative to the **você** format, to be used with close friends and relatives and when talking to children.

> **Você estava** no aeroporto! Eu não **o** vi lá.   (general approach)
> **Tu estavas** no aeroporto! Eu não **te** vi lá.   (familiar approach)
> *You were at the airport! I didn't see you there.*

In Latin American Portuguese, in principle, this distinction is not made. However, particularly in colloquial speech, the tu-approach object (oblique) pronoun **te** is used in conjunction with the **você** subject pronoun and respective conjugation ending.

> **Você estava** no aeroporto! Eu não **te** vi lá.
> *You were at the airport! I didn't see you there.*

In colloquial Latin American Portuguese the following is also heard:

- **tu** subject pronoun with the você conjugation ending.

> **Tu vai** lá agora? *Are you going there now?*
> (Instead of **tu vais** or **você vai**)

- tu conjugation ending and no subject pronoun present.

> **Olha!** *Look!* (The **-a** in **olha** is the ending for the tu-approach in the so-called 'command form' for orders, instructions and requests)

Most adult learners of Portuguese find that they do not need to use the **tu** verb forms. However, these forms play a role in the Portuguese language, and you may wish to have at least a passive knowledge of them. There is a section in this book devoted to the tu-approach under the heading 'The Other Second Person'. The respective tense endings are also shown in the Verb Tables.

If you are a self-taught learner, you may wish to make a decision at this stage in the course. If you opt for learning the **tu** tense endings, study the contents of section 'The Other Second Person' in parallel with the different units in the book. If you opt out, then just carry on through the units without practising this other second person.

The tense endings for the **vós** second person may be of interest to you for specific purposes, for example if you intend to read Portuguese medieval literature. In addition to being plural to **tu**, they were also used to address someone of high standing. You can find these forms in the Verb Tables. They appear in brackets due to their very limited use today.

Madam and Sir

For politeness, in Portuguese you say 'sir' (**o senhor**) and 'madam' (**a senhora**) instead of **você** (*you*), for example when talking to a stranger. These are actually 'nouns', i.e., naming words. It is like saying 'the gentleman' and 'the lady'.

Você vira à esquerda na próxima esquina…
You turn left at the next corner…
or, being very courteous,
O senhor vira à esquerda na próxima esquina…
You (sir) turn left at the next corner…
Literally,
The gentleman turns left at the next corner…

Similarly, **vocês** can be replaced with plural **os senhores / as senhoras**.

As senhoras viram à esquerda na próxima esquina…
You (madams) turn left at the next corner…
Literally,
The ladies turn left at the next corner…

Note: The masculine plural form – **os senhores** – is used both for more than one male and jointly male and female.

o João e a Maria

Particularly in European Portuguese, it is also the practice to use a person's name preceded by the definite article, so that 'o João' (when addressing João) means *you*.

O João prefere café?	*John, do you prefer coffee?*
A Maria está bem?	*Are you well, Mary?*

Literally,
Does (the) John prefer coffee?
Is (the) Mary well?

It

In English, we often say 'she' when we talk about a ship, or a car. Well, in Portuguese, all nouns (naming words) are either masculine or feminine. This is called 'grammatical gender'.

We saw that **ele/ela** translates English 'he/she'. Because of grammatical gender, it also translates 'it'.

Talking about a ship, **navio** (which is masculine in Portuguese):
Ele ……   *It / he* …..
Talking about a car, **carro** (masculine in Portuguese):
Ele …..   *It / he* …..
Talking about a plant, **planta** (feminine in Portuguese):
Ela ...   *It / she* ...

In fact the name itself tends to be used in preference to **ele / ela**, (and **eles / elas** for 'they').

O navio é grande.	*The ship is big.*
O carro está sujo.	*The car is dirty.*
A planta cresce rapidamente.	*The plant grows quickly.*

(See also 'Dispensing with the subject' below)

Dispensing with the subject

In Portuguese the subject word is not always expressed. In some cases its use is optional; in others it is not used at all.

(A) Optional use

(1) For people

When you say

eu compro   *I buy*
nós part**imos**   *we leave*
eles vend**em**   *they sell*

you are showing in duplicate what person you mean. Both **eu** and verb ending **-o** show you mean 'I'; both **nós** and verb ending **-imos** show you mean 'we'; both **eles** and verb ending **-em** show you mean 'they'.

As a result, you may find out that native speakers often dispense with the subject, that is, with **eu** (*I*), etc. and they rely on the verb ending for meaning.

compr**o**   *I buy*
part**imos**   *we leave*
vend**em**   *they sell*

Of course, you can't always do this. In some instances, there might be ambiguity, as between 'you' and 's/he', where the verb ending is the same.

você compra   *you buy*
ele/ela compra   *s/he buys*

On the other hand, context often rules out ambiguity. If someone looks at you and asks 'Fala Português?', it should be clear that the question you are being asked is *Do you speak Portuguese?* not *Does s/he speak Portuguese?*

Omitting the second person subject word is an easy solution when you are not sure whether to address someone as 'sir / madam' (**o senhor / a senhora**) or as 'you' (**você**). You can simply dispense with the subject. For example, when asking *'How are you?'*:

Como vai?   *How are you?* (literally, *how are you going?*)

(2) For something unsexed, plants and sometimes animals

Where the meaning is clear from the context, **ele** / **ela** for 'it' (and **eles** / **elas** for 'they') is often omitted.

(Ele) está sujo.	*It is dirty.* (the car)
(Ele) fica próximo.	*It is near.* (the hotel)
(Ela) fica em frente.	*It is straight ahead.* (the beach)
(Ela) cresce rapidamente.	*It grows quickly.* (the plant)

(B) Subjectless cases

(1) Where in English 'it' is used for a subject that has no personal identity, the Portuguese verb takes the ending for the third person (s/he, it; they) but the subject pronoun is omitted.

É domingo.	*It is Sunday.*
É dia 15.	*It is the 15th. (day of the month)*
São três horas.	*It is three o'clock. (they are three ...)*
Está bem.	*It's all right.*
É difícil.	*It is hard, difficult.*
Vale a pena.	*It is worthwhile.*
Dói aqui.	*It hurts here.*
Há vários hotéis perto daqui.	*There are several hotels nearby. (it exists...)*

(2) Where in English 'it' is used with weather verbs, and for other natural phenomena, the Portuguese verb takes the third person ending, usually singular (s/he, it), but the subject pronoun is omitted.

Está quente hoje.	*It is hot today.*
Chove muitas vezes.	*It rains often.*
Aqui faz muito calor no verão.	*Here it is very hot in summer.* *(it makes much heat ...)*

(3) Where the Portuguese verb takes the third person plural ending ('they') but no one is specifically meant, English often uses a construction called 'passive voice', which is explained in Unit 16.

Pagam bem naquela firma.
(They) pay well in that company.
Dizem que esta fruta é venenosa.
(They) say this fruit is poisonous. /
This fruit is said to be poisonous.

21

Dizem que a moda agora é cabelo comprido.
(They) say that long hair is the current fashion. (long hair is said ...)
Falam sempre bem de você.
(They) always speak highly of you. (you are always ...)
Fazem um pão delicioso naquela padaria.
(They) make delicious bread in that bakery. (delicious bread is ...)

a gente

You can reduce the number of verb endings to learn if you use **a gente** instead of **nós**.

a gente compra / vende / parte = nós compramos / vendemos / partimos
　　　　　　we buy / sell / leave

Although this is a very colloquial construction, it works like English 'one', in 'one buys / sells / leaves'. This means that you are using the same verb ending as you would for 's/he' (**ele / ela**) which, in turn, is the same as for 'you' when talking to one person (**você**).

você, ele/ela, a gente will all take the same verb ending.

você compra / vende / parte　　*you buy / sell / leave*
ele/ela compra / vende / parte　*s/he buys / sells / leaves*
a gente compra / vende / parte　*we buy / sell / leave*

However, this is a colloquialism. In more careful speech, preference is given to the **nós** construction.

nós compr**amos** / vend**emos** / part**imos**　　*we buy / sell / leave*

A gente toma um táxi.
= Nós tomamos um táxi.　　*We are taking a taxi.*
A gente pode conversar depois.
= Nós podemos conversar depois.　*We can talk later.*
A gente usa essa palavra muitas vezes.
= Nós usamos essa palavra muitas vezes.　*We use that word quite often.*

Defective verbs

Due to their meaning or their structure, some verbs do not have all the usual forms. They are said to be 'defective'.

(A) Defective by meaning

Only the third person (s/he, it; they) is used in the following cases:

▪ verbs for natural phenomena, like the weather

Está frio hoje.	*It is cold today.*
Chove poucas vezes.	*It seldom rains.*
No verão anoitece mais tarde.	*In summer it gets dark later.*

▪ verbs in impersonal expressions

É domingo.	*It is Sunday.*
Dói aqui.	*It hurts here.*
Acontece muitas vezes.	*It happens often.*
Há uma farmácia perto daqui. (*)	*There is a chemist's nearby.*

(*) 'há' from irregular verb 'haver' when used in the sense of 'to exist', 'there to be'.

▪ verbs for the voice of animals

Os gatos miam.	*Cats miaow.*
As galinhas cacarejam.	*Hens cluck.*

(B) Defective by structure

In a small number of verbs, some forms tend to be omitted because they are awkward to pronounce or may be confused with other words. The missing forms are then replaced with other verbs that have an equivalent meaning – e.g., nós abolimos, *we abolish* (*from* abolir, *to abolish*), but, for the first person singular, preferably another verb, for example, eu anulo, *I cancel, abolish* (*from* anular, *to cancel, abolish*).

Exercises

3.1 Complete the 'Person and Subject' puzzle with the words you need to fill in the gaps in the sentences below. Nr. 1 across has been done for you.

Across:

1 __Eu__ estou com pressa.
I am in a hurry.

2 _____ querem ir a pé.
They (female) *want to go on foot.*

23

3 _____ podem tomar um táxi.
You (female) *can take a taxi.*

4 _____ é um homem simpático.
He is a gentleman (... nice man).

5 _____ estamos perdidos.
We are lost.

6 _____ é uma alternativa familiar de "você".
"..." is a familiar alternative to "você".

7 _____ dança muito bem.
You dance very well (... are a good dancer).

8 _____ está hospedado no melhor hotel da cidade.
You (male) *are staying at the best hotel in town.*

Down:

1 _____ podem estacionar aqui.
You (male) *can park here.*

2 _____ parece estar contente.
He appears to be happy.

3 _____ é uma forma de tratamento antiga.
"..." is an old form of address.

4 _____ quero este.
I want this one.
5 _____ gosto do hotel.
I like the hotel.
6 _____ fala Português muito bem.
You (female) *speak Portuguese very well.*
7 _____ estamos cansados.
We are tired.
8 _____ têm duas praias perto do hotel.
You have two beaches near the hotel.

3.2 You have learned that in Portuguese the personal pronouns subject (*I,
you, s/he, it, etc.*) are often dispensed with and in some cases not used at all.
Below you have some **no-*it*** and **no-*they*** sentences. Complete them using the
correct form of the verb in brackets. The first one has been done for you.

(A)
1 _Está_ bem.   **(estar)**   *It is all right.*   *((It) is ...)*
2 _____ fácil.   **(ser)**   *It is easy.*
3 _____ uma hora.   **(ser)**   *It is one o'clock.*
4 _____quente hoje.   **(estar)**   *It is hot today.*
5 _____aqui.   **(doer)**   *It hurts here.*

(B)
1 _____ muito caro naquela loja.
That is a very expensive shop ((They) sell very expensive *...).*
                                                          (vender)
2 _____ um prato de peixe delicioso naquele restaurante.
That restaurant serves a delicious fish dish ((They) serve *...).*
                                                          (servir)
3 _____ que essa fruta é muito boa para a saúde.
That fruit is supposed to be very good for your health ((They) say *...).*
                                                          (dizer)

Present Continuous and Perfect

The idea of PRESENT is variable. It depends on one's standpoint. We can view the present as a period of time around the moment at which we are speaking. We can also view it as the very moment at which we are speaking. In addition to the simple present you learned in Unit 2, other verb tenses are used to reflect different ways of looking at the present time.

Present Continuous

Although there are some important differences, the Portuguese present continuous tense translates its English counterpart in its basic meaning.

Eu estou comprando flores.	I am buying flowers.
Eles estão vendendo uma casa.	They are selling a house.

FORM

In **eu estou comprando** and **eles estão vendendo**, both **estou** and **estão** are forms of the simple present of verb **estar**, to be, which you learned in Unit 2. This is used as a helping, or 'auxiliary', verb in the formation of the present continuous.

The other element (**comprando, vendendo**) corresponds to the English *-ing* form of the main verb. This is known in English as 'present participle' and in Portuguese as 'gerund' (gerúndio).

The Portuguese gerund of a regular verb is very easy to form. Simply remove the infinitive ending -**ar**, -**er** or -**ir**, and add respectively -**ando**, -**endo**, -**indo**.

comprar:	compr	→	compr**ando**
vender:	vend	→	vend**endo**
partir:	part	→	part**indo**

Learning aid: For an even easier way of forming the Portuguese gerund, remove the final -**r** of the infinitive ending and add -**ndo**. This is a shortcut that also applies to irregular verbs.

pôr:	po (no accent)	→	po**ndo**

26

Summing up, the present continuous consists of the simple present of **estar** followed by the **-ndo** form of the main verb.

In Portugal, another formation has become popular and taken over as first choice. Instead of the gerund, **a** + infinitive is used. There is, therefore, an alternative present continuous which consists of the simple present of **estar** followed by **a** + infinitive.

I am buying / selling / leaving etc.
eu estou compr**ando** / vend**endo** / part**indo** etc.
eu estou a compr**ar** / vend**er** / part**ir** etc. (Eur.)

subject	present of 'estar'	main verb (1st / 2nd / 3rd conj.)
eu	**estou**	
você, ele/ela	**está**	**-ando** / **-endo** / **-indo**
nós	**estamos**	*or*
vocês, eles/elas	**estão**	**a** + **-ar** / **-er** / **-ir**

For other 'you' forms see Unit 3 and 'The Other Second Person'.

USE

As in English, the Portuguese present continuous is used:

(a) To stress that an action is happening now, at the time of speaking.

Eu estou escrevendo uma carta.   *I am writing a letter.*
Eu estou a escrever uma carta. (Eur.)
Ela está fazendo o almoço.   *She is cooking lunch.*
Ela está a fazer o almoço. (Eur.)

Note: For the time of speech, for example when reporting that some appliance is out of order, often Latin American Portuguese prefers using the present continuous – a máquina não está funcionando, *the machine is not working* – while European Portuguese will just use the simple present – a máquina não funciona, *the machine does not work.*

(b) To convey the idea of continuity and progression over a period of time in the present.

Ele está escrevendo um livro.   *He is writing a book.*

Ele está a escrever um livro. (Eur.)
Ela está aprendendo Português.   *She is learning Portuguese.*
Ela está a aprender Português. (Eur.)

(c) To convey the idea that a current situation is, or may be, transitory.

Agora eu estou trabalhando na cidade.   *Now I am working in town.*
Agora eu estou a trabalhar na cidade. (Eur.)

Unlike English, the Portuguese present continuous is not normally used for the future. However, it is used:

⊙ (d) To stress that something is about to happen.

O céu está cada vez mais escuro; daqui a pouco está chovendo.
O céu está cada vez mais escuro; daqui a pouco está a chover. (Eur.)
The sky is getting darker and darker; it will soon be raining.

Unlike English, the Portuguese present continuous can cover the past, as follows:

⊙ (e) With an expression indicating elapsed time – like **há**, *for*, or **desde**, *since* – to stress that something started in the past is still in progress.

Eu estou fazendo isto desde o meio-dia.   *I have been doing this*
Eu estou a fazer isto desde o meio-dia. (Eur.)   *since noon.*
Eu estou fazendo isto há quatro meses.   *I have been doing this*
Eu estou a fazer isto há quatro meses. (Eur.)   *for the past four months.*

Present Perfect

Similarly to its English counterpart, the Portuguese present perfect bridges time spans between the past and the present. It can translate the English present perfect – *have/has (been)* or *(done)* –, but more often it translates the present perfect continuous – *have/has been (do)ing.*

Este verão tem sido muito quente.   This summer has been very hot.
                                          This has been a very hot summer.
Tem chovido muito nos últimos dias.   It has been raining a lot in the
                                          past few days.
          (the present heat and rain may not be over yet)

FORM

The present perfect tense is formed with the present tense of **ter**, to have, which you learned in Unit 2. This is used as a helping, or 'auxiliary', verb.

The other element in the present perfect (**sido**, been, **chovido**, rained) is known as the 'past participle'. Regular past participles are very easy to form. Simply remove the infinitive ending of the verb (-**ar**, -**er** or -**ir**) and add these endings:

	-**ar** verbs	-**er** and -**ir** verbs
	+ **ado**	+ **ido**
comprar:	compr →	comprado
vender:	vend →	vendido
partir:	part →	partido

Briefly, the present perfect consists of the simple present of **ter** followed by the -**do** form of the main verb.

I have been buying / selling / leaving etc.
eu tenho comprado / vendido / partido etc.

subject	present of 'ter'	main verb (1st / 2nd / 3rd conj.)
eu	**tenho**	
você, ele/ela	**tem**	-**ado** / -**ido**
nós	**temos**	
vocês, eles/elas	**têm**	

For other 'you' forms see Unit 3 and 'The Other Second Person'.

USE

(a) The Portuguese present perfect translates English *have/has (been)* to indicate a state (physical, mental or emotional) that is either continuous or has recurred frequently in the recent past and may or may not continue into the future.

Este verão tem sido muito quente. *This has been a very hot summer.*

With an expression of time like **desde** (*since*) it can also emphasize a state that began at a specific point in the past, is either continuous or has recurred frequently in the recent past and may or may not continue into the future.

29

Ele tem estado doente desde o ano passado.	*He has been ill since last year.*

(b) The Portuguese present perfect translates English *have/has been (do)ing* to indicate an action that is either continuous or has recurred frequently in the recent past and may or may not continue into the future.

Tem chovido muito nos últimos dias.	*It has been raining a lot in the past few days.*
Aquele homem tem trabalhado demais.	*That man has been working too hard.*

With an expression of time like **desde** (*since*) it can also emphasize an action that began at a specific point in the past, is either continuous or has recurred frequently in the recent past and may or not continue into the future.

Nós temos trabalhado nesta firma desde o ano passado.	*We have been working for this company since last year.*

Learning aid:

The English language uses the present perfect, and the present perfect continuous, much more widely than Portuguese. If what you want to say is not covered in (a) and (b) above, then follow these guidelines for the appropriate Portuguese tense:

(1) When the time of the past action or state is indefinite – e.g., Eu já visitei essa companhia. *I have visited that firm before.* – use the Portuguese preterite (Unit 5).

(2) For an activity completed in the immediate past (where *just* is often used) – e.g., O correio chegou agora mesmo. *The post has just come.* – use the Portuguese preterite (Unit 5).

(3) For an activity just concluded when the resulting effect is still present – e.g., Eu perdi a caneta. *I have lost my pen* (now I am unable to write this letter). – use the Portuguese preterite (Unit 5).

Note: In (1), (2) and (3) above, in English the focus is on the open time period, in Portuguese the focus is on the completion of the action or state.

(4) For the duration of an action or state (or the duration of its absence) which was begun in the past, continued to the present and may continue into

the future – e.g., Eu moro aqui há dez anos, *I have lived here for ten years.* – use the Portuguese simple present (Unit 2).

Note: In this case, both English and Portuguese focus on the open time period, but Portuguese does so using the simple present.

Irregular past participles

Some verbs have an irregular past participle. The most common cases are listed below (for a full list of verb forms, see Verb Tables, at the end of the book).

abrir, *to open*	aberto, *open*
cobrir, *to cover*	coberto, *covered*
dizer, *to say*	dito, *said*
fazer, *to do, to make*	feito, *done, made*
pôr, *to put*	posto, *put*
ver, *to see*	visto, *seen*
vir, *to come*	vindo, *come* (same as the present participle
	or Portuguese 'gerund', i.e., the *-ing* form)

In general, compound verbs belonging to the family of any of the above share the same features. E.g., **reaberto**, from **reabrir**, *to reopen*, like **abrir**; **composto**, from **compor**, *to compose*, like **pôr**.

(Some verbs have both a regular and an irregular past participle. This is explained in Unit 13)

Graphic accents

Although being regular, a few past participles have an acute accent (′), as follows:

-oer verbs → **-oído**: m**oer** (*to grind*) → m**oído** (*ground*)

-air verbs → **-aído**: s**air** (*to go/come out*) → s**aído** (*gone/come out*)

-uir verbs → **-uído**: distrib**uir** (*to share out*) → distrib**uído** (*shared out*)
  constr**uir** (*to build*) → constr**uído** (*built*)

(For a chart of root and spelling changes, see Verb Tables at the end of the book)

31

Exercises

4.1

(A) Complete the sentences by entering the Portuguese verbs in brackets in their equivalent to English *-ing*.

1 Eu estou _____ disto. (**gostar**)
I am enjoying this.

2 Você está _____ muito. (**trabalhar**)
You are working hard.

3 Ela está _____ em ordem o apartamento. (**pôr**)
She is tidying up the apartment.

4 Silêncio! O menino está _____. (**dormir**)
Quiet! The little boy is sleeping.

5 Nós estamos _____ cartas. (**escrever**)
We are writing letters.

6 Vocês estão _____ um bom jantar. (**preparar**)
You are preparing a nice dinner.

7 Eles estão _____ isso há muito tempo. (**fazer**)
They have been doing that for a long time.
It's taking them a long time...

(B) Say the same as in (A) above but word the sentences in a way that is more popular in Portugal (**a** + infinitive).

4.2

Complete the puzzle with the correct form of the verb TER for the gaps in the sentences below.

Across:

1 Este inverno _____ sido muito frio.
This has been a very cold winter.

2 Vocês _____ trabalhado demais.
You have been working too hard.

3 O céu _____ estado muito escuro.
The sky has been looking quite dark.

4 Eu _____ comido mais fruta ultimamente.
I have been eating more fruit lately.

5 Nós _____ comprado menos pão esta semana.
We have been buying less bread this week.

Down:

1 _____ chovido muito nas últimas semanas.
  It has been raining a lot these past few weeks.

2 Eu _____ trabalhado nesta firma desde o ano passado.
  I have been working for this company since last year.

3 Eles _____ estado doentes desde o verão passado.
  They have been unwell since last summer.

4 Nós _____ vindo à praia todos os dias desde o princípio das férias.
  We have been coming to the beach every day since the beginning of our holiday.

5 Essa menina _____ crescido muito nos últimos meses.
  That girl has been growing up fast these past few months.

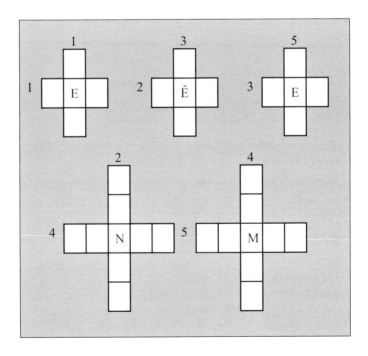

Tenses for the Past

There are different ways of recalling the PAST. An action or a state can be brought back to memory as a whole that happened at a point in time. Equally one can take a close-up at a past event, and concentrate on its details or unfolding. Shades of meaning such as these can be conveyed through different verb tenses.

Preterite

In Portuguese the preterite is the most widely used past tense. It translates two English tenses, the preterite (better known as 'simple past') and the present perfect.

Eles venderam a casa ontem.	They sold their house yesterday.
Eu comprei um carro novo.	I have bought a new car.

FORM

To form the preterite, remove the infinitive final **-ar**, **-er** or **-ir** and add the endings shown in the box below.

I bought / sold / left etc.
I have bought / sold / left etc.
eu comprei / vendi / parti etc.

subject	1st conj.	2nd conj.	3rd conj.
eu	-ei	-i	-i
você, ele/ela	-ou	-eu	-iu
nós	-amos *or* -ámos	-emos	-imos
vocês, eles/elas	-aram	-eram	-iram

For other 'you' forms see Unit 3 and 'The Other Second Person'.

Note: The 'we' form of the preterite is identical with the 'we' form of the present tense. However, for the **-ar** verbs, some speakers make a distinction

34

by pronouncing an open 'a' which is shown with an acute accent ('):
compramos also spelt **comprámos**.

Learning aid:

Note the following:

(1) **-ir** verbs have an **i** in all endings; **-er** verbs have an **e** in most endings;
and **-ar** verbs have an **a** in some endings.

(2) The endings have the same last letter(s) across the three conjugations: **-i,
-u, -mos, -ram.**

USE

As with the English preterite (simple past), the Portuguese preterite
is used:

(a) To indicate a past action or state (physical, mental or emotional) which
occurred at a well-defined time in the past.

Álvares Cabral descobriu o Brasil em 1500.	*Alvares Cabral discovered Brazil in 1500.*
Eu nasci há trinta anos mas ela nasceu há vinte e oito anos.	*I was born thirty years ago but she was born twenty eight years ago.*

(b) To narrate a sequence of single events which occurred at a well-defined
time in the past (this happened, then that, then that, etc.).

Ela chegou a casa, tirou a chave e abriu a porta.	*She got home, took out her key and opened the door.*

(c) For actions or states over a long period in the past, when the beginning
and end of that period are clearly defined.

Dom Manuel I reinou de 1495 a 1521.	*King Manuel I reigned from 1495 to 1521.*
Eu morei em São Paulo durante dez anos.	*I lived in São Paulo for ten years.*

Note: In (a), (b) and (c) above the Portuguese preterite is often used with a
date or time indicator such as last year, yesterday, for a week, etc. However,
in some cases the time reference is understood, not stated, because it has
been mentioned before or is obvious from the situational context.

Ela chegou a casa, tirou a chave   *She got home, took out her key*
e abriu a porta.   *and opened the door.*
(part of a story where a time reference was given at the beginning)
Eles falaram somente Inglês.   *They spoke only English.*
(when they were in England)

As with the English present perfect tense (not the simple past), the Portuguese preterite is used:

(d) When the time of a past action or state is undefined. In this meaning the verb is frequently preceded by **já** (literally, 'already').

Eles deram licença.   *They have given permission.*
Eles compraram uma casa   *They have bought a house near*
perto da praia.   *the beach.*
Eles já chegaram.   *They have arrived. (already arrived)*
Eu já visitei essa companhia.   *I have visited that firm before.*

(e) For an activity completed in the immediate past, when, in English, *just* is often used.

O correio chegou agora mesmo.   *The post has just come.*
Ele telefonou agora mesmo.   *He has just phoned.*

just (now) = **agora mesmo**

Note: **acabar de**, *to have just* (done something) is an alternative way of expressing this meaning.

Ele acabou de chegar.   *He has just arrived.*

(f) For a recent activity when the resulting effect is still being felt.

Eu perdi a caneta.   *I have lost my pen.* (now I can't write)
Eles esvaziaram o pneu   *They have deflated a tyre on my car.*
do meu carro.   (now I have a flat tyre)

Learning aid:
In (d) (e) and (f) above, the English present perfect tense focuses on the open time period while the Portuguese preterite focuses on the action or condition being over and done with.

Verbs with orthographic changes

(For a chart of root and spelling changes, see Verb Tables at the end of the book)

In the preterite, first conjugation verbs (-**ar** verbs) with root ending in **c**, **ç** or **g** change before **e**, for '*I*' forms, as follows:

c   changes to   **qu**
ç   changes to   **c**
g   changes to   **gu**

ficar (*to stay*)   eu fiquei (*I stayed / have stayed*)
começar (*to start*)   eu comecei (*I started / have started*)
pagar (*to pay*)   eu paguei (*I paid / have paid*)

In general, compound verbs belonging to the family of any of the above share the same features.

recomeçar (*to restart*)   eu recomecei (*I restarted, have restarted*)
(like começar)

Graphic accents

-**oer** verbs take an acute accent (´) in the '*I*' form.

moer (*to grind*): eu moí

-**air** and -**uir** verbs take an acute accent (´) on the forms for '*I*', '*we*', '*you, they*'.

sair (*to go/come out*): eu saí, nós saímos, vocês, eles/elas saíram
influir (*to have an influence*):   eu influí, nós influímos, vocês, eles/elas influíram

Irregular verbs

Below is a list of the most common irregular cases in the preterite (for a full list of verb forms, see Verb Tables, at the end of the book).

caber, *to fit*
eu **coube**, você, ele/ela **coube**, nós **coubemos**, vocês, eles/elas **couberam**
crer, *to believe*
eu **cri**, você, ele/ela **creu**, nós **cremos**, vocês, eles/elas **creram**

37

dar, *to give*
eu **dei**, você, ele/ela **deu**, nós **demos**, vocês, eles/elas **deram**
dizer, *to say*
eu **disse**, você, ele/ela **disse**, nós **dissemos**, vocês, eles/elas **disseram**
estar, *to be*
eu **estive**, você, ele/ela **esteve**, nós **estivemos**, vocês, eles/elas **estiveram**
fazer, *to do, to make*
eu **fiz**, você, ele/ela **fez**, nós **fizemos**, vocês, eles/elas **fizeram**
haver, *to exist, there to be, to have*
eu **houve**, você, ele/ela **houve**, nós **houvemos**, vocês, eles/elas **houveram**
ir, *to go*
eu **fui**, você, ele/ela **foi**, nós **fomos**, vocês, eles/elas **foram**
(Note: verbs 'ir' and 'ser' share the same forms in the preterite)
ler, *to read*
eu **li**, você, ele/ela **leu**, nós **lemos**, vocês, eles/elas **leram**
medir, *to measure*
eu **medi**, você, ele/ela **mediu**, nós **medimos**, vocês, eles/elas **mediram**
ouvir, *to hear*
eu **ouvi**, você, ele/ela **ouviu**, nós **ouvimos**, vocês, eles/elas **ouviram**
pedir, *to ask for*
eu **pedi**, você, ele/ela **pediu**, nós **pedimos**, vocês, eles/elas **pediram**
perder, *to lose*
eu **perdi**, você, ele/ela **perdeu**, nós **perdemos**, vocês, eles/elas **perderam**
poder, *can, may, to be able*
eu **pude**, você, ele/ela **pôde**, nós **pudemos**, vocês, eles/elas **puderam**
pôr, *to put*
eu **pus**, você, ele/ela **pôs**, nós **pusemos**, vocês, eles/elas **puseram**
querer, *to want*
eu **quis**, você, ele/ela **quis**, nós **quisemos**, vocês, eles/elas **quiseram**
rir, *to laugh*
eu **ri**, você, ele/ela **riu**, nós **rimos**, vocês, eles/elas **riram**
saber, *to know*
eu **soube**, você, ele/ela **soube**, nós **soubemos**, vocês, eles/elas **souberam**
ser, *to be*
eu **fui**, você, ele/ela **foi**, nós **fomos**, vocês, eles/elas **foram**
(Note: verbs 'ir' and 'ser' share the same forms in the preterite)
ter, *to have*
eu **tive**, você, ele/ela **teve**, nós **tivemos**, vocês, eles/elas **tiveram**
trazer, *to bring*
eu **trouxe**, você, ele/ela **trouxe**, nós **trouxemos**, vocês, eles/elas **trouxeram**
valer, *to be worth*

eu **vali**, você, ele/ela **valeu**, nós **valemos**, vocês, eles/elas **valeram**
ver, *to see*
eu **vi**, você, ele/ela **viu**, nós **vimos**, vocês, eles/elas **viram**
vir, *to come*
eu **vim**, você, ele/ela **veio**, nós **viemos**, vocês, eles/elas **vieram**

In general, compound verbs belonging to the family of any of the above share the same features. E.g., contive (**conter**, *to contain*, like **ter**); satisfiz (**satisfazer**, *to satisfy*, like **fazer**); sorri (**sorrir**, *to smile*, like **rir**); supus (**supor**, *to suppose, assume*, like **pôr**).

Imperfect

The Portuguese imperfect can translate the English simple past. It also often expresses meanings corresponding to the English past continuous – *was/were (do)ing* – or the structure *used to (do)* for an ongoing or repeated action in the past.

Ela estava feliz.	She was happy.
Eu morava nessa cidade.	I was living in that town.
Eles vendiam apartamentos.	They used to sell apartments.

FORM

The imperfect is very easy to conjugate. There are only two sets of endings, one for -**ar** verbs, the other for -**er** and -**ir** verbs. To form this tense, remove the infinitive final -**ar**, -**er** or -**ir** and add the endings shown in the box below.

I bought / sold / left etc.
I was buying / selling / leaving etc.
I used to buy / sell / leave etc.
eu compr**ava** / vend**ia** / part**ia** etc.

subject	1st conj.	2nd and 3rd conj.
eu, você, ele/ela	-ava	-ia
nós	-ávamos	-íamos
vocês, eles/elas	-avam	-iam

39

For other 'you' forms see Unit 3 and 'The Other Second Person'.

As a learning aid, note that there are fewer person endings in the imperfect as compared with other tenses. The **eu** (I), **você** (you) and **ele/ela** (s/he, it) verb forms are identical.

USE

(a) The Portuguese imperfect translates the English simple past to describe a state (physical, mental or emotional) or a permanent situation during a certain time in the past.

	That day... / In those days...
O tempo estava lindo.	*the weather was beautiful.*
A casa era grande.	*the house was large.*
Eles sabiam a gramática.	*they knew their grammar.*
Nós gostávamos dele.	*we liked him.*
Ele era criança.	*he was a child.*

(b) It translates the English past continuous – *was/were (do)ing* – to indicate continuity of action during a certain time in the past.

Eu trabalhava nessa escola.	*I was working at that school.* (at the time)
Nós escutávamos enquanto ele falava.	*We were listening while he was talking.*

(c) It translates *used to (do)* and *would (do)*, to indicate habits and repeated events during a certain time in the past.

Eu lia o jornal regularmente.	*I used to read / would read the newspaper regularly.*
Ele ia à escola todos os dias.	*He used to go / would go to school every day.*

costumar - The Portuguese language also has a structure that translates *used to (do)* and *would (do)* more closely. It is formed with the preterite of verb **costumar**, meaning 'to be in the habit of', 'to practise regularly'.

Eu costumava ler o jornal regularmente.	*I used to read / would read the newspaper regularly.*

Ele costumava ir à escola todos os dias.   *He used to go / would go to*
                                              school every day.

(d) It can translate *had (done)*, to indicate something that had happened before something else, i. e., a 'past of the past'. In this meaning the verb is often preceded by **já** (literally, 'already').

Eu já sabia isso há (*)   *I had known that for a long time.*
muito tempo.   *(since long)*
Havia muito tempo que   *We had waited for a long time for*
esperávamos esse fim feliz.   *that happy ending.*

(*) or imperfect 'havia' (grammatically more accurate)

Note a feature in common in (a), (b), (c) and (d) above: the beginning and the end of the action or state are not clearly defined.

Learning aid:

If you are in doubt whether the imperfect is the appropriate tense for what you want to express in the past, check against the following:

(1) In English, you could say *was/were (do)ing*
(2) In English, you could say *used to (do)*
(3) There is no specific starting and ending time or date being mentioned.

If one or more of these conditions apply, then you can use the Portuguese imperfect. If not, look up the other ways of talking about the past in Portuguese.

Verbs with orthographic changes

(For a chart of root and spelling changes, see Verb Tables at the end of the book)

Graphic accents

-oer, **-air** and **-uir** verbs take an acute accent (´) on all persons.

moer (*to grind*): eu moía, você, ele/ela moía, nós moíamos, vocês, eles/elas moíam
sair (*to go/come out*): eu saía, você, ele/ela saía, nós saímos, vocês, eles/elas saíam

41

influir (*to have an influence*): eu influía, você, ele/ela influía, nós influíamos, vocês, eles/elas influíam

Irregular verbs

In general, the imperfect of irregular verbs is regular. There are four exceptions listed below (for a full list of verb forms, see Verb Tables, at the end of the book).

pôr, *to put*
eu, você, ele/ela **punha**, nós **púnhamos**, vocês, eles/elas **punham**
ser, *to be*
eu, você, ele/ela **era**, nós **éramos**, vocês, eles/elas **eram**
ter, *to have*
eu, você, ele/ela **tinha**, nós **tínhamos**, vocês, eles/elas **tinham**
vir, *to come*
eu, você, ele/ela **vinha**, nós **vínhamos**, vocês, eles/elas **vinham**

In general, compound verbs belonging to the family of any of the above share the same features. E.g., continha (**conter**, *to contain*, like **ter**); supunha (**supor**, *to suppose*, *assume*, like **pôr**).

Imperfect continuous

The Portuguese imperfect continuous can translate the English past continuous (*was/were (do)ing*) but its use is more limited.
Bem, como eu estava dizendo...   Well, as I was saying...

FORM

The imperfect continuous parallels the formation of the present continuous you learned in Unit 4 but with the auxiliary **estar** in the imperfect tense.
I was buying / selling / leaving etc.
eu estava compr**ando** / vend**endo** / part**indo** etc.
eu estava a compr**ar** / vend**er** / part**ir** etc. (Eur.)

subject	imperfect of 'estar'	main verb (1st / 2nd / 3rd conj.)
eu	estava	**-ando** / **-endo** / **-indo**
você, ele/ela	estava	*or*
nós	estávamos	**a** + **-ar** / **-er** / **-ir**
vocês, eles/elas	estavam	

42

For other 'you' forms see Unit 3 and 'The Other Second Person'.

USE

The Portuguese imperfect continuous conveys the same meaning as the imperfect but is more precise. It stresses that an action was happening during a certain time in the past.

For

I was working at that school (at the time)

Eu estava trabalhando nessa escola
Eu estava a trabalhar nessa escola (Eur.)

is an alternative to 'Eu trabalhava nessa escola' when you want to place emphasis on the ongoing activity.

Comparing the Portuguese 'pasts'

(1) preterite and imperfect (plus imperfect continuous)

(A) The Portuguese preterite is for:

(i) a single action or state completed in the past.

Ela foi lá e resolveu o problema.	*She went there and solved the problem.*

(ii) a past habit or repeated action seen as a whole (complete and finished).

Ela ajudou na escola todas as semanas durante um ano.	*She helped at the school every week for one year.*

(iii) a past ongoing state seen as a whole (complete and finished).

Eles estiveram doentes de domingo a sábado.	*They were unwell from Sunday to Saturday.*

(B) The Portuguese imperfect is for:
something (state or action) going on in the past, without its beginning or end being specified.

Havia quatro maçãs na fruteira.	*There were four apples in the fruit bowl.*
Ele fazia sempre a mesma coisa.	*He was always doing the same thing / He would always do the same thing.*

43

The imperfect continuous is an alternative for stressing an ongoing activity.

Ele estava sempre fazendo a mesma coisa.
Ele estava sempre a fazer a mesma coisa (Eur.).
He was always doing the same thing / He would always do the same thing.

(C) The Portuguese imperfect and preterite are frequently contrasted in the same way as the English past continuous, *was/were (do)ing*, and simple past, (*did/was*), to describe something as 'background' information at a time when something else happened – 'foreground' action.

Eu trabalhava nessa escola quando casei.	*I was working at that school when I got married.*

For emphasis on the ongoing activity, the imperfect continuous can be used.

Eu estava trabalhando nessa escola quando casei. Eu estava a trabalhar (Eur.) nessa escola quando casei.	*I was working at that school when I got married.*

(D) The Portuguese imperfect and preterite are frequently contrasted (while in English only the simple past is used) to indicate time and age – 'background' information – when something happened – 'foreground' action.

Eram duas horas quando eles chegaram. Eu tinha cinco anos quando a minha irmã nasceu.	*It was two o'clock when they arrived. I was five years old when my sister was born.*

(2) preterite and present perfect

(As we saw in Unit 4, the present perfect bridges time spans between the past and the present)

(A) The Portuguese preterite is for a state, single action or series of repeated actions, when this is over, even if it has just happened and / or its effect continues to be felt.

Ele aprendeu Inglês quando esteve em Inglaterra. Ele já comeu. Ele chegou agora mesmo.	*He learned English when he was in England. He has eaten. He has just arrived.*

44

(B) The Portuguese present perfect is for a state, sustained action or series of repeated actions, when this may not be over.

Este verão tem sido muito quente.	*This summer has been very hot.*
Ele tem estado doente desde o ano passado.	*He has been ill since last year.*
Eu tenho feito o possível.	*I have been doing my best.*
Tenho viajado muito nos últimos meses.	*I have been travelling a lot in the past few months.*

Exercises

5.1

In the sentences below, the verbs in square brackets have been left in the infinitive but need conjugating. Help yourself to the right verb out of the box and rewrite the sentences.

> **foram   cuidava   choveu   foram
> era   fiquei   estava   lavava   fui
> jantaram   cheguei   fizeram   vivia
> vivi   parou   morávamos   era   leu**

1 O relógio [parar]. *The clock has stopped.*

2 Eles [ir] passear a pé. *They have gone for a walk.*

3 [Chover] durante a noite toda. *It rained all night.*

4 A porta [estar] aberta quando eu [chegar].
   The door was open when I arrived.(was standing open)

5 Enquanto eu [cuidar] das crianças, ele [lavar] a louça.
   While I looked after the children, he washed the dishes.

6 Ele [ler] esse livro do começo ao fim.
   He has read that book from beginning to end.

7 Ontem eu [ir] para a praia e [ficar] lá o dia inteiro.
   Yesterday I went to the beach and stayed there all day.

8 No sábado, de manhã, eles [fazer] compras, à tarde, [ir] ao clube e, à noite, [jantar] fora com amigos.
   Saturday, they did some shopping in the morning, went to the club in the afternoon and went out for dinner with friends in the evening.

9 Quando [ser] criança, eu [viver] nos Estados Unidos. [Viver] lá dez anos.
When I was a child, I used to live in the United States. I lived there for ten years.

10 Naquela época nós [morar] numa casa perto da estação. A casa [ser] muito grande.
At that time we lived in a house near the station. The house was very big.

5.2

(A) In each of the following sentences, replace **Neste momento** (*This moment*) with **Quando vocês chegaram** (*When you arrived*) and change the verb forms in bold accordingly. The first sentence has been done for you.

Neste momento ...	This moment ...
1 eu **estou** almoçando.	*I am having lunch.*
2 ela **está** telefonando.	*she is phoning.*
3 eles **estão** dormindo.	*they are sleeping.*
4 nós **estamos** lendo o jornal.	*we are reading the paper.*

1 Quando vocês chegaram, eu estava almoçando.
When you arrived, I was having lunch.

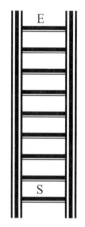

If your new verb forms are right, you can use them to climb down the letter ladder.

The word in the first two sentences will take you to the 6th step down. One more sentence and you are on the 7th step down. The final sentence will take you safely to the bottom of the ladder.

The first and last letters have been entered for you.

(B) Now rewrite both the **Neste momento** and the **Quando vocês chegaram** sentences in a way that is very popular in Portugal (**a** + infinitive).

Tenses for the Future

Expectations, will, sense of duty or obligation are all factors that play a role in the way we talk about the FUTURE. Highly probable events are often presented as a certainty. The speaker's involvement in a future event can range from asserting one's determination to make it happen to accepting, or rejecting, compliance with an imposed duty. Different verb tenses can convey these and other nuances of meaning.

Future

Generally speaking the Portuguese future tense is similar in meaning to the English future with *shall* and *will*.

Eu comprarei um carro novo.   I shall buy a new car.
Eles venderão a casa.   They will sell their house.

FORM

The future is a very easy tense to conjugate. There is just one set of four endings which are added on to the infinitive of the verb.

I shall buy / sell / leave etc.
eu comprarei / venderei / partirei etc.

subject	1st / 2nd / 3rd conj.
eu	-ei
você, ele/ela	-á
nós	-emos
vocês, eles/elas	-ão

For other 'you' forms see Unit 3 and 'The Other Second Person'.

Learning aid:
Note that the endings for the future tense are almost the same as the present of irregular verb **haver** (Unit 2) without the 'h', which is not pronounced:
(h)**ei**, (h)**á**, (hav)**emos**, (h)**ão**.

47

USE

As in English, the Portuguese future tense is used:

(a) To express mere futurity.

A reunião será aqui.　　　　*The meeting will be here.*

As in English, the Portuguese future tense may be tinged with feelings and mental stances associated with the future and the unknown, and as such it can be used:

(b) To express conjecture and doubt.

Elas terão seus trinta anos.　　　*They will be about thirty years old.*
Quem sabe se ele virá.　　　　*Who knows whether he will come.*
　　　　　　　　　　　　　　(I wonder whether...)

(c) To express a stipulated requirement.

O prazo para entrega do documento　*This document shall be submitted*
será de 30 dias.　　　　　　　*in no later than 30 days.*

Note: Unlike English, the Portuguese future forms are fixed and there is no equivalent to the interplay of *will* and *shall* to denote volition and obligation (although this distinction does not necessarily apply in American English). For further detail see 'Expressing volition and obligation' later in this unit.

Irregular verbs

Only three verbs have an irregular future: **dizer**, **fazer** and **trazer**. Although they take the regular endings, these verbs have special contracted roots in the future tense: **dir-**, **far-**, **trar-** (for a full list of verb forms, see Verb Tables, at the end of the book).

dizer, *to say*
eu **direi**, você, ele/ela **dirá**, nós **diremos**, vocês, eles/elas **dirão**
fazer, *to do, to make*
eu **farei**, você, ele/ela **fará**, nós **faremos**, vocês, eles/elas **farão**
trazer, *to bring*
eu **trarei**, você, ele/ela **trará**, nós **traremos**, vocês, eles/elas **trarão**

In general, compound verbs in the same family share the same features. E.g., condirá (**condizer**, *to match*, like **dizer**); satisfarão (**satisfazer**, *to satisfy*, like **fazer**).

Note:

Irregular verb **pôr**, *to put*, and its compounds have a regular future tense but **pôr** loses its circumflex accent (^) before the future endings: porei (**pôr**, *to put*); suporei (**supor**, *to suppose, assume*, like **pôr**).

Colloquial future

This way of expressing the future in Portuguese is similar to the future with *going to* in English.

| **Eu vou comprar um carro.** | I am going to buy a car. |
| **Eles vão vender a casa.** | They are going to sell their house. |

FORM

The colloquial future is formed with the present of **ir**, to go, which you learned in Unit 2. This auxiliary verb is followed by the infinitive of the main verb.

I am going to buy / sell / leave etc.
eu vou comprar / vender / partir   etc.

subject	present of 'ir'	main verb (1st / 2nd / 3rd conj.)
eu	vou	
você, ele/ela	vai	-ar / -er / -ir
nós	vamos	
vocês, eles/elas	vão	

For other 'you' forms see Unit 3 and 'The Other Second Person'.

Note:

The colloquial future is not normally used with verb **ir**. The common practice is to say simply 'eu vou' (not 'eu vou ir').

| Amanhã eu vou à cidade. | *Tomorrow I am going (to go) to town.* |

USE

The Portuguese colloquial future is close in meaning to the English construction *(to be) going to*, but with a shift in emphasis. In English there is a stronger sense of intention and certainty as opposed to mere futurity.

Nós vamos ficar aqui.	*We are going to stay here.*
	or *We are staying here.*
Eu vou viajar no domingo.	*I am going to travel on Sunday.*
	or *I am travelling on Sunday.*
Vou fazer trinta anos no ano que vem.	*I shall be thirty years this coming year.*

The Portuguese colloquial future is often interchangeable with the present tense (see use (h) of the simple present in Unit 2). However this is not the case where movement and dramatic action is the focus.

Cuidado! O telhado vai cair. *Watch out! The roof is falling (about to fall).*

Emphatic future

This way of conveying the future indicates strong will and determination on the part of the speaker, who may, or may not, be the doer of the action.

Eu hei de comprar um carro novo.   I will buy a new car.
Eles hão de vender o carro velho.   They are to sell their old car.

FORM

To form this tense you need the present of verb **haver**, which you learned in Unit 2. This auxiliary verb is followed by **de** and the infinitive of the main verb.

I will buy / sell / leave etc.
eu hei de comprar / vender / partir etc.

subject	present of 'haver'	link word	main verb (1st / 2nd / 3rd conj.)
eu	hei		
você, ele/ela	há	de	-ar / -er / -ir
nós	havemos		
vocês, eles/elas	hão		

For other 'you' forms see Unit 3 and 'The Other Second Person'.

USE

(a) The Portuguese emphatic future can translate English *will* and *shall* constructions as follows:

(i) *will* with *'I'* to express determination.

| Eu hei de consertar este aparelho | *I will repair this machine* |
| a qualquer custo. | *at any cost.* |

(ii) *will* with *'you; s/he, it; they'* to indicate predictability.

| Ele há de fazer sempre o contrário | *He will always do the opposite* |
| do que eu peço. | *to what I ask.* |

(iii) *shall* with *'I'* to express resolution.

| Eu hei de fazer o que quero. | *I shall do what I like.* |

(iv) *shall* with *'you; s/he, it; they'* to denote promise or threat.

Você há de receber o dinheiro	*You shall have the money*
assim que possível.	*as soon as possible.*
Ele há de pagar o que nos deve.	*He shall pay what he owes us.*

(v) *shall* with *'I'* or *'we'* for expressions such as *What shall I do?*

| O que é que nós havemos de fazer? | *What shall we do?* |
| O que é que eu hei de dizer? | *What shall I say?* |

(b) The Portuguese emphatic future can also translate English *to be (supposed) to (do / be)*, as follows:

| Ele há de falar amanhã. | *He is (supposed) to speak tomorrow.* |

Comparing the Portuguese 'futures'

(1) future and colloquial future

Generally speaking, the colloquial future is equivalent in meaning to the future tense but more informal.

51

Ele fará um discurso hoje à noite.
He will make a public speech tonight.
                    =
Ele vai fazer um discurso hoje à noite.
He is going to make a public speech tonight. (*He is making...*)

However, the future tense and the colloquial future are not entirely interchangeable.

(A) The future tense (not the colloquial future) is used for conjecture.

Quem sabe onde ele estará agora.   *Who knows where he may be now.*

(B) The future tense (not the colloquial future) is used for a stipulated requirement.

O pagamento será feito dentro   *Payment shall be made within*
de sessenta dias.   *sixty days.*

(C) Preference is given to the future tense for events seen as remote in the future and / or uncertain.

Daqui a setenta anos farei   *Seventy years from now I shall be*
noventa anos.   *ninety years old.*

(D) The colloquial future is more for events in the immediate future or not too far in the future.

Daqui a dois anos vou   *Two years from now I shall be*
fazer trinta anos.   *thirty years old.*

(2) future, colloquial future and emphatic future

Connotations of volition and determination can be added to the future tense and the colloquial future through tone of voice.

Eu <u>farei</u> isso.   *I will do that.*
Eu <u>vou</u> fazer issso.   *I am going to do that.*

Situational context also plays a role. The future and the colloquial future can be used to give an order where no resistance is expected, that is, a future occurrence seen as a fact.

Ninguém falará durante a prova   *No one will talk during the written*
escrita.   *exam.* (*you will not talk...*)

Ninguém vai falar durante a prova escrita. *No one is going to talk during the written exam.*

but

The emphatic future provides a very explicit way of indicating the speaker's strong will over a future event.

Eu hei de fazer isso. *I will do that.* (this is a promise)

Ninguém há de falar durante a prova escrita. *No one is to talk during the written exam.* (this may be a threat)

Expressing volition and obligation

The English future often expresses additional meanings of volition and obligation through the interplay of *will* and *shall* (although this distinction does not necessarily apply in the USA and other English speaking areas). This feature is part of the English complex system for the expression of volition and obligation which includes constructions with will-would, shall-should, must, have/has to, ought to. The Portuguese language uses other devices to gain the same effect.

In Portuguese volition and obligation can be indicated as follows:

(A) With the construction **ter de** (or **ter que**).

The construction **ter que** or **ter de** translates both 'must' and 'to have to'. In English, with 'must' the feeling of compulsion comes from the speaker; with 'have to' the compulsion is usually from external circumstances. Portuguese **ter de** / **que** covers both meanings.

Eu tenho de estudar o dia todo. *I must study all day.*

Os candidatos têm de preencher um formulário. *The candidates have to fill in a form.*

Eu tenho que ler esse livro; parece ser muito interessante. *I have to read that book; it looks very interesting.*

Ter de or **ter que**?

Ter que is the colloquial version, **ter de** is used in more careful speech and writing. Strictly speaking, this is a better option, grammatically. Why? **De** is a link word known as 'preposition'. Prepositions are often added to verbs to modify their original meaning: **ter** means 'to have' (ownership) but **ter de** means 'to have to', 'must' (obligation). **Que** is not a preposition; it belongs to another grammatical category, that of 'conjunctions'. Therefore, grammatically **ter de** is a preferable choice.

(B) With the verb **dever**.

Eu devia acabar este trabalho hoje.	*I ought to complete this work today.*
Eu devia telefonar para ele mas não me apetece.	*I should phone him but I don't feel like it.*
Os senhores passageiros que se destinam ao centro da cidade devem sair nesta estação.	*All passengers for the town centre are advised to leave the train at this station. (must leave the train here)*

Although verb **dever can express obligation,** as shown above, its use is limited. It tends to be a choice mainly for moral obligation (ought to / should) rather than suggest a command (you must), in which case other options are available.

In public instructions and announcements:

(i) with a 'comand' form (as we shall see in Unit 7)

Por favor utilizem a porta da esquerda.	*Please use the door on the left.*
Os senhores passageiros que se destinam ao centro da cidade por favor saiam nesta estação.	*All passengers for the town centre are advised to leave the train at this station. (must leave the train here)*

(ii) with the verb in the infinitive (as we shall see in Unit 14).

Por favor utilizar a porta da esquerda.	*Please use the door on the left.*
É favor saírem pela porta de trás.	*Please leave by the back door.*

On a personal basis, with **não se esqueça(m) de...**, *do not forget to...*

Não se esqueça de limpar os pés antes de entrar.	*You must wipe your feet before coming in.* (literally, *don't forget to ...*)

(C) With the construction **haver de**, i.e., the 'Emphatic future' explained earlier in the present unit.

See also use (c) of the simple future above and use (i) of the simple present in Unit 2.

Exercises

6.1
Work out the correct verb forms and find the words to solve this puzzle.
(Nr. 1 across has been done for you)

Across:
1 Eu ___indicarei___ o caminho. (**indicar**)
   I shall give directions.
2 Nós _____ ficar em casa. (**ir**)
   We are going to stay at home.
3 Nós _____ aqui. (**estar**)
   We shall be here.
4 O presidente _____ ao norte do país. (**ir**)
   The president will go to the north of the country.
5 Eles _____ de saber que eu estive aqui. (**haver**)
   They shall know that I was here.

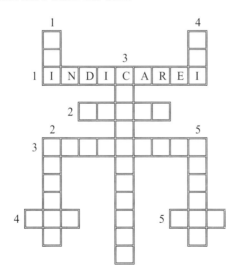

Down:
1 Ela _____ ver o que pode fazer. (**ir**)
   She is going to see what she can do.
2 Ninguém _____ acordado a estas horas. (**estar**)
   No one will be awake at this time.

3 Na próxima vez nós _____ um carro novo. (**comprar**)
Next time we shall buy a new car.
4 Eu _____ de descansar o dia todo. (**haver**)
I will rest all day.
5 Vocês _____ da sala no fim da prova. (**sair**)
You will leave the room after the exam.

6.2
Fill the squares on either side of the diagonal staircase with the correct form of the verb in the future tense so as to match the person shown. Nr. 5 (a) has been done for you.

5 (a) TRAREMOS : nós traremos (*we shall bring*)

1 (a) você… (**fazer**)	(b) nós…	(**trazer**)
2 (a) eu… (**fazer**)	(b) nós…	(**dizer**)
3 (a) eles… (**trazer**)	(b) eu…	(**trazer**)
4 (a) nós… (**fazer**)	(b) vocês…	(**dizer**)
5 (a) nós… (**trazer**)	(b) ele…	(**dizer**)

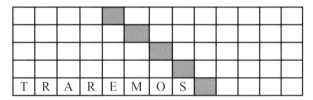

1 (a)→ (b)→
2 (a)→ (b →
3 (a)→ (b)→
4 (a)→ (b)→
5 (a)→ (b)→   T R A R E M O S

Command Forms

What is meant by 'command' is simply the way you tell someone to do (or not to do) something.

Entre !   Come in !

FORM

In English we recognize a written 'command' in two ways: normally there is no subject word and sometimes there is an exclamation mark (!) at the end of the sentence. A spoken 'command' is recognized by the tone of the voice.

In Portuguese, there are special command forms. The verb of the action you wish to happen (or not) will also change its ending according to whether you are talking to one person or a group. These are the 'recipients' of your 'command'.

Talking to one person:

compr**e**, *buy*, vend**a**, *sell*, part**a**, *leave*

Talking to two or more people:

compr**em**, *buy*, vend**am**, *sell*, part**am**, *leave*

recipient	1st conj.	2nd and 3rd conj.
(você)	**-e**	**-a**
(vocês)	**-em**	**-am**

For other 'you' forms see Unit 3 and 'The Other Second Person'.

Learning aid:
Note that the command endings in the box above are the same **você(s)** endings as for the simple present, but swapped over.

-a(m) pres. 1st conj.   → -a(m) command 2nd + 3rd conj.

-e(m) pres. 2nd + 3rd conj.   → -e(m) command 1st conj.

(Negative commands are explained in Unit 15)

USE

As in English, Portuguese 'commands' convey orders, requests or advice.

Abra a janela.	*Open the window.*
Fechem a porta.	*Shut the door.*
Tome cuidado.	*Take care, be careful.*

Equally as in English, Portuguese commands can be toned down, which is done normally for politeness.

Por favor fale mais devagar.	*Please speak more slowly.*

In English we also use expressions such as *Could you please...* or *Would you please...* before the command verb (*Could you please open the window*). In Portuguese you use expressions of request such as **Faça o favor de ...** or **Por favor queira ...** followed by the infinitive of the command verb.

Faça o favor de abrir a janela.	*Could you please open the window.* (literally, *do the favour...*)
Faça o favor de falar mais devagar.	*Could you please speak more slowly.*
Por favor queiram fechar a porta.	*Would you please shut the door.*

See 'Please' later in this unit.

Verbs with orthographic and radical changes

(For a chart of root and spelling changes, see Verb Tables at the end of the book)

First conjugation verbs (-**ar** verbs) with root ending in **c**, **ç** or **g** change before **e** as follows:

c changes to **qu**
ç changes to **c**
g changes to **gu**

fi**c**ar (*to stay*)	fi**qu**e, fi**qu**em (*stay*)
come**ç**ar (*to start*)	come**c**e, come**c**em (*start*)
pa**g**ar (*to pay*)	pa**gu**e, pa**gu**em (*pay*)

Second and third conjugation verbs (-**er** and -**ir** verbs) with root ending in **c**, **g** or **gu** change before **a** as follows:

c   changes to   **ç**
g   changes to   **j**
gu changes to   **g**

conhe**c**er (*to know*)   conhe**ç**a, conhe**ç**am (*get to know*)
des**c**er (*to climb down*)   des**ç**a, des**ç**am (*get down*)
fu**g**ir (*to flee*)   fu**j**a!, fu**j**am! (*run!(flee)*)
er**gu**er (*to lift*)   er**g**a, er**g**am (*lift*)

Third conjugation verbs (-**ir** verbs) with **e** or **o** in the core part of the root change as follows:

e   changes to   **i**
o   changes to   **u**

rep**e**tir (*to repeat*)   rep**i**ta, rep**i**tam (*do/say it again*)
s**e**ntir (*to feel*)   s**i**nta, s**i**ntam (*feel*)
progr**e**dir (*to progress*)   progr**i**da, progr**i**dam (*progress*)
c**o**brir (*to cover*)   c**u**bra, c**u**bram (*cover*)
d**o**rmir (*to sleep*)   d**u**rma, d**u**rmam (*sleep*)

Some verbs have a root change and an additional spelling change.

s**e**guir (*to follow, carry on, go*)   s**i**ga, s**i**gam (*follow, carry on, go*)
                        e → i and **gu → g**

In general, compound verbs in the same family share the same features.

desc**o**brir (*to discover*)   desc**u**bra, desc**u**bram (*discover*)
(like c**o**brir)
recome**ç**ar (*to restart*)   recome**c**e, recome**c**em (*start again*)
(like come**ç**ar)
reconhe**c**er (*to admit*)   reconhe**ç**a, reconhe**ç**am (*you must admit*)
(like conhe**c**er)

Other cases

A number of verbs have an **ei** or **ai** before the ending. These are, respectively, first conjugation verbs in -**ear** and third conjugation verbs in -**air**.

passe**ar** (*to stroll, take a walk*)   passeie, passeiem (*take a walk*)
s**air** (*to go/come out*)   saia, saiam (*get out*)

First conjugation verbs in -**iar** are usually regular but the few listed in Unit 2 follow the same pattern as -**ear** verbs.

remed**iar** (*to put right*)   remedeie, remedeiem (*put (that) right*)

Irregular verbs

Below is a list of the most common irregular cases in the command forms explained in this unit (for a full list of verb forms, see Verb Tables, at the end of the book).

caber, *to fit*	**caiba, caibam**
crer, *to believe*	**creia, creiam**
dar, *to give*	**dê, deem**
dizer, *to say*	**diga, digam**
estar, *to be*	**esteja, estejam**
fazer, *to do, to make*	**faça, façam**
haver, *to exist, there to be, to have*	**haja, hajam**
ir, *to go*	**vá, vão**
ler, *to read*	**leia, leiam**
medir, *to measure*	**meça, meçam**
ouvir, *to hear*	**ouça, ouçam**
pedir, *to ask for*	**peça, peçam**
perder, *to lose*	**perca, percam**
poder, *can, may, to be able*	**possa, possam**
pôr, *to put*	**ponha, ponham**
querer, *to want*	**queira, queiram**
rir, *to laugh*	**ria, riam**
saber, *to know*	**saiba, saibam**
ser, *to be*	**seja, sejam**
ter, *to have*	**tenha, tenham**
trazer, *to bring*	**traga, tragam**

valer, *to be worth*   **valha, valham**
ver, *to see*   **veja, vejam**
vir, *to come*   **venha, venham**

Note: Command forms are not normally used with some of these verbs due to their meaning. This is the case with **caber** (*to fit*) and **poder** (*can, may, to be able*).

In general, compound verbs belonging to the family of any of the above share the same features. E.g., contenha (**conter**, *to contain*, like **ter**); sorria (**sorrir**, *to smile*, like **rir**); suponha (**supor**, *to suppose, assume*, like **pôr**).

Command form alternatives

As you learned in Unit 2, instructions and orders can be given in the simple present, as a description of the course of action to be taken (see use (f) of the simple present). This means that the same instruction or order can be expressed as a 'command' or in the present – **Faça** isso *or* **Você faz** isso, *(You) do that*. In regular verbs these two options (command or present tense) are formally quite close, particularly when subject **você** is not used (as explained in Unit 3, 'Dispensing with the subject').

Simple present
        Você vira à direita na próxima esquina. *or*
        Vira à direita na próxima esquina.
        You turn right at the next corner.

instead of command form
        Vire à direita na próxima esquina.
        Turn right at the next corner.

Simple present
        (**Você**) lava o carro antes do almoço.
        You wash the car by lunch time.

instead of command form
        Lave o carro antes do almoço.
        Wash the car by lunch time.

The same applies to invitations, requests, and reprimands, which can be expressed in the present, often as a question, when you want to avoid a more direct approach.

61

Simple present
 (**Você**) deseja tomar alguma coisa?
 Would you like something to drink? (literally, *do you wish...?*)
instead of command form
 Tome alguma coisa.
 Have something to drink.

(invitation)

Simple present
 (**A senhora**) **quer** dar alguma coisa para... ?
 Would you like to give something for...? (lit., *do you want...?*)
instead of command form
 Dê alguma coisa para ...
 Give something for...

(request)

Simple present
 (**Vocês**) **querem** falar mais baixo?
 Will you speak more quietly? (lit., *do you want...?*)
instead of command form
 Falem mais baixo.
 Speak more quietly.

(reprimand)

See also Unit 6 for ways in which future tenses can be used to convey an order, as a prospective obligation or a future occurrence when no resistance is anticipated, and Unit 14 for orders given in the infinitive.

Note:
For extra politeness, you can always use **o senhor** / **a senhora** (sir / madam) and respective plural forms you learned in Unit 3.
For *You turn right at the next corner.*
Você vira à direita na próxima esquina. or
O senhor vira à direita na próxima esquina. (talking to a man)
For *Would you like to give something for...?*
Você quer dar alguma coisa para...? or
A senhora quer dar alguma coisa para...? (talking to a woman)

Commands with a subject

As explained above, the present tense, in a statement or question, can be an alternative to a command form.

Where the present tense is the option taken, a subject word can be expected to be used, e.g., **você** or **o senhor** / **a senhora** (for a more courteous approach).

Você toma a segunda rua à esquerda.
You take the second road on your left.
A senhora toma a segunda rua à esquerda.
You take the second road on your left. (courteous)

What may cause surprise to an English native speaker is that in Portuguese a subject word can also be present with a command form. In other words, the recipient of your command can be expressed as the subject of the action you wish to happen, or not to happen.

Você tome a segunda rua à esquerda.
(You) take the second road on your left.
A senhora tome a segunda rua à esquerda.
(You) take the second road on your left. (courteous)

This is as if you were saying 'I suggest / recommend that you take the second road on your left', but the first part of your sentence is understood, not expressed. In Unit 8 you will find out more about this feature in section 'Present subjunctive and command forms'.

Please

Polite expressions of request follow the same grammatical pattern as 'commands' in general.

Faça(m) favor   *Excuse me please* (drawing attention, etc.)

Faça(m) o favor de |
Faça(m) favor de | +   infinitive
Por favor **queira(m)** ... |
Queira(m) ..., por favor |

Faça favor de entrar.	*Could you please come in.*
Por favor queira sentar-se.	*Would you please take a seat.*
Por favor queiram sair agora.	*Would you please leave now.*

In **faça(m)** and **queira(m)** you are actually using the command forms of **fazer** and **querer**. There is thus a shift of emphasis from the command action to a request for willingness to carry it out (will you kindly...).

These are all elegant ways of drawing attention and/or introducing a request. In relaxed colloquial speech, the ordinary present is often used instead of the command form, but they are not entirely interchangeable.

Faz(em) favor   *Excuse me please* (drawing attention, etc.)

Faz(em) o favor de	|	
Faz(em) favor de	|	+ infinitive
Por favor **quer(em)** ...	|	
Quer(em) ..., por favor	|	

Faz favor de entrar.	*Could you please come in.*
Por favor quer sentar-se?	*Would you like to take a seat?*

but

Por favor querem sair agora?	*Will you please leave now?*
(this may sound like a threat)	

Exercises

7.1

(A) A lady has asked for the supermarket – Onde fica o supermercado? – and is being shown the way.

A senhora **toma** a primeira rua à direita, no cruzamento **vira** à esquerda e depois **segue** em frente. O supermercado fica a uns vinte metros à esquerda. *You take the first road on your right, at the crossroads turn left and then carry on straight ahead. The supermarket is about twenty metres on your left.*

           (verbs   **tomar**,   **virar**,   **seguir**)

1 Give the same directions, but change the words in bold to the verb forms you learned in this unit. Start with **Tome**.

2 What would you have said (instead of **Tome**, etc.) if the lady had a friend with her and you would be talking to two people instead of one?

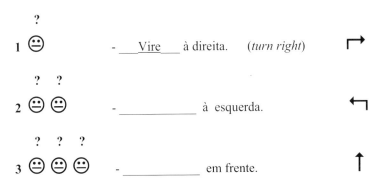

(B) Complete the sentences and give directions to these people. Nr. 1 has been done for you.

You are
talking to

1 ☺   - ___Vire___ à direita.   (*turn right*)   ⌐►

2 ☺ ☺   - _____ à esquerda.   ◄⌐

3 ☺ ☺ ☺   - _____ em frente.   ↑

7.2

Fill in the gaps with the appropriate form of the verb shown in brackets. You are talking to one individual. Nr. 1 has been done for you.

(A) You can't quite catch what someone is saying to you.

1 Por favor ___fale___ mais devagar. (**falar**) *Please speak more slowly.*
2 _____ o favor de repetir. (**fazer**) *Could you please say it again.*

(B) You want to alert someone of danger.

1 _____! (**parar**) *Stop!*
2 _____! (**correr**) *Run!*
3 _____ daqui depressa! (**sair**) *Get out of here quickly!*

(C) You are enjoying being looked after at the hotel and the restaurant.

1 _____ a bagagem para cima, por favor. (**levar**)
                              Take the bags upstair, please.
2 _____ o prato do dia, por favor. (**trazer**)
                              Bring the dish of the day, please.

Present Subjunctive

The present subjunctive indicates that something is:
• not taken for granted or certain
• not accepted as believable, or welcomed
• expressed as hope or a wish
• expressed as someone's request

Eu penso que nós talvez mudemos de casa daqui a dois anos.	I think that we may be moving house two years from now.
Eu duvido que ele trabalhe muito.	I doubt that he will work hard.
Nós sentimos muito que ela esteja triste.	We are very sorry that she may be feeling sad.
Eu espero que chova amanhã.	I hope that it will rain tomorrow.
Ele pede que vocês venham já.	He asks for you to come straight away.

FORM

The present subjunctive is quite easy to learn when you know the command forms we saw in Unit 7. The only new ending you need to learn is that for the first person plural, i.e., 'we' (**nós**): **-emos**, for **-ar** verbs and **-amos**, for both **-er** and **-ir** verbs.

(that) I will, may buy / sell / leave   etc.
(que) **eu** compre / venda / parta   etc.

subject	1st conj.	2nd and 3rd conj.
eu, você, ele/ela	-e	-a
nós	-emos	-amos
vocês, eles/elas	-em	-am

For other 'you' forms see Unit 3 and 'The Other Second Person'.

Note that the present subjunctive is often introduced by **que** (that).

Eu duvido **que** ele trabalhe muito.
Eu espero **que** chova amanhã.

67

USE

The Portuguese present subjunctive is for actions and states that are not assumed to be, or become, a fact, or are not acknowledged as a credible or desirable fact. It includes the expression of uncertainty, probability, possibility; wishes and emotions such as hope and sorrow; someone's request; and necessity or imperative need.

What is expressed with the Portuguese present subjunctive is often conveyed in English with the help of *will, may, can* or *must* and *have/has to.* It is also conveyed with present tense forms or the constructions *to (do)* and *for ... to (do).*

É possível que tudo acabe bem.	*It may all end well.*
	(It is possible that all will end well)
É provável que chova amanhã.	*It may well rain tomorrow. (It is probable that...)*
Tomara que chova amanhã.	*I hope that it rains tomorrow.* or *I hope that it will rain tomorrow.*
Nós esperamos que ele venha hoje.	*We hope that he comes today.* or *We hope that he will come today.*
Eu duvido que ele saiba Português.	*I doubt that he can speak Portuguese.*
Nós desejamos que você faça boa viagem.	*We hope that you may have a good journey.* *We wish you a pleasant journey.*
Nós receamos que tudo acabe mal.	*We fear that it may all end up badly.*
Eu sinto muito que ela esteja tão doente.	*I am very sorry to hear that she is so ill.* or *I am very sorry that she may be that ill.*
É necessário que ele trabalhe mais.	*He must work harder.* *He has to work harder.* *(It is necessary that...)*
Ele pede que vocês venham já.	*He asks / is asking for you to come straight away. (that you come ...)*
Ele quer que vocês venham já.	*He wants you to come straight away. (that you come ...)*

Verbs with orthographic and radical changes

(For a chart of root and spelling changes, see Verb Tables at the end of the book)

The same applies as for the command forms explained in Unit 7, with the same changes in the first person singular (*'I'* form) or plural (*'we'* form).

ficar (*to stay*)	fique, fiquemos	(*(that) I / we stay, etc.*)
começar (*to start*)	comece, comecemos	
pagar (*to pay*)	pague, paguemos	
conhecer (*to know*)	conheça, conheçamos	
descer (*to climb down*)	desça, desçamos	
fugir (*to flee*)	fuja, fujamos	
erguer (*to lift*)	erga, ergamos	
repetir (*to repeat*)	repita, repitamos	
sentir (*to feel*)	sinta, sintamos	
progredir (*to progress*)	progrida, progridamos	
cobrir (*to cover*)	cubra, cubramos	
dormir (*to sleep*)	durma, durmamos	

seguir (*to follow, carry on, go*)   siga, sigamos

descobrir (*to discover*)   descubra, descubramos (*(that) I/we discover*)
(like cobrir)
recomeçar (*to restart*)   recomece, recomecemos (*(that) I/we start again*)
(like começar)
reconhecer (*to admit*)   reconheça, reconheçamos (*(that) I/we admit*)
(like conhecer)

Other cases

Verbs in **-ear** and the **-iar** verbs listed in Unit 2 have **ei** before the *'I'* ending (in addition to the você(s), ele(s) / ela(s) forms).

passear (*to stroll, take a walk*): eu passeie; *but* nós passeemos
remediar (*to put right*): eu remedeie; *but* nós remediemos

-air verbs retain the **i** both before the *'I'* and the *'we'* ending (in addition to the você(s), ele(s) / ela(s) forms).

sair (*to go/come out*): eu saia, nós saiamos

69

Irregular verbs

Below is a list of the most common irregular cases in the present subjunctive (for a full list of verb forms, see Verb Tables, at the end of the book).

caber, *to fit*
eu, você, ele/ela **caiba**, nós **caibamos**, vocês, eles/elas **caibam**
crer, *to believe*
eu, você, ele/ela **creia**, nós **creiamos**, vocês, eles/elas **creiam**
dar, *to give*
eu, você, ele/ela **dê**, nós **dêmos**, vocês, eles/elas **deem**
dizer, *to say*
eu, você, ele/ela **diga**, nós **digamos**, vocês, eles/elas **digam**
estar, *to be*
eu, você, ele/ela **esteja**, nós **estejamos**, vocês, eles/elas **estejam**
fazer, *to do, to make*
eu, você, ele/ela **faça**, nós **façamos**, vocês, eles/elas **façam**
haver, *to exist, there to be, to have*
eu, você, ele/ela **haja**, nós **hajamos**, vocês, eles/elas **hajam**
ir, *to go*
eu, você, ele/ela **vá**, nós **vamos**, vocês, eles/elas **vão**
ler, *to read*
eu, você, ele/ela **leia**, nós **leiamos**, vocês, eles/elas **leiam**
medir, *to measure*
eu, você, ele/ela **meça**, nós **meçamos**, vocês, eles/elas **meçam**
ouvir, *to hear*
eu, você, ele/ela **ouça**, nós **ouçamos**, vocês, eles/elas **ouçam**
pedir, *to ask for*
eu, você, ele/ela **peça**, nós **peçamos**, vocês, eles/elas **peçam**
perder, *to lose*
eu, você, ele/ela **perca**, nós **percamos**, vocês, eles/elas **percam**
poder, *can, may, to be able*
eu, você, ele/ela **possa**, nós **possamos**, vocês, eles/elas **possam**
pôr, *to put*
eu, você, ele/ela **ponha**, nós **ponhamos**, vocês, eles/elas **ponham**
querer, *to want*
eu, você, ele/ela **queira**, nós **queiramos**, vocês, eles/elas **queiram**
rir, *to laugh*
eu, você, ele/ela **ria**, nós **riamos**, vocês, eles/elas **riam**
saber, *to know*

eu, você, ele/ela **saiba**, nós **saibamos**, vocês, eles/elas **saibam**
ser, *to be*
eu, você, ele/ela **seja**, nós **sejamos**, vocês, eles/elas **sejam**
ter, *to have*
eu, você, ele/ela **tenha**, nós **tenhamos**, vocês, eles/elas **tenham**
trazer, *to bring*
eu, você, ele/ela **traga**, nós **tragamos**, vocês, eles/elas **tragam**
valer, *to be worth*
eu, você, ele/ela **valha**, nós **valhamos**, vocês, eles/elas **valham**
ver, *to see*
eu, você, ele/ela **veja**, nós **vejamos**, vocês, eles/elas **vejam**
vir, *to come*
eu, você, ele/ela **venha**, nós **venhamos**, vocês, eles/elas **venham**

In general, compound verbs belonging to the family of any of the above share the same features. E.g., contenha (**conter**, *to contain*, like **ter**); sorria (**sorrir**, *to smile*, like **rir**); suponhamos (**supor**, *to suppose*, *assume*, like **pôr**).

How the present subjunctive works

The following guidelines will take you through the general role of the present subjunctive in the Portuguese verb system.

(A) In sentences that require a present subjunctive **que** often marks the dividing line between two distinct parts. First comes the leading part of the sentence, known as 'main clause'. Then comes the guided part, known as 'subordinate clause'. The subjunctive is used in the subordinate clause.

leading clause	que	present subjunctive

Eu espero **que** ele **venha** hoje.   *I hope that he will come today.*
Eu tenho esperança **que** isso **dê** certo.   *I am hopeful (that) that will work out.*
Eu desejo **que** vocês **sejam** felizes.   *I wish that you may be happy.* or *I wish you to be happy.*
Eles preferem **que** você **venha** agora.   *They would rather you come now.*
Ele quer **que** vocês **falem** mais baixo.   *He wants you to speak more quietly.*

71

The main clause can be worded in impersonal terms (it is possible / regrettable / good / better…).

You will need to use the subjunctive after the following impersonal main clauses:

It is …

É possível	*possible*	É bom	*good*
É provável	*probable*	É melhor	*better*
É de esperar	*to be expected*	É pena	*sad, a shame*
É necessário	*necessary*	É lamentável	*regrettable*
É preciso	*necessary*	Basta	*enough*
É importante	*important*	Convém	*convenient*

É possível **que** ele **telefone** hoje.	*He may phone today.(It is possible that…)*
É provável **que** ele **vá** lá hoje.	*He may well go there today.* *(It is probable that…)*
É de esperar **que** ela **melhore** depressa.	*It is to be expected that she will recover quickly.*
É necessário **que** eu **saiba** isso.	*I must know that / it is necessary for me to know that. (It is necessary that …)*
É importante **que** eu **vá** à festa.	*I must go to the party. (It is important that …)*
É lamentável **que** eles não **venham**.	*It is regrettable that they are not coming.*
Basta **que** nós **assinemos** o contrato amanhã.	*All that is needed is for us to sign the contract tomorrow.*
Convém **que** eles **acabem** esse trabalho esta semana.	*They must finish that job this week. (It is convenient that…)*
É pouco provável **que** as coisas **mudem**.	*It is unlikely that things will change.*

(B) In some cases the leading word(s) will not necessarily be a clause, as with the following:

Talvez	*Perhaps*	Tomara	*I hope*
Oxalá	*Let's hope*	Que pena	*How sad*

leading expression	que	present subjunctive

Talvez **que** ele **venha** amanhã.	*Perhaps he will come tomorrow.*
Talvez **que dê** certo.	*Perhaps things will work out.*

Oxalá **que** eles **estejam** bem.   *Let's hope (that) they are well.*
Tomara **que chova** amanhã.   *I hope (that) it rains tomorrow.* or
                                    I hope (that) it will rain tomorrow.
Que pena **que** ela **prefira** ficar   *How sad that she will rather stay*
em casa.   *at home.*

Note:
With 'talvez' and 'oxalá', 'que' is not always used: Talvez ele **venha** amanhã. Oxalá eles **estejam** bem.

(C) Sometimes not even a leading word is present. With a strong wish, **que** can be the starting word.

————————————	que	present subjunctive

Que faça boa viagem!   *(I wish) you a pleasant journey.*
Que sejam felizes!   *(I wish) you to be happy.*

(D) Further still, the **que** may be left out but the sense of the wish remains.

————————————	———	present subjunctive

Faça boa viagem!   *Have a nice journey!*
Sejam felizes!   *The best of happiness!*

For further information on the present subjunctive see also Units 11 and 19.

Desculpe

Desculpe! – The Portuguese for 'Sorry!' (apologizing) is the second person ('you' form) of the present subjunctive of verb 'desculpar' (to pardon, forgive) and follows the pattern shown in (D) of the above section.

Desculpe means literally 'Pardon', 'Forgive', the following being understood: Eu desejo / espero / peço que você / o senhor / etc. desculpe… (*wish / hope / ask that you may forgive*). It is therefore appropriate to use the plural form when talking to more than one person.

You walked into a couple:

Ah! desculpem   *Oh! Sorry* (literally, *Pardon, Forgive*)

Desculpe? – With a rising intonation, this is a polite means of seekimg clarification.

Desculpe?   *Pardon?*

(These are the same verb forms as the 'commands' explained in Unit 7)

Present subjunctive and command forms

From transmitting an order to giving an order

In the following sentences the speaker is transmitting a request or an order:

Ele pede que **vocês venham já**. *He is asking for you to come straight away.*
                          (*that you come…*)
Ele quer que **vocês venham já**. *He wants you to come straight away.*
                          (*that you come …*)

In the following sentence the speaker is making a direct request or giving an order:

Venham já! *Come straight away!*

The verb form – **venham** – is the same. This is so because the 'command' forms explained in Unit 7 are in fact 'borrowed' from the present subjunctive. See also 'Use' of the present subjunctive earlier in this unit.

Let's…

Equally from the present subjunctive comes the Portuguese equivalent to English *let's* as an expression of incitement. To communicate this meaning simply use the first person plural ('we' form).

Vamos!   *Let's go!*
Esperemos! *Let's wait!*

The subjunctive-'command' form interplay

In the Portuguese language there is the option of omitting the subject word where the meaning remains clear from context, as you learned in Unit 3.

Ele pede / quer que **vocês venham** já.

   or

Ele pede / quer que **venham** já.

Conversely, a subject word is sometimes used with a command form (which is a subjunctive present form).

Venham já!   or   **Vocês venham** já!
Vamos!   or   **Nós vamos**!

This tendency to include a subject word in a 'command' sentence is reinforced by the practice of giving instructions and orders in the ordinary present tense (see use (f) of the simple present, Unit 2, and 'Commands with a subject', Unit 7).

Bossy or courteous?

In English we may sound too bossy if we just use the verb when we make a request.

Come straight away!

For politeness we normally include the word 'please'.

Please come straight away!
Could you please come straight away?

In contrast, the Portuguese 'command' forms do not sound half as bossy as the English translation may suggest.

Venham já! *Come straight away*!

As pointed out above, the 'commands' you learned in Unit 7 are 'borrowed' from the present subjunctive. In other words, the same word is used for an order and for the expression of a wish or hope. The shared forms correspond to a conceptual link that reduces the harshness of an order, making it less authoritarian. Actually these 'command' forms are often referred to as 'polite imperative'.

The inbuilt element of politeness in the Portuguese 'command' forms has two implications for English-speaking learners. Firstly, you must not think that Portuguese speakers are being rude to you if they do not say a 'favor' (please) expression each time they make a request. Secondly, remember that they are usually being very courteous when they use expressions like 'faça favor' or 'queira'. (See 'Please' in Unit 7)

Os senhores **façam o favor** de entrar.	*Could you please come in.* *Would you please come in.*
Os senhores **queiram fazer o favor de** entrar.	*Would you kindly come in.*

Exercises

8.1

(A) Change the infinitives in brackets to the right verb forms for the gaps in the sentences. Nr. 1 has been done for you.

1 Duvido que ele ___acabe___ esse trabalho ainda hoje. (**acabar**)
   I doubt that he will finish that job today.
2 Convém que eles _____ a situação. (**compreender**)
   They must appreciate the situation.
3 É importante que você _____ essa exposição. (**ver**)
   You must see that exhibition.
4 Receio que ele _____ com você. (**ralhar**)
   I fear that he may tell you off.
5 É pena que o leite _____ tão depressa. (**azedar**)
   It is a shame that milk goes sour so quickly.
6 Espero que o jantar _____ a todos. (**agradar**)
   I hope that dinner will please everyone.
7 Desejo que você _____ a carteira. (**encontrar**)
   I hope that you may find your wallet.
8 Talvez _____ tudo na mala. (**caber**)
   Perhaps it will all fit into the suitcase.
9 Tomara que eles _____. (**telefonar**)
   I hope that they will phone.
10 É possível que eles _____ a construção da piscina. (**permitir**)
   They may authorize the swimming pool to be built.
11 É necessário que ele _____ esta semana. (**viajar**)
   He has to travel this week.
12 Oxalá que _____ amanhã. (**chover**)
   Let's hope it will rain tomorrow.
13 É provável que eu _____ ir lá mais cedo. (**poder**)
   I may well be able to go there earlier.

14 Quero que você _____ a carta sem mais demora. (**receber**)
I want you to get the letter without any further delay.

(B) With the right answers from (A) you will be able to solve this puzzle. As you do so, two names will be revealed in the shaded vertical columns. One is a giant river in Brazil, the other a popular holiday area in Portugal. What are they?

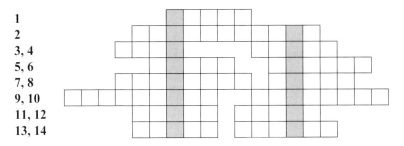

1
2
3, 4
5, 6
7, 8
9, 10
11, 12
13, 14

8.2

The sentences below express wishes, hopes and pressing demands. Extract from them what you could say directly to the person or persons they refer to, as a wish, request or order.

1 Desejo que ele faça boa viagem.
I wish him a good journey. (I wish that he may have a good journey)
2 Espero que eles durmam bem.
I hope that they may sleep well.
3 Desejo que eles tenham um bom fim de semana.
I wish them a good weekend. (I wish that they may have ...)
4 Espero que ela esteja à vontade.
I hope that she will make herself at home.
5 Quero que eles venham já.
I want them to come straight away. (I want that they come ...)
6 É necessário que ele faça esse trabalho.
He must get on with that work. (It is necessary that ...)
7 É preciso que eles esperem mais um pouco.
They must wait a bit longer. (It is required / needed that ...)

Conditional

The Portuguese conditional is close in meaning to the English *would (do/be)* construction.

Seria bom!	It would be nice!
Eu pensava que você viria hoje.	I thought that you would come today.
Eu compraria um carro novo, mas não tenho dinheiro.	I would buy a new car, but I haven't got the money.

FORM

The conditional is even easier to conjugate than the future (Unit 6). There is just one set of three endings, which are added on to the infinitive of the verb.

I would, should buy / sell / leave etc.

eu compra**ria** / vende**ria** / parti**ria** etc.

subject	1st / 2nd / 3rd conj.
eu, você, ele/ela	-ia
nós	-íamos
vocês, eles/elas	-iam

For other 'you' forms see Unit 3 and 'The Other Second Person'.

Learning aid:

Note that the endings for the conditional are the same as the imperfect tense for **-er** and **-ir** verbs (Unit 5) though added to the infinitive.

USE

As in English, the Portuguese conditional is used:

(a) For hypothesis making, often expressing a wish, opinion or advice.

Eu adoraria dar a volta ao mundo.	*I would love to travel around the world.*
Isso seria uma boa solução.	*That would be a good solution.*

78

Seria um erro comprar uma casa mais cara.	*It would be a mistake to buy a more expensive house.*

(b) With verbs of wishing, will and wanting, to express a tentative enquiry or request.

Eu gostaria de ficar no Hotel Central.	*I would like to stay at Hotel Central. / I wonder whether I could please stay at Hotel Central.*
Eu precisaria da sua ajuda.	*I would need your help. / I wonder whether you could please help me.*

This tentative approach can also be used just for politeness.

O senhor poderia dizer-me as horas.	*I wonder whether you could please tell me the time.*

(c) To express futurity in the past. When used for this purpose, the conditional is often given the name of 'future-in-the-past'.

Eu sabia que ele viria domingo.	*I knew that he would come Sunday.*

(d) To express something that might happen if a current impediment could be removed or if an improbable event could make it possible.

Eu iria à festa, mas estou doente.	*I would go to the party, but I am ill.*
Imagine que você ficaria milionário.	*Imagine that you would become a millionaire.*

See also Units 11 and 19 for sentences that require a verb in the conditional.

Irregular verbs

Only three verbs have an irregular conditional: **dizer**, **fazer** and **trazer**. Although they take the regular endings, these verbs have special contracted roots in the conditional: **dir-**, **far-**, **trar-**, as you learned for the future tense in Unit 6 (for a full list of verb forms, see Verb Tables, at the end of the book).

dizer, *to say*
eu, você, ele/ela **diria** nós **diríamos**, vocês, eles/elas **diriam**
fazer, *to do, to make*
eu, você, ele/ela **faria**, nós **faríamos**, vocês, eles/elas **fariam**
trazer, *to bring*
eu, você, ele/ela **traria**, nós **traríamos**, vocês, eles/elas **trariam**

79

In general, compound verbs in the same family share the same features. E.g., condiria (**condizer**, *to match*, like **dizer**); satisfariam (**satisfazer**, *to satisfy*, like **fazer**).

Note:

Irregular verb **pôr**, *to put*, and its compounds have a regular conditional tense but **pôr** loses its circumflex accent (^) before the conditional endings: poria (**pôr**, *to put*); suporia (**supor**, *to suppose, assume*, like **pôr**).

The imperfect for the conditional

Particularly in conversational Portuguese, the imperfect (Unit 5) is often used instead of the conditional.

Isso era (*for* seria) uma boa solução.
That would be a good solution.
Eu gostava (*for* gostaria) de ficar no Hotel Central.
I would like to stay at Hotel Central.
/ *I wonder whether I could please stay at Hotel Central.*
O senhor podia (*for* poderia) dizer-me as horas.
I wonder whether you could please tell me the time.
Eu sabia que ele vinha (*for* viria) domingo.
I knew that he would come Sunday.
Imagine que você ficava (*for* ficaria) milionário.
Imagine that you would become a millionaire.

I would like...

In English, we use the conditional *I would like...* for a polite request, for example when asking for a service in a shop. In Portuguese, the approach is fundamentally the same, but two things are different:

1. The verb used is normally **querer** (*to want, will*); not **gostar** (*to like*).

2. The tense used is normally the imperfect you learned in Unit 5, as a substitute for the conditional.

Eu queria...

Por favor, eu queria dois quilos de feijão.	*I would like two kilos of beans, please.*
Eu queria dois cafés, por favor.	*I would like two coffees, please.*

| Eu queria ficar no Hotel Central, por favor. | *I would like to stay at Hotel Central, please.* |

Eu gostaria...

Earlier in this unit you came across the use of 'Eu gostaria...' translating 'I would like...' / 'I wonder whether I could please...'.

Eu gostaria de ficar no Hotel Central.
I would like to stay at Hotel Central. (I should like ...)
/ I wonder whether I could please stay at Hotel Central.

What is the difference between (a) **Eu queria...** and (b) **Eu gostaria...**?

It is a matter of emphasis. The speaker in (a) is making a polite but assertive request, the speaker in (b) may be making a tentative enquiry or may be expecting difficulties and anticipating a negative response.

| Eu queria ficar no Hotel Central. | *I would like to stay at Hotel Central, please.* |
| Eu gostaria de ficar no Hotel Central. | *I would like to stay at Hotel Central (but I appreciate that there may be no vacancies and I shall have to consider an alternative).* |

Exercises

9.1

Find in the word search the verb forms that are missing in the sentences below. The first sentence has been done for you.

1 ___Seria___ difícil mas não impossível. (**ser**)
   It would be difficult but not impossible.
2 Eu _____ de conhecer a cidade. (**gostar**)
   I would like to see the city.
3 Nós _____ conhecer a sua família. (**adorar**)
   We would love to meet your family.
4 Os senhores _____ indicar-me o caminho para a estação?
   I wonder whether you could please show me the way to the station.
                                                              (**poder**)
5 Com dois meses de férias, eu _____ três ou quatro países.
   With a two-month holiday, I would visit three or four countries.
                                                              (**visitar**)

6 Eu _____ esse rapaz para o colégio, mas agora não tenho tempo.
I would take that boy to school, but I haven't got the time now.
(**levar**)

7 Nós _____ mais presentes para todos, mas não temos dinheiro.
We would bring more gifts for everyone, but we haven't got the money.
(**trazer**)

G	E	V	I	S	I	T	A	R	I	A
O	T	R	A	Z	E	R	L	U	X	A
S	U	G	O	S	T	A	E	Q	I	O
T	A	P	I	F	E	R	V	O	P	A
A	D	O	R	A	R	Í	A	M	O	S
R	U	D	O	B	A	A	T	E	D	I
I	C	E	S	E	R	M	O	N	E	R
A	I	R	E	U	H	O	Q	I	R	A
A	D	O	R	O	S	S	E	T	I	R
V	I	S	I	T	E	I	O	J	A	Z
L	E	V	A	R	I	A	V	A	M	A

9.2

Using the appropriate form of verb **querer**, make the following tentative enquiries and requests more assertive though still being polite (**Eu queria ...** *I would like ...*).

1 **Phoning Mr. Gama's secretary:**
Eu gostaria de falar com o Sr. Gama.
I wonder whether I could please talk to Mr. Gama.

2 **Phoning for a medical appointment:**
Eu gostaria de marcar uma consulta para amanhã.
I wonder whether I could please see the doctor tomorrow. (*book an appointment*)

3 **In a travel agency:**
Nós gostaríamos de ficar num hotel perto da estação.
I wonder whether we could please stay at a hotel near the station.

4 **At the reception desk of an aparthotel:**
Nós gostaríamos de ter um apartamento de casal.
I wonder whether we could please have an apartment for two.

Imperfect and Future Subjunctive

As subjunctives, these two tenses – imperfect and future – have a fundamental feature in common with the present subjunctive you met in Unit 8. All three express something that may not be, or become, a fact, or may not be welcomed as a fact. We can say that they denote non-factuality.

Imperfect Subjunctive

Talvez eu pudesse falar com eles.   Perhaps I could talk to them.

(The speaker is wondering whether talking to them would be possible, or desirable)

FORM

To form the imperfect subjunctive just remove the final **-ram** of the 'vocês, eles/elas' preterite ending you learned in Unit 5 and add **-sse**, **-ssemos**, **-ssem**.

compr**aram**   vend**eram**   part**iram**
   ↓   ↓   ↓
compr**a**   vend**e**   part**i**
   ↓   ↓   ↓
compr**asse**   vend**esse**   part**isse**
etc.   etc.   etc.

(if) I might buy / sell / leave etc.
(se) **eu** compr**asse** / vend**esse** / part**isse** etc.

subject	1st conj.	2nd conj.	3rd conj.
eu, **você, ele/ela**	**-asse**	**-esse**	**-isse**
nós	**-ássemos**	**-êssemos**	**-íssemos**
vocês, eles/elas	**-assem**	**-essem**	**-issem**

83

Note the written accent in the 'we' form: **á**, **ê**, **í**, for respectively the first, second and third conjugation.

For other 'you' forms see Unit 3 and 'The Other Second Person'.

USE

As compared with the present subjunctive, which you learned in Unit 8, the imperfect subjunctive equally expresses uncertainty, probability, possibility, wishes and emotions such as hope and sorrow; someone's request; and necessity or imperative need. However, the imperfect subjunctive places the expressed action or state at an earlier time, in the past. It can also indicate a more remote chance of the expressed action or state becoming a fact or being accepted as true.

What is conveyed with the Portuguese imperfect subjunctive is often conveyed in English with the help of *would, might, could, must* and *had to*. It is also conveyed with the simple past or the constructions *to (do)* and *for ... to (do)*.

Era possível que tudo acabasse bem.	*It might all end well.* (*It was possible that all would end well*)
Era provável que chovesse no dia seguinte.	*It might well rain the following day.* (*It was probable that...*)
Tomara que chovesse amanhã.	*I wish it would rain tomorrow.*
Eu esperava que ele viesse naquele dia.	*I hoped that he would come that day.*
Eu duvidava que ele soubesse Português.	*I doubted that he could speak Portuguese.*
Era nosso desejo que eles fizessem boa viagem.	*We hoped that they might have a good journey.*
Nós receávamos que tudo acabasse mal.	*We feared that it might all end up badly.*
Tive muita pena que ela estivesse tão doente.	*I was very sorry to hear that she was so ill.*
Era preciso que ele trabalhasse mais.	*He had to work harder.* (*It was necessary that ...*)
Ele queria que vocês viessem já.	*He would like you to come straight away if possible. (He wanted ...)*
Ele pediu que vocês viessem já.	*He has asked for you to come straight away. (that you would come ...) / whether you could please come straight away.*

How the imperfect subjunctive works

The use of the imperfect subjunctive runs parallel to that of the present subjunctive you learned in Unit 8, but only up to a point.

(A) In sentences that require an imperfect subjunctive **que** often marks the dividing line between the 'main clause' (leading part) and the 'subordinate clause' (guided part). The imperfect subjunctive is used in the latter.

Eu esperava **que** ele **viesse** naquele dia.	*I hoped that he would come that day.*
Ele pediu **que** vocês **falassem** mais baixo.	*He asked for you to speak more quietly. (that you would speak ...)*
Era provável **que** ele **fosse** lá naquele dia.	*He might well go there that day. (It was probable that ...)*
Era importante **que** eu **fosse** à festa.	*I had to go to the party. (It was important ...)*
Tomara **que chovesse** amanhã.	*I wish it would rain tomorrow.*

(B) While the present subjunctive can point to the future, detach itself from a main clause and be used as a wish directed at someone or a 'polite imperative', the imperfect subjunctive distances itself from what is to happen in the future and tends to remain attached to a main clause. The imperfect focuses not only on the past but also on what may be expected not to happen at all.

Tomara **que chovesse** amanhã. *I wish it would rain tomorrow.*
(There may be little hope that will happen)

✱  Connotations of meaning can be explored by opting for the present or the imperfect subjunctive.

— Ele pediu **que** vocês **falem** mais baixo.	*He has asked for you to speak more quietly.*
— Ele pediu **que** vocês **falassem** mais baixo.	*He has asked whether you could please speak more quietly. (that you would speak ...) (a more polite request)*
Tomara **que** eles **telefonem** hoje.	*I hope they (will) phone today. I wish they would phone today. (but they may not)*

85

Tomara **que** eles **telefonassem** hoje.   *I wish they would phone today.*
                                             (but they are most unlikely to)
Eu sinto muito **que** ela **esteja** tão   *I am very sorry to hear that she is so*
doente.   *ill / that she may be that ill.*
Eu sinto muito **que** ela **estivesse**   *I am very sorry to hear that*
tão doente. (*)   *she was so ill.*

(*) Depending on context, this can be a genuine comment or a sarcastic comment of disbelief.

For further information on the imperfect subjunctive see also Units 11 and 19.

Verbs with orthographic changes

(For a chart of root and spelling changes, see Verb Tables, at the end of the book)

Graphic accents

-air and **-uir** verbs take an acute accent (´) on all persons.

s**air** (*to go/come out*): eu saísse, você, ele/ela saísse, nós saíssemos, vocês, eles/elas saíssem
infl**uir** (*to have an influence*): eu influísse, você, ele/ela influísse, nós influíssemos, vocês, eles/elas influíssem

Irregular verbs

Below is a list of the most common irregular cases in the imperfect subjunctive (for a full list of verb forms, see Verb Tables, at the end of the book).

Note that these verbs are irregular in the sense that they reflect their irregular 'vocês, eles/elas' preterite source, but they take the regular imperfect subjunctive endings (though often with a change from -ê- to -é-).

caber, *to fit*
eu, você, ele/ela **coubesse**, nós **coubéssemos**, vocês, eles/elas **coubessem**
crer, *to believe*
eu, você, ele/ela **cresse**, nós **crêssemos**, vocês, eles/elas **cressem**

dar, *to give*
eu, você, ele/ela **desse**, nós **déssemos**, vocês, eles/elas **dessem**
dizer, *to say*
eu, você, ele/ela **dissesse**, nós **disséssemos**, vocês, eles/elas
dissessem
estar, *to be*
eu, você, ele/ela **estivesse**, nós **estivéssemos**, vocês, eles/elas
estivessem
fazer, *to do, to make*
eu, você, ele/ela **fizesse**, nós **fizéssemos**, vocês, eles/elas **fizessem**
haver, *to exist, there to be, to have*
eu, você, ele/ela **houvesse**, nós **houvéssemos**, vocês, eles/elas
houvessem
ir, *to go*
eu, você, ele/ela **fosse**, nós **fôssemos**, vocês, eles/elas **fossem** (*)
ler, *to read*
eu, você, ele/ela **lesse**, nós **lêssemos**, vocês, eles/elas **lessem**
medir, *to measure*
eu, você, ele/ela **medisse**, nós **medíssemos**, vocês, eles/elas
medissem
ouvir, *to hear*
eu, você, ele/ela **ouvisse**, nós **ouvíssemos**, vocês, eles/elas **ouvissem**
pedir, *to ask for*
eu, você, ele/ela **pedisse**, nós **pedíssemos**, vocês, eles/elas **pedissem**
perder, *to lose*
eu, você, ele/ela **perdesse**, nós **perdêssemos**, vocês, eles/elas
perdessem
poder, *can, may, to be able*
eu, você, ele/ela **pudesse**, nós **pudéssemos**, vocês, eles/elas
pudessem
pôr, *to put*
eu, você, ele/ela **pusesse**, nós **puséssemos**, vocês, eles/elas
pusessem
querer, *to want*
eu, você, ele/ela **quisesse**, nós **quiséssemos**, vocês, eles/elas
quisessem
rir, *to laugh*
eu, você, ele/ela **risse**, nós **ríssemos**, vocês, eles/elas **rissem**
saber, *to know*
eu, você, ele/ela **soubesse**, nós **soubéssemos**, vocês, eles/elas
soubessem

87

ser, *to be*
eu, você, ele/ela **fosse**, nós **fôssemos**, vocês, eles/elas **fossem** (*)
ter, *to have*
eu, você, ele/ela **tivesse**, nós **tivéssemos**, vocês, eles/elas **tivessem**
trazer, *to bring*
eu, você, ele/ela **trouxesse**, nós **trouxéssemos**, vocês, eles/elas
trouxessem
valer, *to be worth*
eu, você, ele/ela **valesse**, nós **valêssemos**, vocês, eles/elas **valessem**
ver, *to see*
eu, você, ele/ela **visse**, nós **víssemos**, vocês, eles/elas **vissem**
vir, *to come*
eu, você, ele/ela **viesse**, nós **viéssemos**, vocês, eles/elas **viessem**

(*) Verbs 'ir' and 'ser' share the same forms in the imperfect subjunctive.

In general, compound verbs belonging to the family of any of the above share the same features. E.g, contivesse (**conter**, *to contain*, like **ter**); sorrisse (**sorrir**, *to smile*, like **rir**); supusesse (**supor**, *to suppose, assume*, like **pôr**).

Future Subjunctive

Vocês podem fazer como   You can do as you please.
vocês quiserem.

(From the speaker's point of view, action will materialize or not depending on someone else's decision)

FORM

In parallel with what we saw for the previous tense, the future subjunctive equally derives from the 'vocês, eles/elas' form of the preterite (Unit 5). Simply remove the final **-ram** and add **-r, -rmos, -rem.**

compr**aram**   vend**eram**   part**iram**
   ↓   ↓   ↓
compra   vende   parti
   ↓   ↓   ↓
compr**ar**   vend**er**   part**ir**
etc.   etc.   etc.

88

(when) I buy / sell / leave etc.
(quando) **eu** comp**rar** / ven**der** / part**ir** etc.

subject	1ˢᵗ conj.	2ⁿᵈ conj.	3ʳᵈ conj.
eu, **você, ele/ela**	**-ar**	**-er**	**-ir**
nós	**-armos**	**-ermos**	**-irmos**
vocês, eles/elas	**-arem**	**-erem**	**-irem**

Note that the future subjunctive looks like an infinitive (ending **-ar**, **-er**, **-ir**) in all the singular forms above, i.e., for **eu**, **você**, **ele/ela**.

For other 'you' forms see Unit 3 and 'The Other Second Person'.

USE

The future subjunctive is for a future action or state that will determine the viability or purposefulness of another action or state. In English, *may* + infinitive can be used in some cases, but we are more likely to use the simple present.

Faça como quiser.	*Do as you please. (as you may like to)*
Farei tudo o que puder.	*I will do all I can.*
Se você vier, podemos ir jantar juntos.	*If you come, we can go for dinner together.*
Falarei com ela, quando ela chegar.	*I will talk to her, when she arrives.*
Quando chegar ao semáforo, vire à esquerda.	*When you get to the traffic lights, turn left.*

For further information on the future subjunctive see also Units 11 and 19.

Verbs with orthographic changes

(For a chart of root and spelling changes, see Verb Tables, at the end of the book)

Graphic accents

-air and **-uir** verbs take an acute accent (´) on the *'you, they'* form.

s**air** (*to go/come out*): vocês, eles/elas sa**í**rem
infl**uir** (*to have an influence*): vocês, eles/elas influ**í**rem

89

Irregular verbs

Below is a list of the most common irregular cases in the future subjunctive (for a full list of verb forms, see Verb Tables, at the end of the book).

Note that these verbs are irregular in the sense that they reflect their irregular 'vocês, eles/elas' preterite source, but they take the regular future subjunctive endings.

caber, *to fit*
eu, você, ele/ela **couber**, nós **coubermos**, vocês, eles/elas **couberem**
crer, *to believe*
eu, você, ele/ela **crer**, nós **crermos**, vocês, eles/elas **crerem**
dar, *to give*
eu, você, ele/ela **der**, nós **dermos**, vocês, eles/elas **derem**
dizer, *to say*
eu, você, ele/ela **disser**, nós **dissermos**, vocês, eles/elas **disserem**
estar, *to be*
eu, você, ele/ela **estiver**, nós **estivermos**, vocês, eles/elas **estiverem**
fazer, *to do, to make*
eu, você, ele/ela **fizer**, nós **fizermos**, vocês, eles/elas **fizerem**
haver, *to exist, there to be, to have*
eu, você, ele/ela **houver**, nós **houvermos**, vocês, eles/elas **houverem**
ir, *to go*
eu, você, ele/ela **for**, nós **formos**, vocês, eles/elas **forem** (*)
ler, *to read*
eu, você, ele/ela **ler**, nós **lermos**, vocês, eles/elas **lerem**
medir, *to measure*
eu, você, ele/ela **medir**, nós **medirmos**, vocês, eles/elas **medirem**
ouvir, *to hear*
eu, você, ele/ela **ouvir**, nós **ouvirmos**, vocês, eles/elas **ouvirem**
pedir, *to ask for*
eu, você, ele/ela **pedir**, nós **pedirmos**, vocês, eles/elas **pedirem**
perder, *to lose*
eu, você, ele/ela **perder**, nós **perdermos**, vocês, eles/elas **perderem**
poder, *can, may, to be able*
eu, você, ele/ela **puder**, nós **pudermos**, vocês, eles/elas **puderem**
pôr, *to put*
eu, você, ele/ela **puser**, nós **pusermos**, vocês, eles/elas **puserem**
querer, *to want*
eu, você, ele/ela **quiser**, nós **quisermos**, vocês, eles/elas **quiserem**

rir, *to laugh*
eu, você, ele/ela **rir**, nós **rirmos**, vocês, eles/elas **rirem**
saber, *to know*
eu, você, ele/ela **souber**, nós **soubermos**, vocês, eles/elas **souberem**
ser, *to be*
eu, você, ele/ela **for**, nós **formos**, vocês, eles/elas **forem** (*)
ter, *to have*
eu, você, ele/ela **tiver**, nós **tivermos**, vocês, eles/elas **tiverem**
trazer, *to bring*
eu, você, ele/ela **trouxer**, nós **trouxermos**, vocês, eles/elas **trouxerem**
valer, *to be worth*
eu, você, ele/ela **valer**, nós **valermos**, vocês, eles/elas **valerem**
ver, *to see*
eu, você, ele/ela **vir**, nós **virmos**, vocês, eles/elas **virem**
vir, *to come*
eu, você, ele/ela **vier**, nós **viermos**, vocês, eles/elas **vierem**

(*) Verbs 'ir' and 'ser' share the same forms in the future subjunctive.

In general, compound verbs belonging to the family of any of the above share the same features. E.g., conter (**conter**, *to contain*, like **ter**); sorrir (**sorrir**, *to smile*, like **rir**); supuser (**supor**, *to suppose, assume*, like **pôr**).

Please

The future subjunctive is used for a very elegant way of saying 'please': **se fizer favor**, *if you please*.

request / invitation + **se fizer favor**

Entre, se fizer favor.   *Could you please come in.*
                                (if you please)
Sente-se, se fizer favor.   *Could you please take a seat.*
Saiam agora, se fizerem favor. *Could you please leave now.*

In this format you are placing your request, or invitation, in the command forms you learned in Unit 7 (which are 'borrowed' from the present subjunctive, as you learned in Unit 8).

Then you add the 'please' expression – **se fizer favor**, *if you please* – as a proviso to the listener's compliance with your 'command'.

91

In relaxed colloquial speech, this expression is often simplified to **se faz favor**, *if you please,* i.e., the ordinary present.

Entre, se faz favor.　　　　　　*Could you please come in.*
　　　　　　　　　　　　　　　(if you please)
Sente-se, se faz favor.　　　　　*Could you please take a seat.*
Saiam agora, se fazem favor.　　 *Could you please leave now.*

Exercises

10.1

Work out the verb forms for the sentences and enter them onto the grid. If you get them all correct, the letters across the middle spell out the Portuguese word for holidays, vacation. Nr. 1 and Nr. 4 have been done for you.

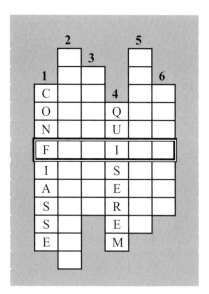

1 Seria bom que você ___confiasse___ mais em mim. (**confiar**)
　It would be nice if you trusted me more. (I wish you would)
2 Ele esperava que nós _____ lá hoje. (**estar**)
　He was expecting us to be there today.
3 Faremos tudo quanto _____. (**poder**)
　We will do all we can.

4 Façam como ___quiserem___. (**querer**)
Do as you please.
5 Seria melhor que vocês _____ o carro. (**comprar**)
It would be better if you bought the car.
6 Eu gostaria que eles _____ amanhã. (**vir**)
I would like them to come tomorrow. or
I would be very happy if they came tomorrow.

10.2

Complete the (b) sentences making them more courteous than the (a) sentences. The first one has been done for you.

1 **(a)** Eu quero que você me ajude.
I want you to help me.
(b) Eu queria que você me ajudasse.
I would like you to help me if you could.

2 **(a)** Eu quero que você me faça um favor.
I want you to do me a favour.
(b) Eu queria que …

3 **(a)** É melhor que você saia agora.
It will be better if you leave now.
(b) Seria melhor que …

4 **(a)** Ele pede que vocês venham já.
He is asking for you to come straight away.
(b) Ele pediu que …

Verb Tenses with *'when'*, *'if'* and Other Cases

In sentences like

> I usually go by car, when I am going shopping.
> I shall go for a walk, if the rain stops.

there are two distinct parts, a leading section, or 'main clause' – *I usually go by car / I shall go for a walk* – and a secondary section, or 'subordinate clause' – *when I am going shopping / if the rain stops.*

Subordinate clauses qualify or modify a main clause. In the examples above they tell us when the main action happens (*when...*) or the condition under which it will happen (*if...*).

The importance of the subordinate clause can be highlighted by placing it before the main clause.

> When I am going shopping, I usually go by car.
> If the rain stops, I shall go for a walk.

Either following or preceding the main clause, the subordinate clause is introduced by a connective, known as 'conjunction', which expresses a relation of time (e.g., *when*), circumstance (e.g., *if*), or other.

The present unit focuses on some verb tenses you need for main and subordinate clauses, particularly where conjunctions **quando** (*when*) and **se** (*if, whether*) are used. Other cases are also explained.

'When' sentences

Sentences with 'when' relate mainly to factual statements but can also be used for hypothesis making.

Present

For a habitual or repeated action or state

main clause	subordinate clause
simple present present continuous	simple present present continuous present of **ir** + infinitive (= colloquial future)

94

Quando o tempo está bom, passo o dia inteiro na praia.
When the weather is fine, I spend the whole day on the beach.
Às vezes eu estou tomando banho, **quando** a campainha da porta toca.
Às vezes eu estou a tomar banho, **quando** a campainha da porta toca. (Eur.)
Sometimes I am having a bath, when the door bell rings.
Às vezes a campainha da porta toca **quando** eu estou tomando banho.
Às vezes a campainha da porta toca **quando** eu estou a tomar banho. (Eur.)
Sometimes the door bell rings when I am having a bath.
Geralmente vou de carro **quando** vou fazer compras.
I usually go by car when I am going shopping.

Past

For a single event (action or state) in the past or a series of past events viewed as a whole

main clause	subordinate clause
preterite	preterite
preterite of **ir** + infinitive	preterite of **ir** + infinitive

Encontrei a Rita **quando** fui ao banco.
I met Rita when I went to the bank.
Quando fui fazer compras, fui de carro.
When I went shopping, I went by car.
Quando morei em Brasília, trabalhei numa escola.
When I lived in Brasília, I worked in a school.
Quando fui para a praia, fui nadar.
When I went to the beach, I went swimming.

For a habitual, repeated or ongoing past event (action or state), in the latter case **enquanto** (*while*) being often used

main clause	subordinate clause
imperfect	imperfect
imperfect continuous	imperfect continuous
imperfect of **ir** or **costumar**	imperfect of **ir** or **costumar**
+ infinitive	+ infinitive

Quando eu era criança, passava as férias com os meus avós.
When I was a child, I used to spend the holidays with my grandparents.
Nós íamos nadar todos os dias, **quando** morávamos perto da praia.
We used to go swimming every day, when we lived near the beach.

95

Quando eu costumava fazer compras ao sábado para toda a semana, ia sempre de carro.
When I used to do the shopping for the whole week on the Saturday, I would always go by car.
Enquanto ele entretinha as crianças, ela arrumava o quarto.
While he was keeping the children occupied, she was tidying up the room.
Enquanto ele estava entretendo as crianças, ela estava arrumando o quarto.
Enquanto ele estava a entreter as crianças, ela estava a arrumar o quarto. (Eur.)
While he was keeping the children occupied, she was tidying up the room.

For something that was going on ('background' information) at a time when something else happened ('foreground' information), when **enquanto** (*while*) can be used in some cases

main clause	subordinate clause
imperfect	preterite
imperfect continuous	imperfect
preterite	preterite of **ir** + infinitive

Ele tinha trinta e cinco anos **quando** casou.
He was thirty five years old when he got married.
Quando entrei na sala, você estava telefonando.
Quando entrei na sala, você estava a telefonar. (Eur.)
When I entered the room, you were on the phone. (phoning)
Vocês ainda dormiam **quando** eu fui almoçar no restaurante.
You were still asleep (sleeping) when I went out for lunch.
Enquanto ela estava no hospital, eles tomaram conta das crianças.
While she was in hospital, they looked after the children.

Future

For a single event (action or state) in the future or a series of future events viewed as a whole, in some cases **enquanto** (*while*) being applicable

main clause	subordinate clause
future	future subjunctive
simple present	future subjunctive of **ir** + infinitive
colloquial future	
emphatic future	

Quando eu for fazer compras, irei de carro.
When I go shopping, I shall go by car.

Nós vamos lá **quando** tivermos tempo.
We will go there when we have time.
Quando eu for acampar, vou calçar botas de borracha.
When I go camping, I am going to wear wellingtons.
Quando nós morarmos em Lisboa, havemos de ir à praia todos os fins de semana.
When we live in Lisbon, we will go to the beach every weekend.
Enquanto ganharmos bem, poderemos viajar muitas vezes no estrangeiro.
While we earn well, we shall be able to travel abroad often.

'Commands'

For a suggestion, order, request or advice, expressed in relation to a specific event, **enquanto** (*while*) being used in some cases

main clause	subordinate clause
command form	future subjunctive future subjunctive of **ir** + infinitive

Pague **quando** puder.
Pay when you can.
Vá de carro **quando** for fazer compras.
Go by car when you go shopping.
Por favor desligue o computador **quando** acabar.
Please turn off the computer when you finish. (have finished)
Quando saírem, fechem a porta.
When you leave, close the door.
Deixem as janelas abertas **enquanto** estiverem em casa.
Leave the windows open while you are in.
Tome cuidado **quando** sair.
Take care when you go out.

Hypothetical statements

For something expressed as a basis for reasoning but without the assumption of it being true, **enquanto** (*while*) also being used in some cases

main clause	subordinate clause
conditional imperfect (*)	imperfect subjunctive imperfect subjunctive of **ir** + infinitive

(*) Rather than temporality, the imperfect in this case expresses something remote from happening.

97

Eu faria as compras **quando** tivesse alguém para tomar conta das crianças.
I would go shopping when I had someone to look after the children.
Eles alugariam um carro **quando** fossem fazer férias.
They would hire a car when they were going on holiday.
Nós combinaríamos a reunião **quando** todos estivessem aqui.
We would arrange the meeting when every one was here.
Eles descansariam / descansavam **enquanto** pudessem. (see Unit 9)
They would rest while they could.

'If' sentences

Sentences with 'if', or 'whether', are usually associated with the expression of uncertainty, probability, possibility, wishes, emotions, necessity, and hypothetical statements.

Present

For a habitual or repeated action or state

main clause	subordinate clause
simple present	simple present
	present of **ir** + infinitive
	(= colloquial future)

Se faz sol, vou à praia, **se** chove, fico em casa.
If it is sunny, I go to the beach, if it rains, I stay at home.
Geralmente vou de carro **se** vou fazer compras.
I usually go by car if I am going shopping.
Se bebo muito café, durmo mal.
If I drink too much coffee, I don't get a good sleep.

Past

For a single event (action or state) in the past or a series of past events viewed as a whole

main clause	subordinate clause
simple present	preterite
preterite	preterite of **ir** + infinitive
preterite of **ir** + infinitive	

Se eles trabalharam aqui durante um mês é coisa que eu não sei.
Whether they worked here for a month is something I don't know.
Se ela telefonou, com certeza que deixou recado.
If she phoned, surely she has left a message.
Se ela foi fazer compras, provavelmente foi de carro.
If she went shopping, she probably went by car.
Com certeza que ele foi nadar se foi para a piscina.
He certainly went for a swim if he went to the swimming pool.

Future

For a single event (action or state) in the future or a series of future events viewed as a whole

main clause	subordinate clause
future	future subjunctive
simple present	future subjunctive of **ir** + infinitive
colloquial future	
emphatic future	

Eu vou com vocês **se** puder.
I will go with you if I can.
Será melhor **se** você atravessar a rua aqui.
It will be better if you cross the road here.
Se for possível, nós havemos de acabar isto hoje.
If at all possible, we will finish this today.
Eu vou fazer compras **se** ela tomar conta das crianças.
I am going shopping if she looks after the children.
Se eu for fazer compras, você tem que ficar a tomar conta das crianças.
If I am going shopping, you will have to stay and look after the children.

'Commands'

For a suggestion, order, request or advice, expressed in relation to a specific event or condition

main clause	subordinate clause
command form	future subjunctive
	future subjunctive of **ir** + infinitive

99

Venham **se** puderem.
Come along if you can.
Vá de carro **se** for fazer compras.
Go by car if you are going shopping.
Se saírem, fechem a porta.
If you go out, close the door.
Toquem a campainha **se** a porta estiver fechada.
Ring the bell if the door is shut.
Tomem cuidado **se** saírem à noite.
Take care if you go out at night.

✦ Hypothetical statements

For something that may be contrary-to-fact, that is to say, supposed but not necessarily real or true

main clause	subordinate clause
conditional	imperfect subjunctive
imperfect (*)	imperfect subjunctive of ir + infinitive

— Seria mais fácil para todos, **se** vocês viessem de carro.
It would be easier for every one if you came by car.
— Eu daria a volta ao mundo **se** tivesse muito dinheiro.
I would travel around the world if I had a lot of money.
— Eu iria de carro **se fosse** fazer compras.
I would go by car if I were going shopping.
— Eu faria isso **se pudes**se sair.
I would do that if I could go out.
— Nós íamos à festa **se** eles nos convidassem. (see Unit 9)
We would go to the party if they invited us.
— **Se** eu fosse milionário, comprava um palácio. — *imperfect*
If I were a millionaire, I would buy a palace.

(*) Rather than temporality, the imperfect in this case expresses something remote from happening.

✦ Sentences with other conjunctions

As explained on the previous pages, some sentences take the imperfect subjunctive and some the future subjunctive after 'quando' (or 'enquanto') and 'se'. Below there is an alphabetical list of other conjunctions that also call for a subjunctive tense. You are likely to see some more often than others.

a fim de que *in order that*	**contanto que** *provided that*
a menos que *unless*	**depois que** *after*
a não ser que *unless*	**desde que** *since, provided that*
ainda que *even if*	**embora** *though, although*
antes que *before*	**logo que** *as soon as*
assim que *as soon as*	**mesmo que** *even if*
até que *until*	**nem que** *even if*
caso *in case*	**para que** *so that*
como *as*	**por mais que** *however much*
conforme *depending on*	**sempre que** *whenever*

Depending on the conjunction and the sentence as a whole, the subordinate clause can take a present, future or imperfect subjunctive, as shown in the right-hand column of the table below. For the main clause, the left-hand column shows a variety of options.

main clause	subordinate clause
simple present	
present continuous	present subjunctive
present perfect	present subjunctive of **ir** + infinitive
future	future subjunctive
colloquial future	future subjunctive of **ir** + infinitive
emphatic future	
commands	
preterite	imperfect subjunctive
imperfect	imperfect subjunctive of **ir** + infinitive
imperfect continuous	
conditional	

Faça isso **como** puder.
Do that as you can.
Vamos para casa **antes que** chova.
Let's go home before it rains.
Telefonarei **assim que** chegar.
I will phone you as soon as I arrive.
Venha comigo **sempre que** for fazer compras.
Come with me whenever you go shopping.
Ficaremos sem saber as notícias **a não ser que** liguemos a TV.
We shall not know the news unless we switch on the TV.

101

Nós havemos de fazer tudo isto **nem que** tenhamos que trabalhar a noite toda.
We will do everything even if we have to work all night.
Vocês podem ficar uns dias no nosso apartamento **desde que** deixem tudo arrumado.
You may stay in our apartment for a few days provided that you leave everything tidy.
Embora eles fossem irmãos, eram muito diferentes.
Although they were brothers, they were very different.
Tivemos uma reunião **para que** todos soubessem o que aconteceu.
We had a meeting so that every one knew what happened.
Nós compraríamos a casa **contanto que** os vendedores baixassem o preço.
We would buy the house provided the sellers dropped the price.

Note:

Conjunction **porque**, *because*, does not usually require a subjunctive, and the same tense is sometimes used in both the main and the subordinate clauses.

Tenho muitos livros **porque** gosto de ler.
I have lots of books because I enjoy reading.
Vou comprar um carro maior **porque** vou ter um emprego melhor.
I am going to buy a bigger car because I am going to have a better job.
Hoje vou de carro **porque** vou fazer compras.
Today I am going by car because I am going shopping.
Bebi a água toda **porque** estava com muita sede.
I have drunk all the water because I was very thirsty.

Sentences with relative pronouns

Look at these two sentences:

(a) That one is the student who speaks Portuguese very well.

(b) The book which I bought yesterday is interesting.

In these sentences, *who speaks Portuguese very well* and *which I bought yesterday* are called 'relative clauses' (also known as 'adjective clauses' or 'attributive clauses'). A relative clause may be at the end of the main clause, as is the case in (a) – ... *who speaks Portuguese very well* – or divide the main clause, as in (b) – ... *which I bought yesterday* ....

Relative clauses are introduced by a relative pronoun – *who* and *which* respectively in our examples – and qualify a noun (naming word) – *student* and *book* – which is in the main clause and is called the 'antecedent'.

In Portuguese some relative clauses require a subjunctive tense, as you can see in example 2 in the following two sets of sentences.

(a, 1) Aquele é o aluno que fala Português muito bem.
        That one is the student who speaks Portuguese very well.

(a, 2) O aluno que falar Português melhor ganhará uma bolsa de estudos.
        The student who speaks Portuguese the best will win a scholarship.(Whoever speaks Portuguese the best ...)

(b, 1) O livro que comprei ontem é interessante.
        The book which I bought yesterday is interesting.

(b, 2) Eu quero comprar um livro que seja interessante.
        I want to buy a book that is interesting.

In sentences (a, 1) and (b, 1) the relative clause refers to a known person or thing. In (a, 2) and (b, 2) it refers to a hypothetical person or thing. In the former the student (aluno) and the book (livro) are existing entities. In the latter they are someone or something that may fit certain conditions – be the best (que falar Português melhor) or be interesting (que seja interessante). They may not even exist.

In English we use an ordinary verb form throughout the four sentences – *speaks* (a 1 and 2) and *is* in (b 1 and 2). In Portuguese a distinction is made. An ordinary (or 'indicative') verb form is applicable where the antecedent is a known person or thing – (a, 1) and (b, 1) – but a subjunctive verb form is the choice where the antecedent is a hypothetical person or thing – (a, 2) and (b, 2). In the examples above, the tenses used are the future subjunctive (falar) and the present subjunctive (seja).

Note 1: English often omits the relative pronoun but Portuguese does not.

*The book **(which / that)** I bought...* O livro **que** eu comprei...

Note 2: Portuguese relative pronoun **que** can translate both 'who' and 'which'. Another relative pronoun is **quem** which can translate a number of meanings: s/he who, anyone who, the one who, whoever.

These chairs are for whoever is tired.
Estas cadeiras são para **quem** esteja cansado.

103

✦ Subjunctive tenses in relative clauses

Use this table as a guideline for the right choice.

MAIN CLAUSE	RELATIVE CLAUSE
the action / state refers to the past	imperfect subjunctive
the action / state refers to the present	present subjunctive
the action / state refers to the future	future subjunctive

Aquelas cadeiras eram para quem estivesse cansado. [past]
Those chairs were for anyone who was tired.
(... whoever might have been tired)

Estas cadeiras são para quem esteja cansado.   [present]
These chairs are for anyone who is tired.
(... whoever is / may be tired (now))

Estas cadeiras são (*) para quem estiver cansado. [future]
These chairs are for anyone who is tired.
(... whoever may get tired)

Estas cadeiras serão para quem estiver cansado.   [future]
These chairs will be for anyone who is tired.
(... whoever may get tired)

(*) present (são) covering the future.

Exercises
11.1
In the box below, for each sentence started on the left there is a matching ending on the right; but they are not in the right order. Can you pair them up and write correct sentences for the following English translations.

1 *When I go to Brasília, I usually take up accommodation at that hotel.*
2 *When I went to Rio de Janeiro, I stayed at a hotel in Copacabana.*
3 *When I lived in Lisbon, I used to go to the beach every weekend.*
4 *When I arrived, you were still sleeping.*
5 *We are going camping with you when we can.* future
6 *If they come along, the party will be more fun.*
7 *If I had a lot of money, I would travel around the world.*
8 *Although it is hard work, they are going to carry on.*

 present

G	1 Quando eu vou a Brasília	**(a)** quando pudermos
d	2 Quando eu fui ao Rio de Janeiro	**(b)** eles vão continuar
f	3 Quando eu morava em Lisboa	**(c)** iria dar a volta ao mundo
h	4 Quando eu cheguei	**(d)** fiquei num hotel em Copacabana
a	5 Nós vamos acampar com vocês	**(e)** a festa ficará mais animada
e	6 Se eles vierem	**(f)** ia à praia todos os fins de semana
c	7 Se eu tivesse muito dinheiro	**(g)** geralmente fico hospedada nesse hotel
x	8 Embora o trabalho seja difícil *present*	**(h)** você ainda estava dormindo /a dormir (Eur.)

11.2

Enter the correct verb form in the sentences below and solve the mini puzzle.

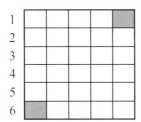

1   Quem quer que ___seja___.
    Be it who it may.   (present subjunctive of **ser**) seja ?

2   O patrão quer uma pessoa que ___saiba___ Inglês.
    The boss wants someone who can speak English.
                                           (present subjunctive of **saber**) saiba .

3   Eu farei tudo o que ___puder___.
    I will do all I can.   (future subjunctive of **poder**)

4   Eu queria alguém que ___fosse___ capaz de fazer isso.
    I wanted someone who would be able to do that.
                                           (imperfect subjunctive of **ser**)

5, 6   ___venha___ o que ___vier___.
    Happen what may. (come what may)
    venha   (present and future subjunctive of **vir**)
                                           vier

    present sub   future sub

105

Verbs Working Together

You can indicate when something happens by simply changing the verb ending. There are different endings for the past, present and future, for example, ele chega, *he arrives*, ele chegou, *he arrived*. A set of verb forms like these (where you just change the ending) is known as a 'simple tense'.

You have learned the following Portuguese simple tenses: present (Unit 2); preterite (Unit 5); imperfect (Unit 5); future (Unit 6); conditional (Unit 9); present subjunctive (Unit 8); imperfect subjunctive (Unit 10); future subjunctive (Unit 10). As we have seen, verb tenses can also express meanings other than time. This is the case with the subjunctive which is used to denote uncertainty, probability, possibility, wishes and emotions, someone's request, necessity or imperative need.

Other verb tenses are formed with an auxiliary (helping) verb combined with the main verb. The auxiliary and the main verb share the same subject (I, you, s/he, it…).

este mês tem sido muito frio	*this has been a very cold month*
	(*it has been…*)
auxiliary: tem (verb 'ter')	*has* (verb *'to have'*)
main verb: sido (verb 'ser')	*been* (verb *'to be'*)

Auxiliaries vary; and so does the way they combine with the main verb. In this unit you will learn a variety of ways in which some verbs can work together to convey different meanings.

Perfect (or compound) tenses

Perfect, or compound, tenses are made up by a combination of the auxiliary verb **ter** (to have) and the past participle of the main verb.

In Unit 4 you learned the present perfect, which consists of the present tense of auxiliary **ter** and the past participle of the main verb.

ele tem estado doente	*he has been ill*
ele tem comprado	*he has been buying*

For other perfect tenses, use the simple tenses of the verb **ter**, following the same model as for the present perfect.

106

◆ present perfect   present of 'ter'
  ele <u>tem</u> comprado
  he ~~has been buying~~
◆ pluperfect (past perfect)   imperfect of 'ter'
  ele <u>tinha</u> comprado
  ~~he had bought~~
◆ future perfect   future of 'ter'
  ele terá comprado
  he will have bought
◆ conditional perfect   conditional of 'ter'
  ele teria comprado
  he would have bought
◆ present perfect subjunctive   present subjunctive of 'ter'
  (que) ele tenha comprado
  (that) he has bought /
  (that) he may have bought
◆ pluperfect subjunctive   imperfect subjunctive of 'ter'
  (se) ele tivesse comprado
  (if) he had bought
◆ future perfect subjunctive   future subjunctive of 'ter'
  (quando) ele tiver comprado
  (when / if) he has bought

Há semanas que eu **tenho praticado** Inglês todos os dias.
For weeks I have been practising English every day.
Parecia que nada **tinha acontecido**.
It looked like nothing had happened.
O concerto já **tinha começado** quando eles chegaram.
The concert had started when they arrived.
Amanhã, a esta hora, eles já **terão embarcado** num cruzeiro de dois meses.
By this time tomorrow they will have boarded the ship on a two-month cruise.
Se eu soubesse, **teria vindo** mais cedo.
If I knew, I would have come earlier.
Espero que todos **tenham entendido** o que ele disse.
I hope that everyone has understood what he said. (may have…)
Se eles **tivessem convidado** mais gente, a festa estaria mais animada.
If they had invited more people, the party would be more fun.
Se eles **tiverem enchido** o tanque, terão combustível suficiente para a viagem toda.
If they have filled the tank, then they will have enough fuel for the whole journey.

Note:

Particularly in old written texts, you may also come across the verb **haver** (equally meaning 'to have') used as the auxiliary for perfect and pluperfect tenses; but, in general, this is no longer in common usage.

ele há comprado (very limited use) = ele tem comprado
he has been buying
se ele houvesse comprado (very limited use) = ele tivesse comprado
if he had bought

The Simple Pluperfect

There is another pluperfect tense, known as 'simple' or 'synthetic' pluperfect. As the name suggests, this is a simple tense, that is to say, it consists of just one word with changed endings.

For **-ar** verbs, endings **-ara, -áramos, -aram**
comprar (*to buy*):
eu, você, ele/ela compr**ara**, nós compr**áramos**, vocês, eles/elas compr**aram**

For **-er** verbs, endings **-era, -êramos, -eram**
vender (*to sell*):
eu, você, ele/ela vend**era**, nós vend**êramos**, vocês, eles/elas vend**eram**

For **-ir** verbs, endings **-ira, -íramos, -iram**
partir (*to leave*):
eu, você, ele/ela part**ira**, nós part**íramos**, vocês, eles/elas part**iram**

Graphic accent

-air and **-uir** verbs have an acute accent (´) on all persons.

sair (*to go/come out*): eu saíra, você, ele/ela saíra, nós saíramos,
                   vocês, eles/elas saíram

influir (*to have an influence*): eu influíra, você, ele/ela influíra,
                   nós influíramos, vocês, eles/elas influíram

The endings for the Simple Pluperfect are shown in the Verb Tables, at the end of the book.

ele comprara = ele tinha comprado
he had bought

A minha avó já **morrera** quando eu nasci.
=
A minha avó já **tinha morrido** quando eu nasci.
My grandmother was dead (had died) when I was born.

The simple pluperfect can be found in written texts but colloquially it has great competition from the compound pluperfect (past perfect) we saw on page 107. This said, it is often used in a number of idiomatic expressions which originate mainly from the verbs **tomar, dar** and **poder.**

Tomara que chova amanhã.	*I hope it rains tomorrow.*
Tomara que tivesse chovido ontem.	*If only it had rained yesterday.*
Quem me **dera** que ele venha amanhã.	*I hope he will come tomorrow.*
Quem me **dera** que ele tivesse vindo ontem.	*If only he had come yesterday.*
Quem nos **dera** que ele venha amanhã.	*We hope he will come tomorrow.*
Pudera!	*Just imagine! / No wonder!*

Learning aid:
(a) The pluperfect tense (compound or simple) is used to refer to an action or state that <u>had</u> occurred before something else happened in the past.
(b) The future perfect and the future perfect subjunctive express a future action or state expected to occur before something else in the future.
(c) The conditional perfect, the present perfect and the pluperfect subjunctive are all tenses used for supposition and hypothesis making.

Continuous (or progressive) tenses

A continuous, or progressive, tense is made up by a combination of the auxiliary verb **estar** (to be) plus the Portuguese **-ndo** form, or gerund (-ing) of the main verb. There is also another formation, in European Portuguese, in which the gerund is replaced with preposition **a** and the infinitive of the main verb.

Ele está comprando/   *He is buying*
Ele está a comprar (Eur.)

You have learned the two most frequently used progressive tenses in the Portuguese language, the present continuous (Unit 4) and the imperfect continuous (Unit 5). Other progressive tenses are not so frequently used but

109

they exist and follow the same model as the present and imperfect continuous.

♦ present continuous   present of 'estar'
   ele está comprando / a comprar (Eur.)
   he is buying
♦ imperfect continuous   imperfect of 'estar'
   ele estava comprando / a comprar (Eur.)
   he was buying
♦ preterite continuous   preterite of 'estar'
   ele esteve comprando / a comprar (Eur.)
   he was buying
♦ future continuous   future of 'estar'
   ele estará comprando / a comprar (Eur.)
   he will be buying
♦ conditional continuous   conditional of 'estar'
   ele estaria comprando / a comprar (Eur.)
   he would be buying
♦ present subjunctive continuous   present subjunctive of 'estar'
   (que) ele esteja comprando /
       a comprar (Eur.)
   (that) he will / may be buying
♦ imperfect subjunctive continuous   imperfect subjunctive of 'estar'
   (se) ele estivesse comprando /
       a comprar (Eur.)
   (if) he were buying
♦ future subjunctive continuous   future subjunctive of 'estar'
   (quando) ele estiver comprando /
       a comprar (Eur.)
   (when) he is buying (in the future)

Vocês **estarão viajando** quando eu acabar este trabalho.
Vocês **estarão a viajar** quando eu acabar este trabalho. (Eur.)
You will be travelling by the time I finish this work.
Eu ficaria muito feliz se ele **estivesse estudando** quando eu chegar.
Eu ficaria muito feliz se ele **estivesse a estudar** quando eu chegar. (Eur.)
I would be very happy if he were studying when I arrive.
... to see him studying when I arrive.

Other auxiliaries

Other auxiliaries play a role in the formation of continuous tenses. They are ordinary verbs that lose their normal meaning when acting as an auxiliary.

- **andar** (to walk, go)

Verb **andar** is used to convey the idea of continuity and progression over a period of time in the present, as opposed to something happening specifically at the time of speaking. Verb **estar** encompasses both meanings.

(a) You want to express something that is happening now, at the very moment you are speaking. Then use 'estar'.

Ele **está escrevendo** uma carta. *He is writing a letter.* (at this moment)
Ele **está a escrever** uma carta. (Eur.)

(b) You want to express something that is happening over a period of time. Then use 'andar' or 'estar'.

Ele **anda escrevendo** um livro. *He is writing a book.* (currently)
Ele **anda a escrever** um livro. (Eur.)

Note:
This meaning can also be expressed by using the present perfect (see Unit 4 and earlier in this unit).

Ele **anda trabalhando** muito. *or* Ele **tem trabalhado** muito.
Ele **anda a trabalhar** muito. (Eur.)
He has been working hard.

- **ir** (to go) and **vir** (to come)

Verbs **ir** and **vir** emphasize effort or incremental development of an action or state of being; and can suggest sustained effort.

In this case use the gerund, that is, the Portuguese **-ndo** form (-ing).

Já **vai amanhecendo**.   *Daylight is breaking.* (dawn)
Ela **vai indo** um pouco melhor. *She is getting a little better.*
                                   (after an illness)
Eu **venho fazendo** progressos.   *I am making progress.*
                                   (in my studies)
Ele **vai piorando** cada vez mais. *He is getting worse and worse.*
                                    (deteriorating health)

111

| Eu **venho procurando** fazer | *I keep trying to do my best.* |
| o possível. | (sustained effort) |

Note:
In continuous tenses with auxiliary **ir** or **vir**, and sometimes also **andar**, European Portuguese uses only the gerund (not 'a' + infinitive) – Já **vai amanhecendo**. *Daylight is breaking.* – as in Latin American Portuguese.

Periphrastic tenses

A periphrastic tense is a construction of auxiliary plus main verb instead of just a simple tense inflection. This is the case with the 'colloquial future' you learned in Unit 6, which is an alternative to the future tense you also learned in Unit 6.

present of **ir** + infinitive of main verb
eu vou comprar (*I am going to buy*)   instead of

future tense
eu comprarei (*I shall buy*)

The imperfect continuous you learned in Unit 5 is another periphrastic construction. It alternates with a simple tense, the imperfect, equally in Unit 5.

imperfect of **estar** + gerund of main verb or **a** + infinitive of main verb (Eur.)

eu estava comprando (*I was buying*)
eu estava a comprar (Eur.)   instead of

imperfect

eu comprava (*I was buying*)

(Though only to a point, the present continuous you learned in Unit 4 also alternates with the present tense you learned in Unit 2)

Nós **estudaremos** mais no ano que vem.
We shall study harder this coming year.
Nós **vamos estudar** mais no ano que vem.
We are going to study harder this coming year.

Eu **morava** lá nessa época.
I lived / was living there in those days.
Eu **estava morando** lá nessa época.
Eu **estava a morar** lá nessa época. (Eur.)
I was living there in those days.

Modal verbs

A modal auxiliary communicates attitude, intention, or manner, thus affecting the meaning of the verb that follows it.

Compare these two sentences:

They work hard.
They must work hard.

The relationship between the subject (they) and the main verb (work) has been altered in the second sentence; the modal (must) has brought in the notion of obligation.

In English, we make frequent use of the following modals: can - could, may - might, shall - should, will - would, and must. However, an English modal construction does not necessarily translate into a Portuguese modal construction; and vice-versa.

Also English modals have some special features that differentiate them from ordinary verbs. For example, they have no -s forms and no infinitives (no *to* + verb). Nothing comparable to this happens in Portuguese, where an ordinary verb can both occur as a free standing verb and act as the auxiliary of a modal construction.

We are going to look first at how we can express, in Portuguese, meanings for which we would have used the English modals. Then we shall look into frequently used Portuguese modal constructions and how to express the equivalent meanings in English.

(A) TRANSLATING ENGLISH MODALS

can - could
can (possibility) – **poder**
    *I **can** do that tomorrow when I have more time.*
    Eu **posso** fazer isso amanhã quando tiver mais tempo.
can (ability, knowledge) – **saber**
    *He **can** speak Portuguese very well.*
    Ele **sabe** falar Português muito bem.
can (ability, skills) – **ser capaz de**
    *He **can** do that.*
    Ele **é capaz** de fazer isso.

113

can for **may** (permisssion) – **poder**
You **can** / **may** *speak now.*
Você **pode** falar agora.
can - could (polite request / expressions) – See Units 7 and 9.
could (non-factual, hypothetical) – See Units 10, 11.

may - might
may (permisssion) – See **can** – **could** above.
may - might (non-factual, hypothetical) – See Units 8 – 11.

shall - should
shall (future) – See Unit 6.
shall (commitment) – See Unit 6
shall (wondering: what shall…?) – See Unit 6.
should (duty) – See Unit 6.
should (conditional) – See Unit 9.

will - would
will (future) – See Unit 6.
will (probability) – See Unit 8.
will (volition, promise: I will…) – See Units 2 and 6.
will (order, threat: you will…) – See Unit 6.
will (imperative request: will you…) – See Unit 7.
would (polite request) – See Units 7 – 9.
would (do) (habit, repeated event in the past) – See Unit 5.
would (conditional) – See Unit 9.
would (non-factual, hypothetical) – See Units 9 – 11.

must
must (obligation) – See Unit 6.
must (necessity) – See Unit 8.

(B) TRANSLATING PORTUGUESE MODALS

A Portuguese modal formation will consist of a modal auxiliary and the
infinitive (English *(to) do/be* form) of the main verb. Often a link word
known as 'preposition' (de, por, a) will be used between the auxiliary and
the infinitive of the main verb.

auxiliary + (**de** / **por** / **a**) + infinitive

In some cases the modal auxiliary can be followed by the present participle

114

of the main verb (Portuguese gerund) and no preposition is used.

auxiliary + **-ndo** form

Learning aid:
Note that, unlike English, Portuguese does not use a '-ndo' (*-ing*) form after
a preposition but uses an infinitive instead – Eu comecei **por ler** a carta, *I
started by reading the letter.*

acabar de (+ infinitive) – See Unit 5
Eu **acabei de telefonar** para casa dela.
I have just phoned her home number.
O telephone tocou mal eu **acabei de chegar**.
The phone rang as soon as I had arrived.

acabar por (+ infinitive) *or* **acabar** (+ gerund) – *to end up by (doing / being)*
Eu **acabei por telefonar** para sua casa.
I ended up by phoning your home number.
Ele **acabou por concordar** comigo.
He ended up by agreeing with me.
Ele **acabou concordando** comigo.
He ended up agreeing with me.

chegar a (+ infinitive) – *to come to the point of (doing / being)*
Ele **chegou a desesperar**.
He came / got to the point of despair.(... despairing)
Ela **chegou a chorar**.
She even cried. (came / got to the point of...)
Ele **chegou a ser** primeiro-ministro.
He rose to prime minister.

começar a (+ infinitive) – *to start to (do / be)*
Ele **começou a estudar** ontem.
He started to study yesterday.
Eles **começaram a rir**.
They started laughing. (... to laugh)
Eu **vou começar a fazer** esse trabalho amanhã.
I am going to start doing that work tomorrow.

começar por (+ infinitive) – *to start by (doing / being)*
Ele **começou por ler** o livro.
He started by reading the book.
Eles **começaram por perguntar** o que tinha acontecido.
They started by asking what had happened.

continuar (+ gerund) *or* **continuar a** (+ infinitive) – *to continue (doing / being)*
Ele **continua escrevendo** / **a escrever** artigos para jornais.
He is still writing (continues writing) newspaper articles.
Ele **continua trabalhando** pouco.
He is still not working enough.
Ele **continuou a falar**.
He carried on talking.

costumar (+ infinitive) – *to usually (do / be)*; also see Unit 5
Eu **costumo ler** o jornal regularmente. (= eu **leio**)
I read the newspaper regularly.
Ela **costumava escrever** para ele todos os dias.
She used to write to him every day.

deixar de (+ infinitive) – *to stop (doing / being), cease to (do / be)*
Ele **deixou de jogar** futebol.
He stopped playing soccer. (gave up)
Ela **deixou de trabalhar** para mim.
She no longer works for me.
Embora doente, ele não **deixou de trabalhar**.
In spite of being ill, he did not fail to work.

dever (+ infinitive) – *to be likely to (do / be)*; also see Unit 6
Vocês **devem chegar** bem atrasados hoje.
You are likely to arrive pretty late today.
Ela **deveria ter** uns sessenta anos.
She must have been sixty years old.
Às nove horas **devemos telefonar** para o hospital.
At nine o'clock we must make a phone call to the hospital.
Ela **deveria** / **devia trabalhar** mais. (imperfect for conditional, Unit 9)
She should work harder. (ought to)
Você **deveria** / **devia ser** enfermeira.
You should be a nurse.

ficar a (+ infinitive) – *to stay (doing)*
Os motoristas **ficaram a buzinar**.
The car drivers wouldn't stop tooting their horns. (continued tooting)
Eu **fiquei a trabalhar** em casa.
I stayed at home working.

haver de (+ infinitive) – See Units 6 and 9 (imperfect for conditional)
Eu **hei de escrever** a carta amanhã.
I will write the letter tomorrow.

116

Nós **havemos de vencer** custe o que custar.
We shall win whatever it takes.
Eu **havia de estudar** mais. (imperfect for conditional)
I should study harder.

parar de (+ infinitive) – *to stop (doing)*
Parem de escrever quando a campainha tocar.
Stop writing when the bell rings.
Ele **parou de falar**. Houve um silêncio prolongado.
He stopped talking. There was a long silence.

poder (+ infinitive) – *can, may (do / be)*
Pode entrar.
You may come in.
Você **pode falar** agora.
You may speak now.
Eu **posso devolver** o livro amanhã.
I can return the book tomorrow.
Cuidado! Aquela telha solta **pode cair** e **ferir** alguém.
Watch out! That loose roof tile may fall down and injure someone.

precisar (+ infinitive) *or* **precisar de** (+ infinitive) – *to need (to) (do / be)*
Eu **preciso fazer** compras hoje.
I need to do some shopping today.
Eu **preciso de acabar** este trabalho ainda hoje.
I still need to finish this work today.
Nós **precisamos ser** gratos pelo que eles fizeram.
We need / ought to be grateful for what they did.

saber (+ infinitive) – *can, to know how (to) (do / be)*
Eu **sei falar** Português.
I can (know how to) speak Portuguese.
Eles **sabem fazer** isso.
They know how to do that.

ter de / que (+ infinitive) – See Unit 6
Nós **temos que sair** pela porta de trás.
We have to leave by the rear door.
Eu **tenho de escrever** esta carta ainda hoje.
I must still write this letter today.
Ele **teve que fazer** essa pergunta. Estava morrendo
/ a morrer (Eur.) de curiosidade.
He had to ask that question. He was dying to know.

117

tornar a (+ infinitive) – *to do / be again, anew*
Ela **tornou a escrever** a carta.
She wrote the letter again. (re-wrote)
Eles **tornaram a entrar.**
They walked in again. (walked back in)

vir a (+ infinitive) – *to become; to come to (do / be)*
Ela **veio a ser** famosa.
She became famous.
Ele **veio a fazer** o trabalho, embora tarde.
He eventually did the work, though late.

voltar a (+ infinitive) – *to do / be again, resume*
Ela **voltou a falar.**
She spoke again.
Ela **voltou a estudar.**
She went back to studying, resumed her studies.

In this unit we have seen different ways in which verbs can work together. We have considered perfect, continuous, periphrastic and modal formations. Some of these categories overlap. However, each one makes its own contribution to conveying different shades of meaning.

Verbs with a preposition

When you open an English-Portuguese dictionary, you may find out that some Portuguese verbs are shown followed by a small particle like **de**, **a** or **por** (literally *of, at/to, by*). This particle, known as 'preposition', links the verb to its next word in the sentence.

Compare the two examples below:
(a) Eu gosto **de** café.   *I like coffee.*
(b) Eu gosto **de** tomar café. *I like having coffee.*

In (a) the word after **de** (o café) is a naming word (noun); in (b) the word after **de** (tomar) is an action word (verb).

Note that the verb (tomar) is in the infinitive while its English translation (having) is in the *-ing* form. The infinitive after a preposition makes good sense in the Portuguese verb system, because in the Portuguese language the infinitive can also play the role of a noun, as we shall see in Unit 13.

This is also the formation you saw in several of the cases listed in section 'Modal verbs (B)' in the present unit.

Ele **deixou de jogar** futebol.   *He stopped playing soccer.* (*gave up*)

Ela **voltou a falar**.   *She spoke again.*

Your dictionary may also show a choice of different prepositions for the same verb. With a change of preposition you can change the meaning, as we saw earlier in this unit.

Eu **acabei de telefonar** para casa dela.   *I have just phoned her home number.*

Eu **acabei por telefonar** para casa dela.   *I ended up by phoning her home number.*

Exercises

12.1 In the sentences below the letters for some verbs (**ter**, **ir**, **vir**, **andar**, **estar**) appear as a code number. Crack the code and re-write the sentences. The letters for numbers 2 and 8 have been entered in the grid.

1	2	3	4	5	6	7	8	9	10	11	12
	H						T				

(A) Verb **ter**

1 Há meses que 8-9-11-2-4 falado Português todos os dias.
   For months I have been speaking Portuguese every day.
2 Nós já 8-10-11-2-1-3-4-5 saído quando vocês telefonaram.
   We had gone out when you phoned. (We were no longer in...)
3 Amanhã, a estas horas, eles já 8-9-12-1-4 partido na viagem de férias.
   By this time tomorrow they will have left on their holiday trip.
4 Espero que vocês 8-9-11-2-1-3 gostado da festa.
   I hope that you have enjoyed the party.
5 Se ele 8-10-6-9-5-5-9 estudado mais, saberia esta matéria muito melhor.
   If he had studied harder, he would know the subject much better.
6 Podemos sair, quando eu 8-10-6-9-12 terminado este trabalho.
   We can go out when I have finished this job.

119

(B) Verbs **ir**, **vir**, **andar**, and **estar**

1 Já 10-1 anoitecendo.
Night was falling. (It was getting dark)
2 Essa máquina 6-1-10 funcionando cada vez pior.
The performance of that machine is getting worse and worse.
(That machine is on its way to breaking down)
3 Eu 6-9-11-2-4 conseguindo melhores resultados cada dia que passa.
I am achieving better and better results each day.
4 Ele 1-11-7-1 aproveitando as férias ao máximo.
Ele 1-11-7-1 a aproveitar as férias ao máximo. (Eur.)
He is making the most of his holidays.
5 Amanhã, às oito horas, 9-5-8-1-12-9-10 trabalhando no escritório.
Amanhã, às oito horas, 9-5-8-1-12-9-10 a trabalhar no escritório. (Eur.)
Tomorrow at 10 o'clock I shall be working at the office.

12. 2 Work out the verb forms for the sentences and solve the puzzle. Nr. 1 across has been done for you.

Across:

1 Nós ___precisamos___ de falar com vocês ainda hoje. (**precisar**)
We still need to talk to you today.
2 Eu _____ por aceitar o convite para a festa. (**acabar**)
I ended up by accepting the invitation to the party.
3 Você _____ embrulhar o presente num papel bonito. (**dever**)
You should wrap up the present in a pretty paper.
4 Nós _____ a detestar isso. (**vir**)
We came to dislike that very strongly.
5 Ele _____ a tocar a campainha da porta. (**voltar**)
He rang the door bell again.

Down:

1 Geralmente eles _____ por tratar dos casos mais difíceis.
                                        (**começar**)
They would usually start by dealing with the more difficult cases.
2 Nós _____ ir buscar o pacote amanhã. (**poder**)
We can go and fetch the parcel tomorrow.
3 Nós _____ falar só uma língua estrangeira. (**saber**)
We can speak one foreign language only.
4 Eles _____ achando que tudo está bem. (**continuar**)
They carry on thinking that all is well.

120

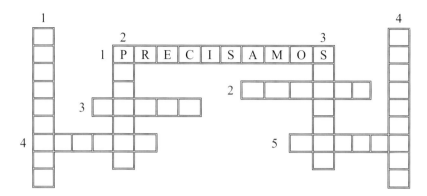

Infinitives and Participles

There are three kinds of verb forms that can be set apart as a group in its own right. They are the following:

the infinitive
to park

the present participle / gerund (*-ing* form)
no one was parking
no parking

the past participle
they have not parked

Although the situation is not exactly the same in English as in Portuguese, two distinct features make these verbal words a separate group. Generally speaking, they are 'non-finite' and they may be 'nominal'.

(A) Non-finite forms

The infinitive, the present participle and the past participle are said to be 'non-finite' forms, because they do not take endings for time (present / past / future), person (I, you, etc.) and other aspects expressed in verb tenses.

infinitive	present participle	past participle
comprar	comprando	comprado
to buy	*buying*	*bought*

This said, the Portuguese language has a second infinitive, a 'personal' infinitive which can be conjugated for I, you, etc., as we shall see in Unit 14.

 (B) Nominal forms

The verb 'nominal' forms are those that can be used as 'nouns', i.e., naming words. Some can also be used as 'adjectives', i.e., describing words.

In English, this is the case chiefly with the *-ing* form and the past participle.

-ing form: no smoking (noun); smoking is bad for you (noun); this is an interesting book (adjective)

past participle: the deceased (noun); she is tired (adjective)

In Portuguese, the infinitive is frequently used as a noun.

fumar pode matar *smoking can kill*
caminhar é bom para a saúde *walking is good for your health*

The Portuguese past participle is often used as an adjective and sometimes also as a noun.

ele está **cansado** *he is tired* (adjective)
o **morto** *the dead person, deceased* (noun)

Infinitive

You were introduced to the Portuguese infinitive in Unit 1. There it is explained that the infinitive is the verb in its basic form, before being manipulated with endings for person (*I walk, he walks*), time (*he walks, he walked*), and other meanings, such as presenting an action or state as a fact or as a supposition.

-ar verbs	**-er verbs**	**-ir verbs**	**-ôr / -or verbs**
(first conjugation)	(second conjugation)	(third conjugation)	(a small extra set)
comprar	vender	partir	pôr

You may wonder why verb **pôr**, *to put*, and its compounds (e.g., com**por**, *to organize*, im**por**, *to impose*) constitute an extra set of verbs in addition to the three conjugations. This is so because modern Portuguese **pôr** is a contracted form of old Portuguese verb **poer**. As a result of this evolution (poer → pôr) the verb no longer ends in -er and, therefore, does not fit in the second conjugation group.

****

Unit 1 of this book gives you an introduction to the infinitive. Now we are going to look into it again, in more detail.

Similarly to what happens in English, Portuguese verbs have both a simple infinitive (comprar, *to buy*) and a perfect, or compound, infinitive (ter comprado, *to have bought*). The latter is formed by combining the auxiliary

123

verb **ter** (to have), in the infinitive, and the past participle of the main verb.

infinitive

simple	perfect
comprar	ter comprado
to buy	*to have bought*
vender	ter vendido
to sell	*to have sold*
partir	ter partido
to leave	*to have left*
pôr	ter posto
to put	*to have put*

Ter passado nos exames recompensou o meu trabalho.
To have passed my exams was the reward I got for my work.
Ter vindo mais cedo teria sido completamente impossível.
To have come earlier would have been absolutely impossible.
Ter comprado uma casa foi a melhor coisa que eu poderia **ter feito**.
To have bought a house was the best thing I could have done.

Note:
Particularly in older texts, you may also come across the auxiliary verb **haver** (equally meaning 'to have').

haver comprado (very limited use) = ter comprado
to have bought

Portuguese and English infinitives compared

Unlike English verbs, the Portuguese infinitive always consists of one word only (comprar, *to buy*). While the English infinitive is usually, but not always, preceded by its marker 'to', the infinitive marker is always present in Portuguese. It is the ending **-ar**, **-er**, **-ir**, **-ôr/-or**.

err**ar** é humano	*to err is human*
ele sabe fal**ar** Português	*he can speak Portuguese*

As in English, the Portuguese infinitive can:

(a) follow another verb form

ele sabe **falar** Português	*he can speak Portuguese*

eu quero **ler** este livro   *I want to read this book*

(b) stand alone in the sentence

errar é humano   *to err is human*
ser ou não **ser**   *to be or not to be*

Unlike English, where the *-ing* form is used, Portuguese uses the infinitive after link words such as *before* and *after*, known as 'prepositions':

antes de falar   *before talking*
depois de comer   *after eating*

Unlike English, the Portuguese language has an inflected, or 'personal', infinitive in addition to the general infinitive explained in the present unit. For the Portuguese personal infinitive, see Unit 14.

The Portuguese infinitive after another verb form

An infinitive can be introduced, or guided, by another verb in the sentence.

(1) Verb form + infinitive

An infinitive may appear directly after another verb form, as it might be the case in English.

nós **queremos ir** à praia   *we want to go to the beach*
ela **prefere ficar** em casa   *she prefers to stay at home*
eu **devia concluir** este trabalho hoje   *I should complete this work
                                             today*

In some cases this joint formation may acquire a meaning of its own, as with verb **mandar**, to order.

eu **mandei buscar** o pacote   *I have sent for the parcel*
eles **mandaram chamar** as crianças *they have sent for the children*
ela **mandará dizer** o que se passa *she will send word of what is
                                       happening*

(2) Verb form + preposition + infinitive
(the preposition often being **de** (*of*) or **a** (*at, to*))

Some verbs take a preposition (e.g. **de** in **gostar de**, *to like*). This preposition

125

will stand between the conjugated verb form and a following infinitive.

eu **gosto de ir** à praia   *I like going to the beach*
eu **aprendi a falar** Português   *I have learned to speak Portuguese*

(3) Expression of judgment + preposition + infinitive

Preposition **de** also appears between an expression of judgment and an infinitive in cases such as 'it is easy', 'it is difficult': fácil (*easy*), difícil (*difficult*), duro (*hard*), bom (*good*), mau, ruim (*bad*), agradável (*pleasant, pleasing*), desagradável (*unpleasant*).

este livro **é difícil de ler**   *this book is difficult to read*
isso é um osso **duro de roer**   *that's a hard nut to crack*
                                         (literally, .. *a bone hard to gnaw at*)

Note:
In (2) and (3) above the preposition (**de** / **a** / etc.) belongs to the preceding verb form or expression. It does not correspond literally to the 'to' that appears in the English translation before the English infinitive.

The Portuguese infinitive on its own

An infinitive can stand on its own in a sentence, as a verb itself, a noun, or an adjective.

(1) As just the verb itself

The Portuguese infinitive can naturally be used for a general reference to an action or state of being.

errar é humano   *to err is human*
ser ou não **ser**   *to be or not to be*
querer é **poder**   *to have the mind is to have the power*
                               (literally, *'to want to' is' to be able to'*)

(2) As a noun

The Portuguese infinitive often functions like a noun with, or without, the masculine form of the definite article (**o**, *the*). This usually corresponds to the English *-ing* form.

modo de **pensar**   *way of thinking*

modo de **escrever**	*style of writing*
(o) fumar pode matar	*smoking can kill*
(o) fumar faz mal à saúde	*smoking damages your health*
(o) nadar faz bem à saúde	*swimming is good for your health*
recordar é **viver**	*re-living your past* (lit., *'recalling'* *(the past) is (re-)'living' (that past)*)
querer é **poder**	*to have the mind is to have the power* (lit., *'to want to' is 'to be able to'* or *'wanting to' is 'being able to'*)
ver e **crer**	*seeing is believing* (lit., *to see and to believe*)

(3) As an adjective

The Portuguese infinitive can also function as an adjective, again usually translating the English *-ing* form.

sala **de jantar**	*dining room* (lit., *room of dining*)
sala **de estar**	*living room, lounge*
tábua **de passar** (roupa)	*ironing board*

The Portuguese infinitive after prepositions

preposition + infinitive

This Portuguese sequence differs considerably from English practice. For a better grasp of this formation, the different cases explained earlier in this unit are brought together below.

In English, the *-ing* form of the verb is used after prepositions, i.e., link words such as after, before, for, by, from, at, with, without, of. (Though originally a preposition, 'to' plays a special role as the sign of the infinitive)

In Portuguese, the infinitive appears after a preposition in a variety of situations, as shown in different sections of the present unit:

• in some phrases

antes de comer	*before eating*
depois de dormir	*after sleeping*
sem pensar	*without thinking*

127

• describing a noun
   máquina **de filmar**   *cine-camera*
   (See 'The Portuguese infinitive on its own')

• with some verbs
   eu **gosto de ir** ao clube   *I like going to the club*
   (See 'The Portuguese infinitive after another verb form')

• with some expressions of judgment
   isso **é fácil de fazer**   *that is easy to do*
   (See 'The Portuguese infinitive after another verb form')

Present participle

The Portuguese 'present participle' is known in Portuguese grammar as 'gerund' (gerúndio), a term that comes from Latin grammar, and corresponds to the English -*ing* form when this functions as part of a verb – e.g., he is smoking.

The Portuguese present participle is formed simply by removing the final **-r** of the infinitive ending (**-ar, -er, -ir, -ôr / -or**) and adding this ending:

-ndo

comprando   vendendo   partindo   pondo

   Relaxando na praia é como eu gosto de passar os domingos.
   Relaxing on the beach is the way I like to spend my Sundays.

You used the present participle earlier in this course as a component of continuous tenses (Units 4, 5 and 12).

****

Similarly to what happens with the English verb '-ing' form, Portuguese verbs can have both a simple '-ndo' form (comprando, *buying*) and a perfect, or compound, '-ndo' form (tendo comprado, *having bought*). The latter is formed by combining the auxiliary verb **ter** (to have), in its '-ndo' form, and the past participle of the main verb.

128

-ndo form

simple	perfect
comprando	tendo comprado
buying	*having bought*
vendendo	tendo vendido
selling	*having sold*
partindo	tendo partido
leaving	*having left*
pondo	tendo posto
putting	*having put*

Tendo estudado bem a matéria, passei no exame sem dificuldade.
Having studied the subject well, I passed the exam without difficulty.
Tendo enchido o tanque do carro antes de partir, tive combustível suficiente
para a viagem inteira.
Having filled the tank in the car, I had enough fuel for the whole journey.

Note:

Particularly in older texts, you may also come across the auxiliary verb
haver (equally meaning 'to have').

havendo comprado (very limited use) = tendo comprado
having bought

English *-ing* and Portuguese *-ndo* compared

In English traditional grammar, the term 'gerund' (from Latin grammar) is
the name given to the '-ing' form when used in a nounlike way – as in *no
smoking* – in contrast with the same form used as a 'present participle' – as
in *he was smoking* – where it functions as part of a verb.

'-ING' WORD AS A VERB (ENGLISH PRESENT PARTICIPLE):

The Portuguese 'gerund' is the '-ndo' form of the verb. It translates English
'-ing' where this appears as a 'present participle', as is the case in the
continuous (or progressive) tenses – e.g., *he was smoking*, ele estava
fumando. These tenses are explained in more detail in Units 4, 5 and 12.

Similarly to the English '-ing' form, the Portuguese '-ndo' form of the verb
also performs other roles, adding to the main verb of the sentence extra

129

meanings of time, manner, cause, or other. For further detail see 'Portuguese -ndo for extra meaning', next in this unit.

'-ING' WORD AS A NOUN OR ADJECTIVE (ENGLISH GERUND):

An '-ing' noun or adjective translates often into a Portuguese infinitive – e.g., *smoking can kill*, (o) fumar pode matar; *way of thinking*, modo de pensar; *dining room*, sala de jantar. For a more detailed explanation, see 'The Portuguese infinitive on its own', earlier in this unit.

A number of '-ing' adjectives can also translate into a '-nte' Portuguese adjective – *interesting*, interessante; *growing*, crescente; *living*, vivente. This is a result of old Latin gerund forms that have survived in Portuguese only as adjectives and some also as nouns (e.g., amante, *lover*).

Learning aid:

Remember that the Portuguese '-ndo' form does not normally translate English adjectives in '-ing'.

dining room	sala de jantar
wedding ring	aliança de casamento
drinking water	água potável

Portuguese *-ndo* for extra meaning

The Portuguese '-ndo' form suggests the notion of 'ongoing'. It can be used adverbially, i.e., to convey the idea of a circumstance surrounding the main action or state of being in the sentence. It can do so in different ways, mainly by expressing a relation of time (when?), purpose (what for?), reason (why?, due to what?), or manner (how?, by what means?).

WHEN?

entrando, vi a mãe sentada junto à janela
walking in, I saw my mother sitting by the window
(the moment I walked in, ...)
or
quando entrei, vi a mãe sentada junto à janela
when I walked in, ...

voltando do trabalho, achei esta carteira
coming back from work, I found this wallet
(on my way back from work, ...)
or
quando voltei do trabalho, achei esta carteira
when I came back from work, ...

WHAT FOR?

ele telefonou **pedindo** ajuda
he phoned asking for help
or
ele telefonou para pedir ajuda
he phoned to ask for help

WHY? DUE TO WHAT?

estando sem emprego, não posso comprar um carro novo
being without a job, I can not buy a new car
or
não posso comprar um carro novo porque estou sem emprego
I can not buy a new car as / because I am out of a job

tendo perdido o emprego, não posso comprar um carro novo
having lost my job, I can not buy a new car
or
não posso comprar um carro novo porque perdi o emprego
I can not buy a new car as / because I have lost my job

WHEN? WHY?

deparando com um homem morto, ela deu um grito de pavor
coming across the body of a dead man, she screamed in horror
or
ela deu um grito de pavor quando / porque deparou com um homem morto
she screamed in horror when / because she came across the body of a dead man

HOW? WHEN?

ela saiu da sala **agradecendo** a todos
she left the room thanking everyone
or
ela agradecia a todos no momento em que saiu da sala
she was thanking everyone as she left the room

131

BY WHAT MEANS?

caminhando 2 km por dia, eu mantenho a forma
walking 2 km per day keeps me fit
(by walking 2 km per day, I keep fit)
or
eu caminho 2 km por dia e assim mantenho a forma
I walk 2 km per day and thus I keep fit

Note that, in general,

(1) the '-ndo' word can be on its own or is the key element in a phrase which is usually independent in construction from the rest of the sentence;

(2) the '-ndo' word or phrase can be replaced with a clause, which is often the case colloquially.

> voltando do trabalho, achei esta carteira
> ⟨phrase⟩   ⟨clause⟩

or

> quando voltei do trabalho, achei esta carteira
> ⟨clause⟩   ⟨clause⟩

or

> achei esta carteira, quando voltei do trabalho
> ⟨clause⟩   ⟨clause⟩

Past participle

The Portuguese 'past participle' corresponds to the English *-en* (or *-ed*) form of the verb – e.g., she had eaten the apple; this car was washed yesterday.

Except for irregular past participles, the Portuguese past participle is quite easy to obtain. Simply remove the infinitive ending (**-ar, -er, -ir**) and add the following endings:

-ado	**-ido**
for '-ar' verbs	for '-er' and '-ir' verbs
comprado	vendido partido

Combinado! *Agreed!*

You used the past participle earlier in this course as a component of the perfect tenses (Units 4 and 12).

Double past participles

Some English past participles appear in one of two different forms depending on the role they play in the sentence, e.g., *shaved* and *shaven* – *he has shaved twice* but *he is clean shaven*.

A similar situation can be found in the Portuguese language, with a regular and an irregular version for some past participles. Where two past participles coexist, the regular version is normally used in perfect (or compound) tenses – ele tinha acendido a luz, *he had switched on the light* – and the other elsewhere – a luz estava acesa, *the light was (switched) on*.

The two options are used with a certain degree of flexibility. In some instances the irregular past participle gradually takes over and the regular one falls into disuse. In Unit 4 you have a number of cases in which only an irregular past participle is available.

verb	regular participle	irregular participle
aceitar, *to accept*	aceitado	aceito, aceite (*)
acender, *to light*	acendido	aceso
eleger, *to elect*	elegido	eleito (*)
entregar, *to deliver*	entregado	entregue (*)
enxugar, *to wipe dry*	enxugado	enxuto
escrever, *to write*	escrevido	escrito (**)
expressar, *to express*	expressado	expresso
exprimir, *to express*	exprimido	expresso
expulsar, *to expel*	expulsado	expulso (*)
extinguir, *to extinguish*	extinguido	extinto
frigir, *to fry*	frigido	frito
ganhar, *to earn, win*	ganhado	ganho (**)
gastar, *to spend*	gastado	gasto (**)
imprimir, *to print*	imprimido	impresso
inserir, *to insert*	inserido	inserto
limpar, *to clean*	limpado	limpo
matar, *to kill*	matado	morto
morrer, *to die*	morrido	morto
omitir, *to omit*	omitido	omisso
pagar, *to pay*	pagado	pago (**)
pegar, *to catch*	pegado	pego (Am.) (***)

133

prender, *to fasten, arrest*	prendido	preso
romper, *to tear*	rompido	roto
salvar, *to rescue, save*	salvado	salvo (*)
secar, *to dry*	secado	seco
soltar, *to set free*	soltado	solto
suspender, *to suspend*	suspendido	suspenso
tingir, *to dye*	tingido	tinto

(*)   preferred form
(**)   dominant form
(***) dominant form in Latin American Portuguese. Otherwise the
      regular participle (pegado) is generally used.

English -*en*/-*ed* and Portuguese -*ado*/-*ido* compared

The English -*en*/-*ed* form and the Portuguese -*ado*/-*ido* form are equally
known as 'past participle'. The English and the Portuguese past participles
have much in common in the way they are used. There are differences too.

'-EN/-ED' WORD AS A VERB:

Both the English and the Portuguese past participles are used in the
formation of the perfect tenses – e.g., *he had bought*, ele tinha comprado.
For the Portuguese perfect (or compound) tenses see Units 4 and 12.

Both the English and the Portuguese past participles are used in the
formation of the passive voice – e.g., *this apartment was sold yesterday*, este
apartamento foi vendido ontem. For the Portuguese passive voice see Unit
16.

Similarly to what happens in English, the Portuguese past participle can be
used to add an extra meaning to the main verb of the sentence. This is
explained in 'The Portuguese past participle for extra meaning', later in this
unit.

Note:
The same way that there are exceptions to the '-en/-ed' ending in the English
past participle (e.g., *bought*, *sold*), there are also exceptions to the
Portuguese '-ado/-ido' ending. For these irregular forms see 'Irregular past
participles' in Unit 4 and 'Double past participles' earlier in the present unit.

134

'-EN/-ED' WORD AS AN ADJECTIVE OR NOUN:

Some English past participles are also used as an adjective (e.g., *a broken chair*) or a noun (e.g., *a drunk*). The same happens in Portuguese. However, an English past participle does not necessarily translate into a Portuguese past participle, and vice-versa.

a broken chair	uma cadeira quebrada
a cracked safe	um cofre arrombado
the bereaved	os enlutados
the dead	os mortos
'lost and found', 'lost property'	'perdidos e achados'
I have got some small change	eu tenho (dinheiro) trocado

The past participle and agreement

The past participle can be 'variable' or 'invariable'. In other words, in some cases the past participle changes its ending (-ado/-ido) according to number (singular or plural) and gender (masculine or feminine). In other cases its ending never changes. The invariable form and the masculine singular form share the same final two letters (-do).

do	masculine singular	**da**	feminine singular
dos	masculine plural	**das**	feminine plural

(a) The past participle will not change its ending when it is used as part of a perfect (or compound) tense.

ela tinha vendid**o** os apartamentos	*she had sold the apartments*
eles tinham pag**o** a conta	*they had settled the bill*

(See Units 4 and 12)

(b) The past participle will change its ending (masculine/feminine; singular/plural) when it is used as part of a passive voice.

a cont**a** foi pag**a** por ele	*the bill was settled by him*
	(feminine singular)
as cas**as** foram vendid**as** ontem	*the houses were sold yesterday*
	(feminine plural)

(See Unit 16)

(c) The past participle will change its ending (masculine/feminine; singular/plural) when it is used as an adjective or noun.

est**es** homen**s** estão cansad**os**	*these men are tired*
	(masculine plural)
as loj**as** estão abert**as**	*the shops are open*
	(feminine plural)
uma cadeir**a** quebrad**a**	*a broken chair*
	(feminine singular)
'perdid**os** e achad**os**'	*'lost and found (items)'*
	(masculine plural)

(See sub-section '-en/-ed word as an adjective or noun' earlier in this unit)

(d) The past participle will not change its ending when it is used as an adjunct to the main action or state of being expressed in the sentence.

(See section 'The Portuguese past participle for extra meaning' below)

The Portuguese past participle for extra meaning

The past participle conveys the notion of 'done' or 'been'. It can be used as an adjunct (an extension) to the main action or state of being expressed in the sentence in order to add a relation of time (once done…) and / or cause (because…).

dito e **feito**, eles realizaram os seus planos
no sooner said than done, they implemented their plans

resolvido o problema, fomos para casa
the problem solved, we went home
(once the problem had been solved…)

cansado de um pesado dia de trabalho, ele adormeceu profundamente
tired after a heavy day's work, he fell into a deep sleep
(because he was tired …)

Exercises

13.1 The infinitives missing in these sentences are all in the box below. Find which word goes where and complete the sentences.

1 Eu comprei uma máquina de _____.
I have bought a cine-camera.
2 Nós gostamos do modo de _____ dele.
We like his manner. (his way of being)
3 É melhor apagar a luz antes de _____.
It is better to switch off the light before going out.
4 _____ aprendido Português sem dúvida que tem sido muito útil.
To have learned Portuguese has proved to be very useful.
5 _____ e _____ é bom para a saúde.
Singing and dancing does you good.
6 Eu prefiro _____ em casa e _____ um livro.
I would rather stay at home and read a book.
7 _____ ou não _____ um carro novo, isso é uma decisão difícil.
To buy or not to buy a new car, that is a hard decision to make.

> ler filmar ter ser
> dançar sair ficar
> comprar cantar comprar

13.2 In the bow tie, the words on your left are Portuguese gerunds (-ndo forms) and those on your right are past participles, some regular (-ado / -ido) others irregular.

(A) Use the words on the left to complete the sentences. These words will contribute meanings such as when, why or how something is or was done.

1 Ela entrou na sala_____.
She walked into the room laughing.
2 Ele ganha a vida _____ Português.
He earns a living by teaching Portuguese.
3 _____, nós partiremos.
At day break we shall set off.

4 _____ pela praia, tropecei num seixo.
As I was walking on the beach I tripped over a stone.

5 Ele trouxe um presente, _____assim a sua gratidão.
He brought a gift as a token of his gratitude. (expressing this way his gratitude)

6 _____ terminado os exames, pude gozar as férias.
Having finished my exams, I could then enjoy my holiday.

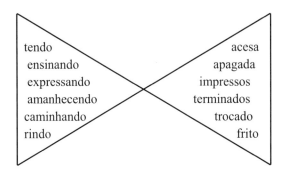

tendo
ensinando
expressando
amanhecendo
caminhando
rindo

acesa
apagada
impressos
terminados
trocado
frito

(B) The words on the right play a variety of roles in the sentences below: naming something; qualifying or describing something; adding more meaning to the main action. Find the right slot for each one.

1 A luz está_____.
The light is on.

2 A luz está _____.
The light is off.

3 Nem toda a gente gosta de peixe _____.
Not every one likes fried fish.

4 Temos que preencher os _____.
We have to fill in the forms.

5 Talvez ele tenha _____.
Perhaps he has some small change.

6 _____ os exames, eu fui viajar.
Once the exams were over, I went travelling.

Personal Infinitive

In addition to the general infinitive explained in Unit 1 and Unit 13, the Portuguese language also has an inflected or 'personal' infinitive.

... para nós comprarmos ...   ... for us to buy ...
... para eles lerem ...   ... for them to read ...

FORM

While the general infinitive (comp**rar**, vend**er**, part**ir**, p**ôr**) has no subject (*I, you, s/he, etc.*) and is invariable in form, the inflected infinitive can take subject words and personal endings. The latter are added onto the general infinitive and therefore are the same for all verbs.

(... for) me to buy / sell / leave etc.
(... para) **eu** comprar / vender / partir etc.

subject	1st / 2nd / 3rd conj.
eu, você, ele/ela	-
nós	-mos
vocês, eles/elas	-em

For other 'you' forms see Unit 3 and 'The Other Second Person'.

Learning aid:

(a) In the table above personal endings are showing only for the plural (nós, vocês, eles/elas). The singular forms (eu, você, ele/ela) look like a general infinitive (comp**rar**, vend**er**, part**ir**).

(b) The subject for the personal infinitive is the Portuguese equivalent to the English '*I*' etc.; not '*me*' etc. (e.g., para **nós** vendermos, *for **us** to sell*).

(c) Irregular verbs form the personal infinitive in the same way as regular verbs, i.e., regularly (e.g., fazer → nós fazermos); but **pôr** loses its circumflex accent ($^\wedge$) (pôr → nós pormos).

(d) -air and -uir verbs take an accent in the 'vocês, eles/elas' form: saírem, influírem.

(e) In regular verbs, the same endings are shared by the personal infinitive and the future subjunctive (Unit 10).

139

USE

DIFFERENT SUBJECTS FOR THE MAIN VERB AND THE INFINITIVE

(1) A subject word and / or personal ending must be used with the infinitive where the main verb and the infinitive do not have the same subject.

Compare these three sentences:

Eu comprei uma revista para ler.
I have bought a magazine to read.
I have bought the magazine + I am reading it
There is only one subject: I

Eu comprei uma revista para eles lerem.
I have bought a magazine for them to read.
I have bought the magazine + they are reading it
There are two different subjects: I and they

Ele comprou uma revista para eu ler.
He has bought a magazine for me read.
He has bought the magazine + I am reading it
There are two different subjects: he and I

In the second and third sentences a subject word (eles; eu) and / or a personal ending (-em) are required.

More examples:

Já está na hora de vocês voltarem para casa.   *or*
Já está na hora de voltarem para casa.
It is time you go back home.
Nós saímos sem (eles) verem.
We left without them knowing. (their knowing)
Vamos comprar um bolo para (vocês) comerem.
We are going to buy a cake for you to eat.

(2) After an impersonal expression, an infinitive may also need a subject word and / or personal ending. It depends on what you mean.

Compare these three sentences:

É preciso ir.	*It is necessary to go.*
É preciso você ir.	*It is necessary for you to go.*
É preciso eles irem.	*It is necessary for them to go.*

In the first sentence, no specific mention is made of the subject (who is to go). In the other two sentences, a subject word (você, eles) and a personal ending (-em) indicate the subject.

The first sentence can also be interpreted as *It is necessary for someone to go* – 'É preciso alguém ir' or 'É preciso a gente ir', where 'a gente' may be a colloquial alternative to 'nós' as explained in Unit 3.

More examples:

É necessário eu saber isso.
It is necessary for me to know that.
É melhor você fazer isso agora.
It is better you do that now.
Foi uma alegria vocês virem à festa.
We were so happy you came to the party. (it was a joy…)
Será tão bom voltarmos a estar juntos.
It will be so nice to be together again. (us to be…)
É urgente vocês acharem a carteira.
It is urgent that you find the wallet.
É urgente (vocês) consertarem o aquecimento central.
It is urgent that you repair the central heating.
The central heating must be repaired without delay.

Note:
The need for a subject word and / or personal ending does not apply when talking about natural phenomena like the weather (see 'Subjectless cases' in Unit 3).

Foi necessário chover durante uma semana inteira para o reservatório ficar cheio.
It was necessary for it to rain for a whole week to fill the reservoir.

THE SAME SUBJECT FOR THE MAIN VERB AND THE INFINITIVE

Where the subject of the main verb and the subject of the infinitive are the same, a subject word and / or personal ending can still be used. This is the normal practice for extra clarity in the following cases:

(1) When the logical subject of the infinitive may not be immediately obvious usually because the infinitive precedes the main verb and / or is far removed from it.

Depois de venderem o apartamento da cidade, eles foram morar na praia.
After selling their apartment in town, they went to live at the seaside.
Ao entrarmos, vimos a mãe sentada junto à janela.
On walking in, we saw our mother sitting by the window.
Note:
For two things happening at the same time, the present participle is often heard instead (see 'Portuguese -ndo for extra meaning', Unit 13).

Ao entrarmos, vimos a mãe sentada junto à janela.   *or*
Entrando, vimos a mãe sentada junto à janela.
On walking in, we saw our mother sitting by the window.

(2) When you wish to stress who does what, or who is who, for emphasis or style.

Eu comprei uma revista para eu ler.
I have bought a magazine for me to read.
(it is exclusively or mainly for <u>myself</u>)
Eles vieram à festa sem serem convidados.
They came to the party without being invited.
(<u>no one</u> invited them)

Personal infinitive replacing other tenses

While indicating the subject of the action or state of being, the personal infinitive also retains the uncharacteristic quality of an infinitive. Thanks to these features, the personal infinitive can fit into different sentence contexts, i.e., indicative or subjunctive (present, past or future) and singular or plural person (I or we, you, s/he, it or they).

The examples below show two different ways of saying the same thing, the first one in the personal infinitive, the second one in another tense. The choice is yours.

Expressing time

Telefonei para casa ao **chegar.**
Telefonei para casa quando cheguei. (preterite)
I phoned home when I arrived.
Vamos jantar depois de vocês **chegarem.**
Vamos jantar depois que vocês cheguem. (present subjunctive)
We are going to have dinner after you arrive.
(we shall wait for you)

Atravessem ao **chegarem** à esquina.
Atravessem quando chegarem à esquina. (future subjunctive)
Cross over when you get to the corner.

Expressing cause or purpose

Não vamos ao cinema por **termos** comido tarde.
Não vamos ao cinema porque comemos tarde. (preterite)
We are not going to the cinema because we ate late.
Comprei este livro para você o **ler**.
Comprei este livro para que você o leia. (present subjunctive)
I bought this book for you to read / so that you may read it.
Eu tinha comprado o livro para ele o **ler**.
Eu tinha comprado o livro para que ele o lesse. (imperfect subjunctive)
I had bought that book for him to read / so that he might read it.

Expressing condition or concession

Vocês engordarão a **comerem** assim.
Vocês engordarão se comerem assim. (future subjunctive)
You will put on weight if you carry on eating this much.
Eles são magros apesar de **comerem** muito.
Eles são magros embora comam muito. (present subjunctive)
They are thin in spite of eating a lot.

With impersonal expressions

É urgente vocês **acharem** a carteira.
É urgente que vocês achem a carteira. (present subjunctive)
It is urgent that you find the wallet.
É possível ela **tomar** uma bebida quente.
É possível que ela tome uma bebida quente. (present subjunctive)
É possível que ela tomasse uma bebida quente. (imperfect subjunctive)
She may well have a hot drink.
She might well have a hot drink.
(it is / may be possible that ...)

Infinitive or subjunctive?

Expressing will

Use the infinitive, when expressing will, if the subject of the second verb is
the same as that of the first verb. (The infinitive does not require a subject
word and / or personal ending)

Ele quer **vir**.   *He wants to come.*
Eu prefiro **ficar** em casa.   *I prefer staying at home. (to stay)*

Use the subjunctive if the subject is not the same, i.e., where there is the imposition of the will of one subject on another.

Ele quer que vocês **venham**.
He wants you to come.
Eles desejam que nós **compareçamos** na reunião.
They wish / want us to attend the meeting.
Nós proibimos que eles **colocassem** o pacote em cima da mesa.
We forbade them to place the parcel on top of the table.

With 'pedir' and 'dizer'

Both verb **pedir**, to ask, and verb **dizer**, to tell, can express will of one subject upon another. Where this is the case a subjunctive tense is recommended for the dependent verb.

Ele pede que vocês **venham** já.   (present subjunctive)
He is asking for you to come straight away.
Ele pediu que você **entrasse**.   (imperfect subjunctive)
He has asked for you to come in.

However, the following formation is also frequently heard, with the dependent verb in the infinitive:

   form of **pedir** / **dizer**   +   preposition **para**   +   infinitive

(For clarity, the infinitive often takes a subject word and / or personal ending)

Ele pede para **vocês virem** já.
He is asking for you to come straight away.
Ele pediu para **você entrar**.
He has asked for you to come in.
Ele disse para **eles entrarem**.
He has asked (said) for them to come in.

Expressing wishes, hope, sorrow

Use the infinitive, when expressing emotion, if the subject of the second verb is the same as that of the first verb. (In some cases, the infinitive can take a subject word and / or personal ending)

Eu espero **fazer** boa viagem.
I hope to have a nice journey. (that I may have)

Eu receio **estarmos** doentes.
I fear we may be ill.

Use the subjunctive, if the subject is not the same.

Eu desejo que (você) **faça** boa viagem.
I wish you to have a good journey. (that you may have a nice journey)
Eu receio que ele **esteja** doente.
I fear he may be ill.

Note:

In some instances a subjunctive is used where both verbs have the same subject. It conveys a slightly different meaning (may…).

Nós sentimos não **podermos** ir à sua festa.
We are sorry we can't come to your party.
Nós sentimos que não **possamos** ir à sua festa.
We are sorry that we may not be able to come to your party.

Instructions in the infinitive

How to give orders and instructions is explained in detail in Units 7 and 8, using the so-called 'command' forms and some alternatives. The infinitive is another possible alternative.

When Portuguese speakers say a sentence like 'Ele pediu para (você) entrar', *He has asked for you to come in* (see 'Infinitive or subjunctive?' above), grammatically, they are one small step away from giving an order or instruction in the infinitive.

Entrar! *Come in!*

Verbally, this format is not used much other than in specific contexts such as the military. However, it is often seen in writing. It is common practice in public instructions. The infinitive is normally shown in the singular, with the subject (você) left unexpressed. The instruction is addressed to the individual as a member of the public, anonymously.

Empurrar   *Push* (opening instruction on a door)
Puxar para abrir   *Pull to open* (machine operating instructions)

Sair pela porta da
esquerda

Exit by the door on the left hand side
(loudspeaker or written instruction)

These instructions can be preceded by **é favor**, a polite expression which grammatically has the same effect in the sentence as the impersonal expressions you learned earlier in the present unit (Use 2 of the personal infinitive). As alternatives you can also say **por favor** or just **favor**.

É favor **sair** pela porta da
direita.

Please exit by the door on the right.

É favor **fechar** a porta.

Please shut the door.

Por favor **fechar** a porta ao sair.

Please shut the door when you leave.
(*on leaving*)

These instructions can equally be preceded by the polite expressions explained in section 'Please', Unit 7.

Faça o favor de **sair** pela
porta da direita.

Please exit by the door on the right.
/ *Could you please exit ...*

Por favor queira **fechar**
a porta ao sair.

Please shut the door when you leave.
/ *Would you please shut ...*

Combined with a polite expression, the infinitive is also often used in speech.

É favor **sairem** pela porta da
direita.

Please exit by the door on the right.

A senhora faça o favor de
sair pela porta da direita.

Please exit by the door on the right.
/ *Could you please exit ...*

This same format is also common practice in business and formal letters in general. In such a case as this, it often appears in the plural, addressing the organization as a collective group of individuals.

É favor **enviarem** a nota de
venda.

Please send the sales receipt.

É favor os senhores **enviarem**
a nota de venda.

Please send the sales receipt.

Exercises

14.1 Work out the verb forms for the sentences and enter them on the grid. If you get them right, the letters down the middle spell out the name of a famous Portuguese song and the name of a famous Brazilian dance. Nr. 1 has been done for you.

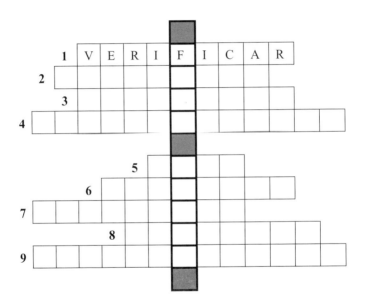

1 É melhor você __verificar__ se tem combustível que chegue para a viagem. (**verificar**)
  It is better you check you have enough fuel for the journey.
2 Será difícil eles _____ tão cedo. (**acordar**)
  It will be difficult for them to wake up that early.
3 É impossível eu _____ nisso. (**acreditar**)
  It is impossible for me to believe that.
4 É melhor nós _____ aqui. (**estacionar**)
  It is better for us to park here.
5 Os pais compraram um computador para o filho _____. (**usar**)
  The parents bought a computer for their son to use.

6 Antes de _____ com eles, temos que combinar o que vamos dizer. (**falar**)
Before talking to them, we have to agree what we are going to say.

7 Ela comprou os selos para nós _____ a carta. (**enviar**)
She has bought the stamps for us to send the letter.

8 Receberemos o pacote depois de eles _____ o cheque. (**cobrar**)
We shall receive the parcel after they have cashed the cheque.

9 Seria perigoso eles _____ nessa estrada. (**ultrapassar**)
It would be dangerous for them to overtake / pass a car on that road.

14.2

(**A**) This is a list of instructions for Internet users.

1 entre (*enter*)
2 clique (*click*)
3 volte (*go back*)
4 navegue (*browse*)
5 digite (*key in, type in*)
6 busque *or* pesquise (*search*)

These instructions are given in the 'command' forms you learned in Unit 7, but when you open a website written in Portuguese you will often see them in the infinitive instead. Can you work out what they will look like on your screen? Remember that they will have one of the following endings: -ar, -er, -ir, -ôr/-or.

(**B**)   You are flying on a Portuguese airliner. Facing you is the following instruction printed on the back of the passenger seat in front of yours:

**MANTER O CINTO APERTADO
QUANDO ESTIVER SENTADO**

fasten seat belt while seated
(*keep your seat belt fastened while you are seated*)

During the flight there is a bit of turbulence and the stewardess is checking that all passengers have their seat belt on. You haven't. The stewardess reminds you that you should be wearing your seat belt, saying: - **Faça o favor de manter o cinto apertado**.

What will she say if she wants to remind both you and the person seating next to you?

Questions, Negatives and Emphasis

In this unit you will learn how to use verbs in questions, negative and emphatic sentences.

'To do'... or no 'to do'...

In English, the verb 'to do' plays a number of roles as an auxiliary verb. We use the help of *do, does, did* for the following:

- Ask questions
  *Where **do** you live?*
- Make 'no' statements
  *He **does** not drink coffee.*
- Give 'no' orders
  ***Do** not do that.*
- Show emphasis
  *It **did** hurt.*

However, with some special verbs we do not need any help from 'to do' – *How are you?*; *He will not come.*

In Portuguese no 'to do' equivalent is used at all. In fact, Portuguese questions, negative and emphatic sentences are quite easy to build.

Negative sentences

The statements 'I want to go out' or 'I am tired' are 'yes' statements, called 'affirmative sentences'. The statements 'I do not want to go out' or 'I am not tired' are 'no' statements, called 'negative sentences'.

In Portuguese, to change from affirmative to negative simply place the word **não** (not) before the verb.

PORTUGUESE	subject + **não** + verb
ENGLISH	subject + verb + ***not*** (+ verb)

Ele **não** é inglês.   *He is not English.*
Ele **não fala** Inglês.   *He does not speak English.*

Learning aid:
Note that Portuguese **não** translates both English 'no' and 'not' – **Não**, eu **não** estou com frio. *No, I am **not** cold.*

Asking and answering questions

The way we word questions normally reflects the kind of information we are seeking. We may be looking for a 'yes' or 'no' reply. Or we want a specific answer about someone (who?), something (what?), time (when?), place (where?), and so on.

Wh- and How questions

Many of the questions we ask in English begin with an 'interrogative', that is, a question word such as who?, what?, where?, when?, how?, etc. The same happens in Portuguese (quem?, (o) que?, onde?, quando?, como?, etc.).

Often **é que** is used in the question. These are filler words that mean literally *(it) is that.*

O que **é que** ele disse?   *What did he say?*

The use of **é que** is optional but has a considerable advantage. In this type of question, Portuguese word order can vary and is quite free in some parts of the Portuguese-speaking world.

For example, for *What did he say?*, the following options are available, all with the same meaning:

O que ele disse?
O que disse ele?
O que **é que** ele disse?

This may be confusing for a foreign learner, but **é que** provides an easy solution, for it helps to fix the word-order in a subject plus verb sequence, as in a simple statement.

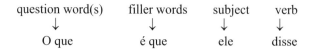

question word(s)	filler words	subject	verb
↓	↓	↓	↓
O que	é que	ele	disse

PORTUGUESE	question word(s) + **é que** + subject + verb
ENGLISH	question word(s) + verb + subject (+ verb)

Com quem **é que** ela vai?   *With whom is she going?*
Que livro **é que** você prefere?   *Which book do you prefer?*
Quando **é que** ele chegou?   *When did he arrive?*
Para onde **é que** ela vai?   *Where is she going to?*
Quanto **é que** esse dicionário custa? *How much does that dictionary cost?*

O que **é que** você está fazendo?   *What are you doing?*
O que **é que** você está a fazer? (Eur.)

Note 1: Where the question word is also the subject, word order is the same with or without 'é que'.

Quem (é que) chegou?   *Who has arrived?*

Note 2: In Portuguese the subject is often omitted, as explained in Unit 3. In this case word order is the same with or without 'é que'.

Quanto (é que) custa?   *How much is (it)?*
Como (é que) vai?   *How are (you)?*

To answer the question, just use a statement as you would in English.

- Que livro é que você prefere?   *- Which book do you prefer?*
- Eu prefiro este.   *- I prefer this one.*

- Com quem é que ela vai?   *- With whom is she going?*
- Eu não sei.   *- I don't know.*

- Como vai?   *- How are you?*
- Vou bem, obrigado. E você?   *- I am well, thank you. And you?*

Pardon?

When you haven't heard what has been said to you, in Portuguese you seek clarification with a 'how' question.

Como disse?   *Pardon? (how did you say?)*
Como é?   *Pardon? (how is it?)*
usually shortened to **Como?**

(See also 'Desculpe' in Unit 8)

Yes-no questions

To turn a Portuguese statement into a question, simply give it a rising intonation; or place a question mark (?) at the end of your question, if you are writing. Unlike English, word order is not normally inverted.

statement		question
Ele é inglês.	→	Ele é inglês?
He is English.		*Is he English?*

PORTUGUESE	subject + verb
ENGLISH	verb + subject (+ verb)

A professora está na sala?	*Is the teacher in the room?*
Você fala Inglês?	*Do you speak English?*
As crianças também vêm?	*Are the children coming too?*
Ela gostou do hotel onde ficou?	*Did she like the hotel where she stayed?*
Tem quartos vagos?	*Do you have any vacant rooms?*
Há uma farmácia perto daqui?	*Is there a chemist's nearby?*
Pode chamar um táxi para mim?	*Can you send for a taxi for me?*
Pode me fazer um favor?	*Can you help me?* (*do me a favour*)

To answer the question, naturally you can say **sim** (yes) or **não** (no), but native speakers prefer to 'echo' the verb in the question.

- Ele é inglês?	*- Is he English?*
- É.	*- Yes.* (lit., *he is*)
- A professora está na sala?	*- Is the teacher in the room?*
- Não, não está.	*- No, she isn't.*
- Você fala Inglês?	*- Do you speak English?*
- Falo.	*- I do.*
- As crianças também vêm?	*- Are the children coming too?*
- Não, não vêm.	*- No, they aren't.*
- Você gostou do hotel onde ficou?	*- Did you like the hotel where you stayed?*
- Gostei.	*- I did.*

You can also 'echo' other elements in the question.

- Ele **já** chegou?	*- Has he arrived?*
- **Já**.	*- Yes.* (lit., *already*)

- Ela **já** chegou?   *- Has she arrived?*
- Ainda não.   *- Not yet.*

- Eles **já** comeram?   *- Have they eaten? / Have they eaten yet?*
- **Já**   *- Yes.*

(For 'já' revise use (d) of the preterite and use (d) of the imperfect, Unit 5)

Question tags

In conversation, we often add a brief question to a statement, i.e., a 'question tag', to check on agreement – *He works in the town centre, **doesn't he?***

In Portuguese, one all-purpose question tag tends to be used: **não é?** (in rapid speech it sounds like */né/*). This can translate a variety of English question tags: isn'it?, aren't you?, don't you?, etc.

To answer the tag question, you can say **sim** (yes) or **não** (no) but you often give an 'echo' reply. (See 'Yes-no questions' above')

- Ele é inglês, não é?   *- He is English, isn't he?*
- É.   *- Yes.*

- Você fala Inglês, não é?   *- You speak English, don't you?*
- É.   *- I do.*

- Ele trabalhava no centro da   *- He used to work in the town*
  cidade, não é?   *centre, didn't he?*
- Não.   *- No.*

You can also opt for more elaborate tag questions and replies, using the same verb as in the statement.

- Você fala Inglês, não fala?   *- You speak English, don't you?*
- Falo.   *- I do.*

- Ele trabalhava no centro da   *- He used to work in the town*
  cidade, não trabalhava?   *centre, didn't he?*
- Não, não trabalhava.   *- No, he didn't.*

153

Negative commands

The Portuguese sequence 'não' + verb that applies to negative statements (see above) equally applies to negative orders and instructions, i.e., how to tell someone not to do, or to be, something. This is the case both with a command form (Unit 7) and the infinitive (Unit 14).

Não entre!	*Don't come in!*
Não feche a porta!	*Don't shut the door!*
Não corra!	*Don't run!*
Não faça isso!	*Don't do that!*
Não seja antipático!	*Don't be unpleasant!*
Não fumar	*No smoking (not to smoke)*
Não usar a porta da esquerda	*The left door is not to be used*

Of course, when an instruction or order is given in the present tense (as explained in Unit 7), then the negative 'command' functions grammatically like a negative statement.

Você não faz isso.	*You don't do that.*
Você não vira à direita.	*You don't turn right.*
Você não sai pela porta da esquerda.	*You don't leave by the left door.*

As you learned in Unit 3, the subject word can be omitted when the meaning remains clear.

(Você) não faz isso.	*You don't do that.*
(Você) não lava o carro.	*You don't wash the car.*

Emphasis

In English we use emphatic verb forms. We combine *do, does, did* with the main verb to indicate special meaning or importance – It **did** hurt.

In Portuguese an emphatic form of the verb is not used. Instead emphasis is obtained by the use of an 'intensifier' external to the verb, i.e., a word or phrase that reinforces meaning but does not interfere with the verb form.

(a) stressed statements

Particularly in the spoken language, **mesmo** is a popular intensifier. This word means literally 'same', 'very', and remains invariable (no change of ending) when used with this function.

Gosto **mesmo**.	*I do like it.*
Doeu **mesmo**.	*It did hurt.*
Ajuda **mesmo**.	*It does help.*
Você está **mesmo** com bom aspecto.	*You do look well.*
Ele não sabe **mesmo** falar Português.	*He cannot speak Portuguese at all.*

Other intensifiers can be used. The following occur frequently in both colloquial and formal situations: **claro que** (clearly, of course); **sem dúvida que** (without doubt, no doubt); **na verdade** (in truth, truthfully); **de facto** / **de fato** (in fact, actually).

For example, for *It does help* you can have the following versions:

Ajuda **mesmo**.
Claro que ajuda.
Sem dúvida que ajuda.
Na verdade ajuda.
De facto / **fato** ajuda.

(b) urgent requests

Command forms can be used for an urgent request rather than an instruction or order (*Do come!*). In Portuguese, this meaning can be conveyed with a polite expression like **por favor** or, more colloquially, with **mesmo**.

Venha **mesmo**!	*Do come!*
Por favor venha!	*Do come (please)!*
Não desapareça **mesmo**!	*Do keep in touch!* (lit., *Don't vanish!*)
Por favor não esteja triste.	*Please don't be sad.*

Note:

Colloquially, mere intonation of the voice and repetition of the verb are also used as intensifying devises.

<u>Gosto</u>!	*I do like it!*
Gosto, gosto!	*I do like it!*
Venha, venha!	*Do come!*

155

Exercises

15.1

(A) Read the following sentences and their English translation.

◊ **Ele é americano.**   *He is an American.*
◊ **Esta loja fica aberta à noite**.   *This shop stays open at night.*
◊ **Você conhece bem esta cidade**. *You know this city well.*
◊ **Eles gostaram da festa ontem**. *They liked the party yesterday.*

Can you ask these questions in Portuguese?

1 Is he an American?
2 Does this shop stay open at night?
3 Do you know this city well?
4 Did they like the party yesterday?

(B) Reword these questions inserting **é que**:

1 O que aconteceu?   *What has happened?*
2 Quem chegou ontem?   *Who arrived yesterday?*
3 Onde trabalha você?   *Where do you work?*
4 Para onde você vai amanhã? *Where are you going to tomorrow?*

(C) What are the mystery words in the middle box?

1	Você concorda, … *You agree, …*		**?**	*don't you?*
2	Você vem de manhã, … *You are coming in the morning,*			*aren't you?*
3	Ele gosta de cerveja, … *He likes beer,*			*doesn't he?*
4	Aquele carro ali é seu, … *That car over there is yours,*			*isn't it?*
5	Eles estão com pressa, … *They are in a hurry,*			*aren't they?*
6	Nós vamos à praia, … *We are going to the beach,*			*aren't we?*
7	Você entendeu, … *You have understood,*			*haven't you?*

15.2

(A) Make the following sentences into negative statements, orders and requests (**não**).

1 Eu quero mesmo sair. *I really want to go out.*
2 Nós vamos fazer isso. *We are going to do that.*
3 Ele foi ao trabalho na semana passada. *He went to work last week.*
4 Até agora, o carro funcionava. *Until now, the car was working.*
5 Claro que isso ajuda. *Of course, that will help.*
6 Isso seria uma boa solução. *That would be a good solution.*
7 Vire à direita. *Turn right.*
8 Abram as janelas. *Open the windows.*
9 Por favor, esperem por mim. *Please wait for me.*

(B) Complete the answers in the mini dialogues. The missing words are hidden in the word search.

1   - Ela provou esse bolo?   *- Has she tasted that cake?*
     -_____.   *- Yes, she has.*

2   - Vamos tomar um cafezinho?   *- Shall we have a coffee?*
     - _____!   *- Yes, let's have it!*

3   - Você já achou a chave?   *- Have you found your key?*
     - _____ não.   *- Not yet.*

4   - Por favor, onde é   *- Excuse me please, where*
       a farmácia?   *is the chemist's?*
     - Eu não _____, não   *- I don't know, I am not*
       _____ daqui.   *from here.*

V	A	M	O	S	L
O	I	M	B	E	H
I	N	Q	D	I	R
U	D	T	J	V	S
C	A	G	Z	F	O
P	R	O	V	O	U

Passive Voice

Look at these two sentences:

They sold the cars.
The cars were sold by them.

The two statements mean fundamentally the same, but the sentence structure is reversed. The first one is said to be in the 'active voice'; the second one in the 'passive voice'.

In the 'active voice' sentence, **they** is the subject that carries out the action: **they sold...**

In the 'passive voice' sentence, **the cars** is the subject, though a passive one, i.e., a subject that receives rather than does the action: **the cars were sold ....** The doer of the action – **they** (**by them**) – is known as the 'agent'.

Generally speaking, the subject of the sentence is the main point of interest. So, when we want to place the emphasis on the performer of the action, we use the active voice; when we want to place the emphasis on the receiver (or sufferer) of the action, we use the passive voice.

Eles venderam os carros.   *They sold the cars.*
    (emphasis on the performer: eles, *they*)
Os carros foram vendidos por eles.   *The cars were sold by them.*
    (emphasis on the receiver: carros, *cars*)
As raposas comem galinhas.   *Foxes eat hens.*
    (emphasis on the performer: raposas, *foxes*)
As galinhas são comidas por raposas.   *Hens are eaten by foxes.*
    (emphasis on the receiver / sufferer: galinhas, *hens*)

To change a sentence from active to passive voice, take the following steps:

(1) Ask the verb the question 'What?'
What did they sell? What do foxes eat?
Answer: **os carros** (the cars); **galinhas** (hens).

The answer – os carros; galinhas – is the receiver of the action, known as the 'object'. In other words, the action of selling passes over from subject 'eles' (they) to object 'os carros' (the cars); and the action of eating passes over from subject 'as raposas' ((the) foxes) to object 'galinhas' (hens).

(2) Use the object (the answer to your 'What?' question) as the new subject in the passive voice.

Os carros foram vendidos por eles.
As galinhas são comidas por raposas.

Note:

Not all verbs lend themselves to switching between an active and a passive voice. It has to be a 'transitive verb', i.e., a verb that takes a direct object, because its meaning implies that the action influences someone or something.

subject	+	form of *ser*	+	past participle	+	by ...
os carros	+	foram	+	vendidos	+	por ...
as galinhas	+	são	+	comidas	+	por ...

What you need for the Portuguese passive voice

For the Portuguese passive voice you need the following:

(1) verb 'ser'

Verb **ser**, to be, is the auxiliary in the formation of the passive voice.

Os carros **foram** vendidos.	*The cars **were** sold.*
As galinhas **são** comidas.	*Hens **are** eaten.*

As with its English counterpart 'to be', Portuguese **ser** can be used in different tenses. These tenses are explained in previous units, but you can also consult the Verb Tables at the end of the book.

(2) past participle

The past participle is the verb form that means 'done' in the sentence (*sold* and *eaten* in our examples).

Os carros foram **vendidos**.	*The cars were **sold**.*
As galinhas são **comidas**.	*Hens are **eaten**.*

159

When used as part of the passive voice construction, the past participle agrees with the subject in gender (masculine or feminine) and number (singular or plural).

Os carr**os** foram vendid**os**.   (masculine plural)
As galinh**as** são comid**as**.   (feminine plural)

The past participle has also other functions and some past participles are irregular, both as explained in Unit 13.

(3) word for '*by*'

The word **por** translates *by* when introducing the doer (agent) in a passive voice formation, though it is not always necessary to show the agent.

Os carros foram vendidos (**por** eles).
*The cars were sold (**by** them).*
Se o convite tivesse sido feito **por** vocês, eu teria aceitado.
*If the invitation had been made **by** you, I would have accepted.*

✳ The word **por**, known as a 'preposition', combines and contracts with the word for *the*, known as the 'definite article', as follows:

por + o = pelo (masculine, singular)
por + os = pelos (masculine, plural)
por + a = pela (feminine, singular)
por + as = pelas (feminine, plural)

Esse quadro foi pintado **pelo** meu amigo João.
That picture was painted by my friend John.
Esta carta foi escrita **pela** minha mãe.
This letter was written by my mother.
A loja tinha sido assaltada **pelos** ladrões que foram apanhados.
The shop had been broken into by the burglars that have been caught.

Verb *estar* with a past participle

We have seen the use of **ser**, to be, with a past participle in the formation of the passive voice.

Os carros **foram** vendidos ontem.
The cars were sold yesterday.

The other Portuguese verb 'to be', **estar**, can also be used with a past participle, though not strictly as part of the passive voice.

Os carros **estão** vendidos. *The cars are sold. (have been sold)*

For guidelines on how to distinguish between **estar** and **ser**, revise the relevant section of Unit 2: Using verbs 'estar', 'ser' and 'ter'.

When to use estar with a past participle:

Use a form of verb **estar** (está, estão, etc.) when you want to describe a state resulting from an action.

The statement 'Os carros **estão** vendidos', *The cars **are** sold*, is applicable when they have been sold, when you see a SOLD notice.

> VENDIDOS

When used with **estar**, the past participle agrees with the subject in gender (masculine or feminine) and number (singular or plural), as an adjective would.

O apartament**o** está vendid**o**.   *The apartment is sold.*
A casa está vendid**a**.   *The house is sold.*
Os carros estão vendid**os**.   *The cars are sold.*

For more on the past participle as an adjective refer to Unit 13.

Portuguese and English passive voice compared

Basically the Portuguese passive voice, explained earlier in the current unit, corresponds to its English counterpart. There are, however, some important differences.

Ontem ele enviou muitas mensagens para ela.
Yesterday he sent lots of messages to her.

In this sentence, subject **ele** (he) carried out an action: **enviou...** (sent...). This action has two 'objects'. It passes over directly to the messages, the 'direct object' – **muitas mensagens** (lots of messages) – and indirectly to her, the 'indirect object' – **para ela** (to her).

In English, either of these objects may become the subject of the passive voice.

161

(a) Lots of messages were sent to her. (by him)
(b) She was sent lots of messages. (by him)

The latter sentence makes the indirect object the subject of the passive voice and is perhaps more usual.

Version (a) has a parallel translation into Portuguese.

Muitas mensagens foram enviadas para ela. (por ele)

Version (b) does not have a Portuguese parallel construction. In Portuguese this is expressed in a different way, in the active voice.

Ela recebeu muitas mensagens. (enviadas por ele)
She received lots of messages. (sent by him)

See also the 'reflexive construction' in the next unit.

Exercises

16.1 Complete the sentences and solve the puzzle with the missing forms of the verb SER.

Across:

1 O hotel _____ avisado ontem.
The hotel was notified yesterday.
2 Os recibos _____ emitidos assim que possível.
The receipts will be issued as soon as possible.
3 A notícia estava _____ lida por todos.
The news was being read by everyone.
4 A notícia estava a _____ lida por todos. (Eur.)
The news was being read by everyone.
5 Eu pensava que o carro _____ alugado mais tarde.
I thought that the car would be hired later.
6 Espero que as malas _____ transportadas por via aérea.
I hope that the suitcases will be carried by air.

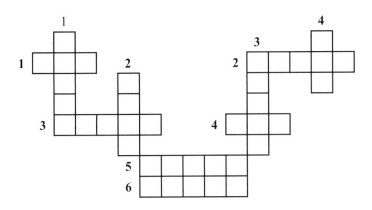

Down:

1 Nós _____ todos convidados.
We have all been invited.
2 As passagens já tinham _____ reservadas.
The travel tickets had already been booked.
3 Penso que _____ levada de táxi para o hotel.
I think I shall be taken to the hotel by taxi.
4 Aqueles pontos turísticos _____ muito visitados por
estrangeiros.
Those tourist spots are very popular with foreigners.
(*... much visited by*)

16.2 Complete the sentences with the missing forms of the verb ESTAR
and solve the puzzle.

1 _____ combinado!
It's agreed!
2 A luz _____ acesa.
The light is (switched) on.
3 Eu _____ hospedado num bom hotel.
I am staying (lodged) at a good hotel.
4 Vocês _____ convidados!
You are invited!
5 O quadro _____ pintado a óleo.
The picture was an oil painting. (painted in oil)

6 O teatro tem _____ encerrado para obras de renovação.
The theatre has been closed for refurbishing.
7 Espero que _____ todos sentados.
I hope that they are all sitting. (*seated*)
8 Estas bebidas são para aqueles que _____ com sede.
These drinks are for those who are thirsty.
(*... whoever may be thirsty*)

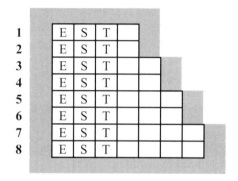

Reflexive Construction

Look at these two sentences:

I wash the car.
I wash myself.

In the first sentence, the action of washing passes over from subject **I** to object **car**. In the second sentence, doer and receiver are the same. The action passes from the subject back again to the subject: **I** and **myself**. This construction is known as 'reflexive'.

Eu lavo o carro.   *I wash the car.*
Eu lavo-me.   *I wash myself.*

To conjugate a verb reflexively you need to know the 'reflexive pronouns' (myself, yourself, etc.).

The following are the Portuguese reflexive pronouns, shown in relation to their respective subject forms which you learned in Units 2 and 3.

Personal pronouns

subject	reflexive	
eu	me	*myself*
você, ele/ela	se	*yourself, him/her/itself*
nós	nos	*ourselves*
vocês, eles/elas	se	*yourselves, themselves*

A verb retains its characteristics – regular, irregular, radical changing, spelling changing – when conjugated reflexively.

For other 'you' forms see Unit 3 and 'The Other Second Person'.

Word order in reflexive sentences:

The position for the reflexive pronoun in the sentence is somewhat flexible but there is a basic pattern.

165

(1)   **main verb + hyphen + reflexive pronoun**
        in affirmative statements and questions

(a) mainly in the written language and formal speech, both in
European Portuguese and Latin American Portuguese.

O presidente **preparou-se** para receber os ministros.
The president got ready (prepared himself) to receive the ministers.

(b) colloquially, in European Portuguese.

Normalmente eu **lavo-me** às 7 horas. (Eur.)
Usually I have a wash (wash myself) at 7 am.
Você **lavou-se** às 7 horas? (Eur.)
Did you have a wash (washed yourself) at 7 am?

(2)   **reflexive pronoun + main verb**

(a) in negative statements / questions and in questions that begin
with a question word, both in European and Latin American
Portuguese.

Normalmente eu não **me lavo** às 6 horas.
Usually I don't have a wash at 6 am.
A que horas é que você **se lava**?
At what time do you have a wash?
O presidente não **se preparou** para receber os ministros.
*The president did not get ready (prepared himself) to receive the
ministers.*

(b) in affirmative statements and questions, colloquially, in
Latin American Portuguese.

Normalmente eu **me lavo** às 7 horas. (Am.)
Usually I have a wash at 7 am.
Você **se lavou** às 7 horas? (Am.)
Did you have a wash at 7 am?

(c) after words such as an adverbial phrase – e.g., **antes de** (*before*)
– a short adverb – e.g., **já** (*already*) – a conjunction – e.g., **que**
(*that*) – or a pronoun – e.g., **que** (*who*) –, on both sides of the
Atlantic, though verb + hyphen + reflexive pronoun can also be
heard.

Antes de (ele) **se lavar**. *or* Antes de **lavar-se**.
Before he had a wash.

Ele já **se lavou**.
He has (already) had a wash.
Eu penso que ele **se lava** às 7 horas.
I think that he has a wash at 7 am.
Penso que ele **se lavou** às 7 horas.
I think that he had a wash at 7 am.
Estas são as pessoas que **se lavaram** cedo.
These are the people who had an early wash.
Claro que o presidente **se preparou** para receber os ministros.
Of course the president got ready to receive the ministers.

For affirmative statements and questions, mainly in the written language, formal speech and European Portuguese colloquial usage,

(subj. pronoun)	**+**	**verb**	**+**	**hyphen**	**+**	**refl. pronoun**
(eu)	+	lavo	+	-	+	me

otherwise,

(subj. pronoun)	**+**	**refl. pronoun**	**+**	**verb**
(eu)	+	me	+	lavo

Note 1:

Although the reflexive pronoun can vary its position in the sentence,

(a) unlike English, it can not follow a past participle.

eu tinha-**me** preparado   *I had prepared myself*
or eu **me** tinha preparado
                    (past participle: *prepared* – preparado)

ele tinha-**se** lavado   *he had washed himself*
or ele **se** tinha lavado
                    (past participle: *washed* – lavado)

Though to a lesser degree, it is also avoided after a present participle.

não **me** estou preparando   *I am not preparing myself*
não estou **me** preparando (Am.)

(b) unlike English it can not follow a future or conditional, but it is placed either between the two parts of the verb (infinitive and the tense ending) or before the verb.

nós preparar-**nos**-emos　　*we will get ready / prepare ourselves*
or nós **nos** prepararemos
nós lavar-**nos**-íamos　　*we would have a wash / wash ourselves*
or nós **nos** lavaríamos

The intercalated format is hardly used in Brazil. The reflexive pronoun before the verb is the preferred format in Latin American Portuguese – nós **nos** prepararemos, nós **nos** lavaríamos.

Note 2:

When the reflexive follows the verb, a change occurs in the 'first person plural' ('we', form). Simply drop the final 's'.

nós **lavamo**-nos (= lavamos + nos)
we have a wash (wash ourselves)
nós **preparávamo**-nos (= preparávamos + nos)
we used to prepare ourselves

This format is avoided in the spoken language in Brazil. The reflexive pronoun before the verb is the preferred format in Latin American Portuguese – nós **nos** lavamos, nós **nos** preparamos.

Losing the reflexive pronoun:

Colloquially, the reflexive pronoun is sometimes omitted. It tends to be dropped when answering a question.

- Você esqueceu-se? (Eur.) / Você se esqueceu? (Am.)
- Esqueci.
- *Have you forgotten it?*
- *I have. (I forgot)*

- Você lava-se às 7 horas? (Eur.) / Você se lava às 7 horas? (Am.)
- Lavo.
- *Do you have a wash at 7 am?*
- *I do. (I wash)*

English equivalents to the Portuguese reflexive construction

In English, we sometimes conjugate a verb reflexively – *I washed myself, I prepared myself* – but we tend to prefer a different form of expression – *I had a wash, I got ready*. In Portuguese, the reflexive construction is used much more frequently. Moreover, it also plays a number of extra roles in addition to expressing a literally 'reflexive' action. It is used in the following cases:

(A) To do with the 'self', and one's body.

(in this case the Portuguese reflexive sometimes translates into English 'get')

Como **se chama**? *What is your name? (How do you call yourself?)*

also:

sentar-se	*to sit down*
levantar-se	*to stand up, get up*
deitar-se	*to lie down, go to bed*
vestir-se	*to get dressed*
despir-se	*to get undressed*
pentear-se	*to do one's hair*
barbear-se	*to have a shave*
preparar-se	*to get ready* (get dressed, etc.)
mudar-se	*to move* (residence)

Todos **se sentaram**. *Everyone sat down.*
Vocês já **se mudaram**? *Have you moved house?*
Ele só **se barbeia** uma vez por dia. *He has a shave once a day.*

(B) To do with one's mind and one's feelings, physical or emotional.

(in this case the Portuguese reflexive sometimes translates into English 'get' and can also translate 'become')

preparar-se	*to get ready* (to face a situation)
lembrar-se	*to remember*
esquecer-se	*to forget*
sentir-se	*to feel*
cansar-se	*to get tired*
chatear-se	*to get upset, bored*
zangar-se	*to get angry, cross*
assustar-se	*to become frightened*

169

ofender-se	*to take offence*
alegrar-se	*to rejoice at / over*
divertir-se	*to enjoy oneself, have a good time*

Não **me sinto** bem.	*I don't feel well.*
Não **se zangue**!	*Don't get cross!*
Desejo que **se divirtam**.	*I hope you enjoy yourselves.*

(C)   For interaction, conveying a reciprocal meaning (each other, one another). The verb is in a plural form (we, you, or they).

A que horas é que **nos encontramos** amanhã?
At what time are we meeting tomorrow?
Penso que eles **se escrevem** de vez em quando.
I think that they write to each other from time to time.
Eles **olharam-se**. (Eur.) Eles **se olharam**.(Am.)
They looked at one another.

(D)   Where there is an unknown, unrevealed or undetermined subject, translating English 'one', 'you', 'they', or 'people'. The verb is in the 's/he', 'it', or 'they' form.

Como é que **se escreve** esse endereço?
How do you / they spell (write) that address?
Como **se dizem** 'fly' and 'butterfly' em Português?
How do you / they say 'fly' and 'butterfly' in Portuguese?
Nunca **se sabe** o que pode acontecer.
One never knows what may happen.

(E)   When we want to lay emphasis on the action itself (rather than its doer and / or receiver). For this purpose, English uses the passive voice – as in 'English (is) spoken here' – or other means of expression – as in 'to let'. In Portuguese the verb is in the 's/he, it', or the 'they' form.

Aqui só **se fala** Português.	*Here only Portuguese is spoken.*
Não **se sabe** o que aconteceu.	*It is not known what happened.*

This format is often seen in written public notices and newspaper advertisements.

Fala-se Inglês	*English (is) spoken (here)*
Aceitam-se encomendas	*Orders (are) accepted / taken*
Precisa-se secretária	*Secretary wanted*
Aluga-se	*To let*

Vende-se	*For sale*
Escritórios **arrendam-se**	*Offices to lease*

Vende-se *or* vendem-se?

You may come across public signs and notices such as these:

Vende-se apartamentos	*Apartments for sale*
Fala-se Inglês, Francês e Alemão	*English, French and German spoken (here)*

In these sentences you have a singular verb – vende; fala – but a plural subject – apartamentos; Inglês, Francês e Alemão. Grammatically this is not in logical agreement. These sentences should really have a plural verb for a plural subject, as follows:

Vend**em**-se apartamentos	*Apartments (are) for sale*
Fal**am**-se Inglês, Francês e Alemão	*English, French and German (are) spoken (here)*

However, the ungrammatical combination is often seen and heard.

The reflexive construction and the passive voice

In some cases there is a close affinity between the reflexive construction and the passive voice. This has much to do with the relative importance given by the speaker to two elements in the sentence: the action, expressed by the verb, and the thing or person that receives that action.

Passive voice in English but 'se' in Portuguese

As explained earlier in this unit, there are instances in which the Portuguese reflexive construction translates the English passive voice. It is so when the main focus is on the action itself.

Fala-se Inglês	*English is spoken (here)*
Aceitam-se encomendas	*Orders are accepted / taken*

Passive voice in English, passive voice or 'se' in Portuguese

Often the Portuguese reflexive construction and passive voice are interchangeable. This means that there is an option when translating from

171

English into Portuguese. For example, *The houses have been sold* can have the following two translations:

(1) As casas **foram vendidas**

(2) **Venderam-se** as casas

Do (1) and (2) mean the same? Fundamentally yes, but there is a shift of emphasis. In (1) the main focus is on the houses – as casas – but in (2) on the action of selling – venderam-se.

More examples:

A casa **foi construída** em menos de seis meses. *or*
Construiu-se a casa em menos de seis meses.
The house was built in less than six months.
Muitas estórias **são contadas** acerca das personagens célebres. *or*
Contam-se muitas estórias acerca das personagens célebres.
Many tales are told about celebrities.

Exercises

17.1 In the sentences below the letters of the alphabet appear as a code number in some verbs. Crack the code and re-write the sentences. The letters for numbers 8 and 13 have been entered in the grid.

1	2	3	4	5	6	7	8	9
							A	

10	11	12	13	14	15	16	17	18
			E					

(A)

1 Como é que a senhora se <u>6-18-8-9-8</u>? (**chamar**)
   What is your name, lady?

2 Como é que se <u>13-2-6-4-13-3-13</u> o seu nome? (**escrever**)
   How do you spell your name?

172

3 Onde é que nós nos <u>13-14-6-11-14-7-4-8-9-11-2</u> hoje à noite?

(**encontrar**)

Where are we meeting tonight?

(B)

1 Por onde se <u>3-8-10</u> para a praia? (**ir**)
What is the way to the beach? (*how do you get to the beach?*)

2 Onde se <u>3-13-14-12-13</u> água mineral? (**vender**)
Where can you buy mineral water? (*where is mineral water sold?*)

3 Onde se <u>8-5-16-17-8-9</u> carros? (**alugar**)
Where can you hire a car? (*where can cars be hired?*)

(C)

1 Eles já se <u>5-13-3-8-14-7-8-4-8-9</u>? (**levantar**)
Have they got up?

2 Então você ainda não se <u>1-8-4-1-13-11-16</u>? (**barbear**)
So you haven't had a shave yet?

3 Eu já me <u>3-13-2-7-10</u> mas ainda não me <u>15-13-14-7-13-13-10</u>.

(**vestir**) (**pentear**)

I have got dressed but haven't done my hair yet.

(D)

1 Nós <u>12-10-3-13-4-7-10-9-11</u>-nos na festa ontem à noite. (Eur.)
Nós nos <u>12-10-3-13-4-7-10-9-11-2</u> na festa ontem à noite. (Am.)

(**divertir**)

We had a good time at the party last night. (*enjoyed ourselves*)

2 As crianças <u>6-11-9-15-11-4-7-8-4-8-9</u>-se bem. (Eur.)
As crianças se <u>6-11-9-15-11-4-7-8-4-8-9</u> bem. (Am.)

(**comportar**)

The children behaved well. (*behaved themselves*)

3 Claro que as crianças se <u>12-13-10-7-8-4-8-9</u> tarde. (**deitar**)
Of course the children went to bed late.

17.2 Change the way the hotel information is given, following the model in the first box.

1 | Arrumam-se os quartos ► Os quartos são arrumados
de manhã. de manhã.

The bedrooms are tidied up in the morning.

2 | Mudam-se as toalhas ►
todos os dias.

The towels are changed every day.

3 | Serve-se o jantar a ►
partir das 19 horas.

Dinner is served starting from 7 pm.

4 | Guardam-se os carros ►
na garagem do hotel.

Cars are kept in the hotel garage.

5 | Chama-se um médico ►
em caso de doença.

A doctor is sent for in the case of illness.

Pronominal Construction

Look at these two sentences:

I washed the car.
I gave the car to Peter.

Ask the question 'what?' to both sentences – what did I wash?; what did I give? – and you will get the same answer: the car. The car is the 'object', or receiver, of the action, be it washing or giving.

In the second sentence we also have another 'object', Peter. He receives the action, not in the sense that the action is done to him, but as the beneficiary.

Therefore we have two 'objects', the car and Peter. Both the action of washing and that of giving pass over **directly** from subject **I** to the **car**. In the second case the action of giving also passes over **indirectly** from subject **I** to **Peter**. To distinguish between the two objects, we say that the car is the 'direct object' and Peter the 'indirect object'.

Now look at these two new sentences:

I washed it.
I gave it to him. or **I gave him it.**

In the first set of sentences above, the objects were expressed by 'nouns', or naming words (**car** and **Peter**). In the new set of sentences, the nouns have been replaced with 'object pronouns', that is, words used instead of the noun that stands for the object. In this case they are the 'direct object pronoun' **it** (for the car) and the 'indirect object pronoun' **him** (for Peter).

Eu lavei o carro.	*I washed the car.*
Eu lavei-o.	*I washed it.*
Eu dei o carro a Pedro.	*I gave the car to Peter.*
Eu dei-o a Pedro.	*I gave it to Peter.*
Eu dei-lhe o carro.	*I gave him the car.*
Eu dei-lho. (=lhe+o)	*I gave it to him. (I gave him it)*

To conjugate a Portuguese verb pronominally you need to know the 'object pronouns', direct and indirect. In the boxes below the Portuguese object pronouns are shown in relation to their respective subject forms which you learned in Units 2 and 3.

Personal pronouns

subject	direct object	indirect object
eu	me *me*	me *(to) me*
você, ele/ela	o/a *you, him/her/it*	lhe *(to) you, him/her/it*
nós	nos *us*	nos *(to) us*
vocês, eles/elas	os/as *you, them*	lhes *(to) you, them*

subject	indirect object	indirect object contracted with direct object o/a, os/as
		him / her / it / them...
eu	me	mo/ma, mos/mas *(to) me*
você, ele/ela	lhe	lho/lha, lhos/lhas *(to) you, him/her/it*
nós	nos	no-lo/no-la, no-los/no-las *(to) us*
vocês, eles/elas	lhes	lho/lha, lhos/lhas *(to) you, them*

A verb retains its characteristics – regular, irregular, radical changing, spelling changing – when conjugated pronominally.

For other 'you' forms see Unit 3 and 'The Other Second Person'.

(For colloquial usage of object pronouns, see 'The Portuguese object pronouns in the spoken language' later in this unit)

Word order in sentences with pronoun objects:

The position for the object pronoun in the sentence is similar to what you learned in Unit 17 for the reflexive pronoun which itself is a kind of object pronoun. Word order varies but there is a basic pattern.

(1)   **main verb + hyphen + object pronoun**

is the general practice for affirmative statements and questions in European Portuguese but has a limited use in colloquial Latin American Portuguese.

Eu **comprei-as.**	*I bought them.* (as flores, *the flowers*)
Eu **dei-as** a Regina.	*I gave them to Regina.* (as flores, *the flowers*)
Você **deu-lhe** as flores?	*Did you give her the flowers?*
Eu **dei-lhas.**	*I gave them to her.* (as flores, *the flowers*)
Ele **disse-me.**	*He told me (it).*

(2)   **object pronoun + main verb**

(a) is the general practice for affirmative statements and questions in Latin American Portuguese.

Eu **as comprei**. (Am.)	*I bought them.* (as flores, *the flowers*)
Você **as deu** a/para Regina? (Am.)	*Did you give them to Regina?*
	(as flores, *the flowers*)
Ele **me disse**. (Am.)	*He told me (it).*

(b) is the general practice for all other cases on both sides of the Atlantic (this includes negative statements and questions; questions that begin with a question word; and after an adverbial phrase, a short adverb, a conjunction or a pronoun), though verb + hyphen + object pronoun can also be heard.

Eu não **as comprei**.	*I did not buy them.*
	(as flores, *the flowers*)
Ninguém **me compreende**.	*No one understands me.*
Quando é que você **o lavou**?	*When did you wash it?*
	(o carro, *the car*)
Já **os lavei**.	*I have (already) washed them.*
	(os copos, *the drinking glasses*)
Depois de **lhe falar**.	*After speaking to you / him / her.*
Penso que ele **a vendeu**.	*I think that he has sold it.*
	(a casa, *the house*)
Esta é a pessoa que **o tinha vendido**.	*This is the person who had sold it.*
	(o carro, *the car*)
Antes de **o comprar**. *or*	*Before buying it.*
Antes de **comprá-lo**.	(o carro, *the car*)

See Note 2 below.

For affirmative statements and questions, in general, in European Portuguese, and mainly in the written language and formal speech, in Latin American Portuguese,

(subj. pronoun)	**+**	**verb**	**+**	**hyphen**	**+**	**obj. pronoun**
(eu)	+	lavei	+	-	+	o

otherwise,

(subj. pronoun)		**+**	**obj. pronoun**	**+**	**verb**
(eu)		+	o	+	lavei

Note 1:

Although the object pronoun can vary its position in the sentence,

(a) unlike English it can not follow a past participle.

ele tinha-**me** dito (*) *or* ele **me** tinha dito   *he had told me (it)*
                    (past participle: *told* – dito)

eu tinha-**lhe** falado (*) *or* eu **lhe** tinha falado   *I had spoken to **him***
                    (past participle: *spoken* – falado)

ele tinha-**o** lavado (*) *or* ele **o** tinha lavado   *he had washed **it***
                    (past participle: *washed* – lavado)

ela tinha-**lho** dado (*) *or* ela **lho** tinha dado   *she had given **it** to **him***
                    (past participle: *given* – dado)

Though to a lesser degree, it is also avoided after a present participle.

ele está-**me**(*) ensinando Inglês   *he is teaching me English*
ele está-**me** a ensinar Inglês (Eur.)
or ele **me** está ensinando Inglês

(*) In Latin American Portuguese the hyphen (-) tends not to be used.

ele **me** tinha dito   *he had told me (it)* (inverted)
ele está **me** ensinando Inglês   *he is teaching me English*

(b) unlike English it can not follow a future or conditional, but it is placed either between the two parts of the verb (infinitive and the tense ending) or before the verb.

eu dar-**lhos**-ei   *I shall give **them** to **him***
or eu **lhos** darei
ele dar-**mo**-ia   *he would give **it** to **me***
or ele **mo** daria
esse carro, eu tê-**lo**-ia comprado   *that car, I would have bought **it***
or esse carro, eu **o** teria comprado

The intercalated format is hardly used in Brazil. The object pronoun before the verb – eu **o** teria comprado – is the preferred format in Latin American Portuguese.

Note 2:

With object pronoun **o/a/os/as**, certain changes occur in the object pronoun and/or the verb in the following situations:

(a) after a verb form ending in a nasal sound, add an 'n' before the pronoun.

elas lavaram-**no**	*they washed it* (o carro, *the car*)
eles dão-**nas**	*they give them* (as flores, *the flowers*)
vocês põem-**nos**	*you place them* (os copos, *the glasses*)

(b) after a verb form ending in a sibilant sound (s, z) drop the 's' or 'z' and add 'l' to the object pronoun.

ele di-**lo** (= diz + o)	*he says it*
você fê-**lo** (= fez + o)	*you did it*
ela fá-**lo** (= faz + o)	*she does it*
nós lavávamo-**lo** (= lavávamos + o)	*we used to wash it* (o carro, *the car*)

(c) after an infinitive, drop the 'r' and add 'l' to the object pronoun.

comprá-**lo** (= comprar + o)	*to buy it* (o carro, *the car*)
vendê-**la** (= vender + a)	*to sell it* (a casa, *the house*)
feri-**lo** (= ferir + o)	*to hurt, wound it* (o braço, *the arm*)
pô-**las** (= pôr + as)	*to place them* (as flores, *the flowers*)

(d) after the first part of a split future or conditional, drop the 'r' and add 'l' to the object pronoun.

eu dá-**la**-ei (= dar + **a** +ei)	*I shall give it* (a flor, *the flower*)
eles senti-**lo**-iam (= sentir + **o** + iam)	*they would feel it* (o frio, *the cold*)
nós vendê-**los**-emos (= vender + **os** + emos)	*we shall sell them* (os carros, *the cars*)

In (b), (c) and (d) above, when the resulting verb form ends in **-a, -e** or **-o** add a graphic accent to show the stress on the syllable (**-á, -ê, -ô**).

The Portuguese object pronouns in the spoken language

The table at the beginning of this unit shows the object forms of the Portuguese personal pronoun in relation to their respective subject forms. Particularly in relaxed speech, the subject forms are often used instead of the object forms. This happens:

(A) After a preposition like **para** (*to*), except for the 'first person', i.e., **mim** (*me*).

Ele disse que ela …   *He said that she phoned ...*
   me telefonou   = telefonou para **mim**(*)   *me*
   lhe telefonou   = telefonou para **você**   *you* (singular)
   lhe telefonou   = telefonou para **ele**   *him*
   lhe telefonou   = telefonou para **ela**   *her*
   nos telefonou   = telefonou para **nós**   *us*
   lhes telefonou   = telefonou para **vocês**   *you* (plural)
   lhes telefonou   = telefonou para **eles**   *them* (masculine)
   lhes telefonou   = telefonou para **elas**   *them* (feminine)

(*) **mim** is simply a 'strong' form of 'weak' object pronoun **me**.

(B) Equally after a preposition, particularly to avoid confusion between **o/a**, **lhe** (and their plurals) because these forms apply to both the 'second person' and the 'third person', i.e., both to someone you are talking to (*you*) and someone or something you are talking about (*him/her/it/them*).

dialogue
- Eu sei que ela **lhe telefonou**.   *- I know that she has phoned.*
                                           (you? or him?)
- Telefonou para quem? Para **ele**?   *- She has phoned whom? Him?*
- Não, para **você**.   *- No, you.*

dialogue
- Ele disse que ela **os viu** ontem.   *- She has said that she saw*
                                        you(?)/them(?) yesterday.
- Que ela **nos** viu?   *- That she saw us?*
- Não, que ela **os** viu, a **eles**.   *- No, that she saw them.*

(preposition **para** and preposition **a** – both meaning 'to'– were used above:
 para ele, **a** ele)

(C) Without a preposition. In this case, **você(s)** is widely used in Latin American Portuguese and sometimes also in European Portuguese.

Eu vi **você** ontem no cinema.   *I saw you at the cinema yesterday.*

In Latin American Portuguese, this practice frequently extends to the 'third person' – **ele(s)**, **ela(s)**.

Eu vi **ele** ontem no cinema.   *I saw him at the cinema yesterday.*

Losing the object pronoun:

Object pronouns are often omitted. Colloquially they tend to be dropped when the meaning remains clear.

- Você lavou o carro?   *Did you wash the car?*
- Lavei.   *I did. (I washed)*

- Gosta?   *Do you like it?*
- Gosto.   *I do. (I like)*

Object nouns, not pronouns

As explained in Unit 3, the word **você** (you) is often replaced with **o senhor** (sir) or **a senhora** (madam) for politeness, for example when talking to strangers. Literally meaning 'the gentleman' and 'the lady', **o senhor** and **a senhora** are nouns, i.e., naming words.

A senhora vira à direita na próxima esquina...
You, lady, turn right at the next corner...

In these road directions, **a senhora** replaces **você** in its role of subject, i.e., the doer of the action (the person who will have to turn right etc. to reach her destination).

By the same token, **o senhor** / **a senhora** can replace **você** when the latter is used as an object pronoun as explained earlier in the present unit.

Eu vi **a senhora** ontem no cinema.
I saw you, lady, at the cinema yesterday.

Also, particularly in European Portuguese, someone's name can be used.

Eu vi **o João** ontem no cinema.
I saw you, John, at the cinema yesterday.

181

Delighted to meet you

As explained above, you have a number of choices for 'you', when addressing someone, like **você**, **o/a**, **o senhor / a senhora**. Using these alternatives, you can say *Delighted to meet you* in the following three different ways when you are introduced to a lady:

Muito prazer em **conhecer você**	(for a relaxed tone)
Muito prazer em **conhecê-la**	(for a neutral tone)
Muito prazer em **conhecer a senhora**	(for a ceremonious tone)

Exercises

18.1 Work out the verb forms for the sentences and solve the puzzle.

Down:

1 Pedimos que nos _____, se puder. (**ajudar**)
   We wonder whether you can help us, if possible.
   (literally, *We are asking that you help us, if you can*)
2 Sei o endereço deles mais ou menos; não o _____ bem. (**saber**)
   I know their address roughly; I don't know it well.
3 Estou com o cabelo molhado. Preciso _____-lo. (**enxugar**)
   My hair is wet. I need to dry it.
4 Eles querem que eu os _____. (**acompanhar**)
   They want me to accompany them.

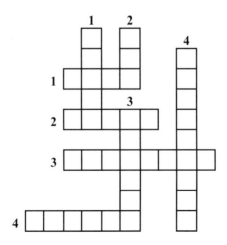

Across:

1 Falem mais alto para que todos possam _____-los. (**ouvir**)
Can you please speak louder so that every one can hear you.
2 Elas gostariam de ir ao clube. _____-nas com vocês. (**levar**)
They would like to go to the club. Take them with you.
3 Eles trouxeram as malas e _____-nas na receção. (**deixar**)
They brought in the suitcases and left them in reception.
4 Esse preguiçoso ainda não apareceu! Vou _____-lo. (**acordar**)
That lazy bones hasn't turned up yet! I am going to wake him up.

18.2

(**A**) The sentences on the right are a colloquial alternative to those on the left, but they are not in the right order. Pair them up.

É verdade que Marta...
It's true that Marta...

1 me comprou um presente. *bought me a gift.*	(**a**) comprou um presente para você.
2 lhe comprou um presente. *bought you a gift.*	(**b**) comprou um presente para mim.
3 lhe comprou um presente. *bought him a gift.*	(**c**) comprou um presente para nós.
4 lhe comprou um presente. *bought her a gift.*	(**d**) comprou um presente para eles.
5 nos comprou um presente. *bought us a gift.*	(**e**) comprou um presente para ela.
6 lhes comprou um presente. *bought you* (plural) *a gift.*	(**f**) comprou um presente para elas.
7 lhes comprou um presente. *bought them* (male) *a gift.*	(**g**) comprou um presente para ele.
8 lhes comprou um presente. *bought them* (female) *a gift.*	(**h**) comprou um presente para vocês.

(**B**) You are being introduced to Ana and João. How can you say to the couple ***Delighted to meet you*** in Portuguese?
Use (a) **los** (b) **vocês** (c) **os senhores**

Indirect Speech

There are two different ways in which we can convey what somebody has said: 'direct speech' and 'indirect speech' (also known as 'reported speech').

Direct speech quotes the exact words of the speaker, normally between quotation marks.

Ela disse: "No próximo ano nós não ficaremos neste hotel nem aqui nesta praia porque o meu marido quer ir ao estrangeiro."
She said: 'Next year we shall not stay at this hotel or here at this seaside resort because my husband wants to go abroad.'

Note that double quotation marks (" ") or angle brackets (« ») are used in Portuguese.

Ela disse: «No próximo ano nós não ficaremos neste hotel nem aqui nesta praia porque o meu marido quer ir ao estrangeiro. »

Indirect speech, or **reported speech**, gives the same meaning but without reproducing the exact words of the speaker.

Ela disse que no ano seguinte eles não ficariam naquele hotel nem lá naquela praia porque o seu marido queria ir ao estrangeiro.
She said that for the following year they would not stay at that hotel or there at that seaside resort because her husband wanted to go abroad.

In direct speech there are two separate parts.

Ela disse:	"No próximo ano ……."
She said:	*'Next year ....'*
└ sentence ┘	└ sentence ┘

In indirect speech the first part flows into the second part. The introductory section is known as the 'main clause'; the reported message is the 'subordinate clause'. They are linked together by a connective, such as 'que', *that*.

Ela disse	**que**	no ano seguinte …
She said	*that*	*for the following year …*
└ main clause ┘		└ subordinate clause ┘

↓
connective
└ ← one single sentence → ┘

184

In indirect speech a number of transformations take place in the subordinate section of the sentence; and words denoting nearness are often replaced by words suggesting remoteness. This may affect:

(1) The references to the people involved, i.e., the subject words – **nós**, *we*, → **eles**, *they* – and verb person – **não ficaremos**, *(we) shall not stay*, → **não ficariam**, *(they) would not stay* – as well as 'possessive' forms – **meu**, *my* → **seu**, *her*.

(2) Time references, through verb tenses – **não ficaremos** (tense for the future), *(we) shall not stay*, → **não ficariam** (conditional), *(they) would not stay*; **quer** (tense for the present), *(he) wants* → **queria** (imperfect), *(he) wanted* – and time expressions – **próximo**, *next* → **seguinte**, *following*.

(3) Place references, through pointing words known as 'demonstratives' – **neste**, *at this* (masculine) → **naquele**, *at that* (masculine); **nesta**, *at this* (feminine) → **naquela**, *at that* (feminine) – and place expressions – **aqui**, *here* → **lá**, *there*.

Reporting statements, questions, orders and requests

What you want to report may be a statement, a question, an order or a request. This will determine the kind of connecting word you need to use. You may need:

(a) a conjunction, i.e., a word used to join words, phrases and clauses – e.g., **que**, *that*, **se**, *if*, *whether;*

(b) a pronoun, i.e., a word that can be used instead of a noun so that we can refer to people or things without really naming them – e.g., **quem**, *who*, **que**, *what;*

(c) an adverb, i.e., a word that we can add to a verb (or a set of words around the verb) to make its meaning clearer, fuller or more exact – e.g., **quando**, *when*, **como**, *how*, **onde**, *where;*

(d) a preposition, i.e., a word that expresses the relationship between another word and a following noun, nounlike word or expression – e.g., **para**, *for*.

Reporting a statement

When reporting a statement, you need conjunction **que**, *that*. The same applies to both affirmative and negative statements.

Ele diz **que** vai estar tudo bem.	*He says (that) everything is going to be fine.*
Elas disseram **que** não viriam à festa.	*They said (that) they would not come to the party.*

(Note that, unlike English practice for 'that', Portuguese 'que' should not be omitted)

Not only someone's own words can be expressed but also someone's own thoughts and feelings.

Eu penso **que** nós talvez mudemos de casa daqui a dois anos.
I think that we may be moving house two years from now.
Nós sentimos muito **que** ela esteja triste.
We are very sorry that she may be feeling sad.

Reporting a question

(a) Wh- and How questions

You may wish to report an open question, i.e., one that starts with an interrogative word such as who?, when?, where?, how?. For that you need a pronoun like **quem**, *who*, or an adverb like **quando**, *when*, **onde**, *where*, **como**, *how*.

Ele perguntou **onde** é que eu pus o livro.	*He asked where I put the book.*
Eu tinha perguntado **quem** queria mais café.	*I had asked who wanted more coffee.*

(b) Yes-no questions

You may wish to report a closed question, i.e., a yes-no question. In this case you need conjunction **se**, *if*, *whether*.

Eu já perguntei várias vezes **se** está tudo bem.	*I have asked several times if everything is fine.*
Ela perguntou **se** nós tínhamos gostado da viagem.	*She asked whether we had enjoyed the journey.*

Reporting an order or request

You need conjunction **que**, *that*, when the reported message expresses a demand.

A lei exige **que** esses documentos sejam apresentados.	*The law demands that those documents be produced.*
Solicita-se **que** os senhores compareçam na reunião.	*You are requested to attend the meeting.*
O patrão manda **que** vocês concluam esse trabalho ainda hoje.	*The boss wants you to complete that task today.* (*that you complete...*)
Ele pede **que** vocês venham já.	*He is asking for you to come straight away.* (*that you come...*)
Ele disse **que** vocês entrassem.	*He has said for you to come in.* (*that you come in...*)

Colloquially, another format is very popular, with preposition **para**, *for*, when the order or request is introduced with verb **pedir**, *to ask*, or **dizer**, *to say*, *tell*.

Ele pede **para** vocês virem já.	*He is asking for you to come straight away.*
Ele disse **para** vocês entrarem.	*He has asked (said) for you to come in.*

See also section 'Infinitive or subjunctive?' in Unit 14.

Verb tenses in indirect speech

There is a certain degree of flexibility in the choice of verb tense for the subordinate clause, i.e., the part of the sentence that actually contains the reported words, thoughts or feelings.

This flexibility enables different meanings to be expressed.

Compare the following sets of sentences:

(a) Ela **diz** que **gosta** de bolos.   *She says she likes cakes.*
(b) Ela **diz** que **gostava** de bolos.   *She says she used to like cakes.*

Both (a) and (b) have the same verb tense in the main clause – **diz**, in the present – but different tenses in the subordinate clause. In (a), **gosta** is in the present and indicates that currently she is fond of cakes. In (b), **gostava** is in the imperfect and suggests that she may no longer like cakes.

(a) Ele **disse** que **visitou** esse país.   *He said he visited that country.*
(b) Ele **disse** que **visitaria** esse país.   *He said he would visit that country.*

Both (a) and (b) have the same verb tense in the main clause – **disse**, in the preterite. As for the subordinate clauses, the verb in (a) – **visitou**, in the preterite – tells us that he has been to that country, while the verb in (b) – **visitaria**, in the conditional – leaves us uninformed on whether or not the visit has taken place.

The following table will give you a basic guideline of appropriate options from which you can choose when reporting words, thoughts and feelings.

MAIN CLAUSE	SUBORDINATE CLAUSE
present present continuous present perfect	present present continuous future colloquial future emphatic future preterite imperfect imperfect continuous present subjunctive future subjunctive
preterite	present preterite imperfect imperfect continuous pluperfect (past perfect) conditional present subjunctive imperfect subjunctive
imperfect imperfect continuous pluperfect (past perfect)	imperfect imperfect continuous pluperfect (past perfect) conditional imperfect subjunctive

Ela **diz** que **gosta** de bolos.
She says she likes cakes.

Ele **pede** que vocês **falem** mais baixo.
He is asking for you to speak more quietly.
Eu **agradeço** que você me **ajude**, se **puder**.
I will appreciate it if you help me, if you can.
Creio que ele **foi** lá hoje.
I believe he went there today.
Nós **prometemos** que **havemos de fazer** isso.
We promise we will do that.
Ele **diz** que **vai escrever** a carta amanhã.
He says he is going to write the letter tomorrow.
Eu **acho** que ele **tomava** café todas as manhãs.
I imagine he used to have coffee every morning.
Eu **penso** que eles **estão dormindo** / **a dormir.** (Eur.)
I think they are asleep. (they are sleeping ...)
Eu **penso** que ele **estava trabalhando** / **a trabalhar** (Eur.) nisso.
I think he was working on that.
Eu **estou pensando** / **a pensar** (Eur.) que isso não **vale** a pena.
I am thinking that is not worth it.
Tenho pensado várias vezes se isso **será** verdade.
I have been wondering a lot whether that is true.

Ela **disse** que **tem** dor de cabeça.
She has said that she has a headache.
Ela **pediu** que eu **faça** as compras para ela.
She has asked me to do the shopping for her.
Ele **disse** que **leu** o livro todo num dia.
He said he read the whole book in one day.
Eles **perguntaram** se nós **estávamos** doentes.
They asked whether we were ill.
Ele **disse** que **estava pintando** / **a pintar** (Eur.) um quadro.
He said he was painting a picture.
Eu **perguntei** se ela **tinha comprado** as flores.
I asked whether she had bought the flowers.
Eles **disseram** que **iriam** lá se **pudessem**.
They said they would go there if they could.

Ela nunca **dizia** que **gostava** de viajar.
She never said she enjoyed travelling.
Ele **costumava dizer** que **tinha dado** a volta ao mundo.
He used to say he had travelled around the world.

Ele **estava dizendo** que **estava trabalhando** muito. /
Ele **estava a dizer** que **estava a trabalhar** muito. (Eur.)
He was saying that he was working hard.
Vocês **tinham pedido** que nós **ajudássemos** se **pudéssemos**.
You had asked us to help if we could.
Nós **tínhamos prometido** que **iríamos** lá.
We had promised we would go there.

Strictly speaking, we can not report something in the future. It hasn't happened yet! However we often anticipate what will be said or asked in the future, either out of someone's own initiative or in compliance with a given order or request.

The following table will give you some more basic guidelines, this time for tense combinations in relation to the future.

MAIN CLAUSE	SUBORDINATE CLAUSE
future colloquial future emphatic future future continuous future perfect	present preterite future colloquial future present subjunctive future subjunctive
command forms	present preterite imperfect future colloquial future emphatic future present subjunctive future subjunctive

Nós **diremos** que **faremos** tudo o que **pudermos**.
We shall say that we will do all we can.
Eu **vou pedir** que você me **ajude**.
I am going to ask you to help me.
Nós **havemos de prometer** que **vamos voltar** quando **tivermos** tempo.
We will promise that we are going to come back when we have the time.
Amanhã a esta hora ele **estará dizendo** / **a dizer** (Eur.) que todos **assinaram** o contrato.
At this time tomorrow he will be saying that everyone signed the contract.

Amanhã a esta hora ele já **terá perguntado** quem **falta** na reunião.
By this time tomorrow he will have asked who is missing from the meeting.

Pergunte se eles **moram** perto daqui.
Ask whether they live nearby.
Pergunte quem já **chegou.**
Ask who has arrived.
Informe o grupo que o barco **vai partir.**
Tell the group that the boat is going to leave.
Anuncie que eles **chegarão** mais tarde.
Make an announcement that they will arrive later.
Peça que eles **ajudem** se eles **tiverem** tempo.
Ask them to help if they can afford the time.

Exercises

19.1 The sentences on the left are a colloquial way of reporting orders and requests. Reword them in the format shown for Nr. 1 and fill the empty spaces on the right.

1	Eles pedem para você esperar aqui.	▶	Eles pedem que você espere aqui.

They are asking for you to wait here.

2	Ela pede para vocês ajudarem.	▶	

She is asking for you to help.

3	Ele diz para eles entrarem agora.	▶	

He says for them to go in now.

4	Eles pediram para nós cantarmos.	▶	

They have asked for us to sing.

5	Eles disseram para você escolher um presente.	▶	

They have said for you to choose a gift.

19.2 Work out the verb forms for the sentences and solve the puzzle. When you have filled in the grid, the letters down the middle will spell out the Portuguese word for CONGRATULATIONS on completing this course.

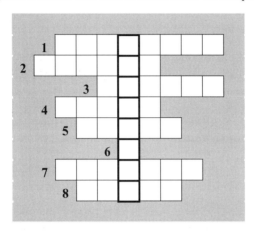

1 Ela diz que aquele músico _____ melodias lindas. (**compor** like **pôr**)

She says that that musician used to compose beautiful melodies.

2 Eu penso que eles _____ de ler romances. (**gostar**)

I think that they like reading novels.

3 Ele explicou que geralmente _____ três páginas por hora. (**traduzir**)

He explained that he usually translates three pages an hour.

4 Ele diz que vocês não se _____ onde não são chamados. (**meter**)

He says for you to mind your own business.
(... not to interfere when you are not called for)

5 Ela pede que vocês não _____ esse vinho. (**beber**)

She has asked for you not to drink that wine.

6 Dizem que a última moda _____ saia comprida. (**ser**)

Apparently the latest fashion is the long skirt. (they say that ...)

7 Ela pede que você _____ que a reunião vai começar. (**anunciar**)

She is asking for you to announce that the meeting is going to start.

8 Eu calculo que ele _____ ter tudo pronto amanhã. (**poder**)

I reckon that he may be able to have everything ready tomorrow.

The Other Second Person

As you learned in Unit 3, the Portuguese language has two second-person systems, **você-vocês** and an older one, **tu-vós**. Out of the older system, **vós** is nowadays archaic in most of the Portuguese-speaking world but you can find its verb tense endings, in brackets, in the Verb Tables. The verb tense endings for **tu** are still in use. They are shown in the Verb Tables, for a more familiar alternative to **você**, as explained in Unit 3. The present section is devoted to the different tense endings for second person **tu**.

When using the **tu**-format, always bear in mind these three points:

(1) The verb endings for **tu** are quite distinctive. In **tu compras**, *you buy*, there is a double indicator for 'you', **tu** and ending **-as**. As a result the word **tu** is often dropped and the speaker relies on the verb ending for meaning: **compras**, *you buy*.

(2) In today's Portuguese, **vocês** is plural to both **você** and **tu**: **você compra** or **(tu) compras**, referring to one person, but **vocês compram**, referring to more than one person.

(3) The command forms you learned in Unit 7 (polite imperative) are 'borrowed' from the present subjunctive. The same applies in the case of **tu** (and **vós**) but only in negative commands – **não entres!**, *don't come in!*. In affirmative commands – **entra!**, *come in!* – the verb ending is that of the imperative, the older tense for commands in the Portuguese language.

You will have noticed that the imperative form for **tu** (**entra!**) looks the same as the **você, ele / ela** form for the present tense (**entra**). Particularly in Latin American Portuguese, there is often interplay between these two forms, with subject pronoun **tu** omitted.

******

193

In the present section you will be given practice in converting **você** verb forms into **tu** verb forms. Each sub-section corresponds to a different unit in the main body of the book.

In the Verb Tables section look up the verb forms you need for **tu** in the present tense. Then follow the model and do the first set of tasks. They correspond to Unit 2 in the main body of the book. Before moving on, check your results in the 'Key to the exercises', for correctness. Carry on in a similar manner for Unit 4 and subsequent units.

Present (Unit 2)

‖ **você compra** *you buy* ⇒ **(tu) compras** *you buy* (**comprar**)
‖ **você conduz** *you lead* ⇒ **(tu) conduzes** *you lead* (**conduzir**)

1 **você vende** *you sell* (verb **vender**)

2 **você sai** *you get out, leave* (**sair**)

3 **você passeia** *you take a walk* (**passear**)

4 **você segue** *you follow, go* (**seguir**)

5 **você sobe** *you climb up* (**subir**)

6 **Você vira** à direita na próxima esquina. (**virar**)
   You turn right at the next corner.

7 **Você fala** Português muito bem. (**falar**)
   You speak Portuguese very well.

8 **Você é** o meu melhor amigo. (**ser**)
   You are my best friend.

9 **Você introduz** as moedas e **pressiona** a tecla.
                                    (**introduzir**; **pressionar**)
   You insert the coins and press the key.

10 **Vocês podem** vir também; **cabem** no carro. (**poder**; **caber**)
   You can come along; there is room for you in the car
   (you fit in the car).

Present Continuous and Perfect (Unit 4)

(A) Present Continuous

> **Você está trabalhando** muito.   (**estar, trabalhar**)
> **Você está a trabalhar** muito. (Eur.)
> $\Rightarrow$
> **(Tu) estás trabalhando** muito.
> **(Tu) estás a trabalhar** muito. (Eur.)
> *You are working hard.*

1 **Você está fingindo**.   (**estar, fingir**)
  Você está a fingir. (Eur.)
  You are pretending.

2 **Você está sofrendo** desnecessariamente.   (**estar, sofrer**)
  Você está a sofrer desnecessariamente. (Eur.)
  You are suffering unnecessarily.

3 **Vocês estão preparando** um bom jantar.   (**estar, preparar**)
  Vocês estão a preparar um bom jantar. (Eur.)
  You are preparing a nice dinner.

(B) Present Perfect

> **Você tem trabalhado** demais.   (**ter, trabalhar**)
> $\Rightarrow$
> **(Tu) tens trabalhado** demais.
> *You have been working too hard.*

1 **Você tem dito** isso muitas vezes.   (**ter, dizer**)
  You have been saying that often.

2 **Você tem feito** muita coisa ultimamente.   (**ter, fazer**)
  You have been doing a lot lately.

3 **Vocês têm emagrecido** muito nos últimos meses.   (**ter, emagrecer**)
  You have been losing a lot of weight in the past few months.

Tenses for the Past (Unit 5)

(A) Preterite

> **Você comprou** um carro muito bom.   (**comprar**)
> $\Rightarrow$
> **(Tu) compraste** um carro muito bom.
> *You have bought a very good car.*

1 **Você aprendeu** Português rapidamente.   (**aprender**)
  You have learned Portuguese quickly.

2 **Você teve** sorte!   (**ter**)
  You were lucky! (had luck)

3 **Você disse** isso na reunião de ontem.   (**dizer**)
  You said that in yesterday's meeting.

(B) Imperfect

> **Você era** um aluno aplicado.   (**ser**)
> $\Rightarrow$
> **(Tu) eras** um aluno aplicado.
> *You were a hard-working pupil.*

1 **Você parecia** feliz na festa.   (**parecer**)
  You looked happy at the party.

2 Naquela época **você trabalhava** no centro da cidade.   (**trabalhar**)
  At that time you were working in the town centre.

3 **Você costumava telefonar** para mim todos os dias.
                                   (**costumar, telefonar**)
  You used to phone me every day.

(C) Imperfect Continuous

> **Você estava trabalhando** nesta escola.   (**estar, trabalhar**)
> **Você estava a trabalhar** nesta escola. (Eur.)
> $\Rightarrow$
> **(Tu) estavas trabalhando** nesta escola.
> **(Tu) estavas a trabalhar** nesta escola. (Eur.)
> *You were working at this school.*

1 **Você estava pensando** que ela não vinha quando a campainha da porta tocou.
Você estava a pensar que ela não vinha quando a campainha da porta tocou. (Eur.)

(**estar**, **pensar**)

You were thinking she was not coming when the door bell rang.

2 **Vocês estavam descalçando** os sapatos quando eu entrei.
Vocês estavam a descalçar os sapatos quando eu entrei. (Eur.)

(**estar**, **descalçar**)

You were taking your shoes off when I walked in.

Tenses for the Future (Unit 6)

(A) Future

Ele não sabe se **você virá**.   (**vir**)

⇒

Ele não sabe se (**tu**) **virás**.

He doesn't know whether you will come.

1 **Você comprará** um carro novo, penso eu.   (**comprar**)
You will buy a new car, I think.

2 **Você saberá** tudo em breve.   (**saber**)
You will know everything soon.

3 De acordo com o horário, **vocês chegarão** às 9 horas.   (**chegar**)
According to the timetable, you will arrive at 9 o'clock.

(B) Colloquial Future

Não há problema, **você vai perceber** tudo.   (**ir**, **perceber**)

⇒

Não há problema, (**tu**) **vais perceber** tudo.

No problem, you are going to understand everything.

1 Cuidado! **Você vai cortar** o dedo.   (**ir**, **cortar**)
Watch out! You are about to cut your finger.

2 **Você vai fazer** quarenta anos dois meses antes dela.   (**ir**, **fazer**)
You will be forty (years old) two months before her.

3 Então **vocês vão ficar** aqui até amanhã.   (**ir**, **ficar**)
I see you are going to stay here until tomorrow.

197

(C) Emphatic Future

> **Você há de conseguir** isso.   (**haver, conseguir**)
>   ⇒
> (**Tu) hás de conseguir** isso.
>
> *You will achieve that.*

1 **Você há de pertencer** ao clube; vou recomendar.   (**haver, pertencer**)
   You will belong to the club; I am going to make a recommendation.
2 **Você há de receber** o dinheiro, eu prometo.   (**haver, receber**)
   You shall have the money, I promise.
3 **Vocês hão de participar** na reunião de amanhã.   (**haver, participar**)
   You are supposed to take part in tomorrow's meeting.

Command Forms (Unit 7)

> **Entre!**   (**entrar**)
>   ⇒
> **Entra!**
> *Come in!*

1 **Abra** a porta!   (**abrir**)
   Open the door!
2 **Feche** a janela, por favor.   (**fechar**)
   Close the window, please.
3 Por favor, **repita**.   (**repetir**)
   Please say it again.
4 **Saia** daí!   (**sair**)
   Get out of there!
5 **Traga** o livro amanhã.   (**trazer**)
   Bring the book tomorrow.
6 (a) Ah, **desculpe**!   (**desculpar**)
   (b) Ah, **desculpem**!
      Oh, sorry!
7 (a) **Suba**!   (**subir**)
   (b) **Subam**!
      Climb up!
8 (a) **Fique** aqui!   (**ficar**)
   (b) **Fiquem** aqui!
      Stay here!

198

9 (a) Boa noite, **durma** bem.   (**dormir**)
  (b) Boa noite, **durmam** bem.
      Good night, sleep well.

Present Subjunctive (Unit 8)

Eu espero que **você goste** do bolo.   (**gostar**)
        ⇒
Eu espero que (**tu**) **gostes** do bolo.
I hope you will like the cake.

1 Eu espero que **você seja** muito feliz.   (**ser**)
    I hope that you will be very happy.
2 Eu desejo que **você faça** boa viagem.   (**fazer**)
    I hope that you may have a good journey.
3 É possivel que **você obtenha** um bom resultado.   (**obter**)
    You may obtain a good result. (it is possible that you will obtain)
4 (a) Eu duvido que **você saiba** isso.   (**saber**)
  (b) Eu duvido que **vocês saibam** isso.
      I doubt that you will know that.
5 (a) Ele pede que **você venha** já.   (**vir**)
  (b) Ele pede que **vocês venham** já.
      He asks for you to come straight away. (that you come)

Conditional (Unit 9)

Eu pensava que **você viria** hoje.   (**vir**)
        ⇒
Eu pensava que (**tu**) **virias** hoje.
I thought that you would come today.

1 Quem sabe se **você ficaria** ou não milionário...   (**ficar**)
    Who knows whether you would or would not become a millionaire....
2 Eu sabia que **você faria** isso.   (**fazer**)
    I knew that you would do that.
3 (a) Você poderia mostrar-me no mapa onde eu estou?   (**poder**)
  (b) Vocês poderiam mostrar-me no mapa onde eu estou?
      I wonder whether you could please show me on the map where I am.

199

Imperfect and Future Subjunctive (Unit 10)

(A) Imperfect Subjunctive

Talvez **você pudesse** falar com eles.   (**poder**)
⇒
Talvez **(tu) pudesses** falar com eles.
Perhaps you could talk to them.

1 Eu pensava que **você apreciasse** essa música.   (**apreciar**)
I thought that you might appreciate that music.

2 Eu gostaria que **você considerasse** esse assunto.   (**considerar**)
I would like you to consider that matter. (that you would consider)

3 (a) Tomara que **você sorrisse**.   (**sorrir**)
  (b) Tomara que **vocês sorrissem**.
     I wish you would smile.

4 (a) Ele pediu que **você falasse** mais baixo.   (**falar**)
  (b) Ele pediu que **vocês falassem** mais baixo.
     He asked for you to speak more quietly. (that you would speak)

(B) Future Subjunctive

Nós faremos como **você quiser**.   (**querer**)
⇒
Nós faremos como **(tu) quiseres**.
We will do as you please .

1 Será melhor se **você verificar** que o carro tem combustível para a viagem.   (**verificar**)
It will be better if you check that the car has enough fuel for the journey.

2 (a) Se **você vier**, podemos ir jantar juntos.   (**vir**)
  (b) Se **vocês vierem**, podemos ir jantar juntos.
     If you come, we can go for dinner together.

3 (a) Vamos dar uma festa quando **você chegar**.   (**chegar**)
  (b) Vamos dar uma festa quando **vocês chegarem**.
     We are going to throw a party when you arrive.

Verb Tenses with *'when'*, *'if'* and Other Cases (Unit 11)

Se **você viesse**, iríamos à praia.　　(**vir**)

⇒

Se (**tu**) **viesses**, iríamos à praia.
If you came, we would go to the beach.

Quando **você chegar**, podemos tomar alguma coisa.　　(**chegar**)

⇒

Quando (**tu**) **chegares**, podemos tomar alguma coisa.
When you come, we can have a drink.

Este é o livro que **você pediu**.　　(**pedir**)

⇒

Este é o livro que (**tu**) **pediste**.
This is the book you asked for.

1　Fico sempre muito contente quando **você vem**.　　(**vir**)
　I am always very pleased to see you. (very happy when you come)

2　Se **você depositasse** esse cheque, o saldo ficaria positivo.　　(**depositar**)
　If you deposited that cheque, the balance would be in credit.

3　Vou preparar o jantar antes que **você tenha** fome.　　(**ter**)
　I am going to prepare dinner before you get hungry.

4 (a) **Pague** quando **puder**.　　(**pagar; poder**)
　(b) **Paguem** quando **puderem**.
　　Pay when you can.

5 (a) **Venha** se **puder**.　　(**vir; poder**)
　(b) **Venham** se **puderem**.
　　Come along if you can.

6 (a) **Você é** o aluno que **fala** Português melhor.　　(**ser; falar**)
　　You are the student who speaks Portuguese the best.
　(b) **Vocês são** os alunos que **falam** Português melhor.
　　You are the students who speak Portuguese the best.

201

Verbs Working Together (Unit 12)

Você tem apresentado um trabalho excelente.   (**ter, apresentar**)

⇒

(**Tu**) **tens apresentado** um trabalho excelente.

You have been producing excellent work.

Você estava dormindo e eu não quis incomodar. (**estar, dormir**)
Você estava a dormir e eu não quis incomodar. (Eur.)

⇒

(**Tu**) **estavas dormindo** e eu não quis incomodar.
(**Tu**) **estavas a dormir** e eu não quis incomodar. (Eur.)

You were sleeping and I didn't want to disturb you.

Você devia estudar mais.   (**dever, estudar**)

⇒

(**Tu**) **devias estudar** mais.

You ought to study harder.

1 Amanhã, a esta hora, você já **terá embarcado** no cruzeiro.

(**ter, embarcar**)

By this time tomorrow you will be on board the ship for your cruise.
(will have boarded the ship)

2 Neste momento **você estaria tomando** banho de sol na praia se o avião
não estivesse atrasado.
Neste momento **você estaria a tomar** banho de sol na praia se o avião
não estivesse atrasado. (Eur.)   (**estar, tomar**)
At this moment you would have been sunbathing on the beach if the
plane were not late.

3 Parabéns! **Você vai falando** Português cada vez melhor.   (**ir, falar**)
Congratulations! You are speaking Portuguese better and better.

4 Por favor **volte a telefonar** em breve.   (**voltar, telefonar**)
Please phone again soon.

5 (a) Discutimos o assunto quando **você tiver reunido** todos os dados.
  (b) Discutimos o assunto quando **vocês tiverem reunido** todos os
       dados.   (**ter, reunir**)
       We will discuss the matter when you have gathered all the data.

202

6 (a) Enquanto **você vai fazer** compras, eu vou arrumar a casa.
(b) Enquanto **vocês vão fazer** compras, eu vou arrumar a casa.

(**ir, fazer**)

While you are going shopping, I am going to tidy up around the house.

Personal Infinitive (Unit 14)

> É melhor **você vir** amanhã.
> ⇒
> É melhor (**tu**) **vires** amanhã.
> *It is better for you to come tomorrow.*
>
> Eu comprei esta revista para **você ler**.
> ⇒
> Eu comprei esta revista para (**tu**) **leres**.
> *I have bought this magazine for you to read.*

1 É necessário **você fazer** isso sem mais demora.
It is necessary for you to do that without further delay.

2 Já está na hora de **você voltar** para casa.
It is time you go back home.

3 Eu cortei uma fatia do bolo para **você experimentar**.
I have cut out a slice of the cake for you to try.

4 É melhor **você cozer** esta carne agora.
It is better for you to cook this meat now.

5 Eu trouxe o caderno para **você corrigir** os erros.
I have brought the exercise book for you to make the corrections.

6 (a) Isto é um questionário para **você responder**.
(b) Isto é um questionário para **vocês responderem**.
This is a questionnaire for you to answer.

7 (a) É favor **você sair** pela porta da direita.
(b) É favor **vocês saírem** pela porta da direita.
You are asked to please leave by the door on the right.

Questions, Negatives and Emphasis (Unit 15)

(A) Negative sentences, questions and emphasis

> **Você não mora** aqui, eu sei...   **(morar)**
> ⇒
> **(Tu) não moras** aqui, eu sei...
> *You don't live here, I know...*
>
> **Você fala mesmo** essa língua?   **(falar)**
> ⇒
> **(Tu) falas mesmo** essa língua?
> *Do you really speak that language?*

1 **Você não sabe mesmo** falar essa língua.   **(saber)**
   You can not speak that language at all.
2 **Você tenciona** fazer isso?   **(tencionar)**
   Are you intending to do that?
3 O que é que **você disse**?   **(dizer)**
   What have you said?
4 (a) Eu sei que **você não frequentou** essa escola.   **(frequentar)**
   (b) Eu sei que **vocês não frequentaram** essa escola.
   I know that you did not attend that school.
5 (a) **Você gostou** do hotel onde **ficou**?   **(gostar; ficar)**
   (b) **Vocês gostaram** do hotel onde **ficaram**?
   Did you like the hotel where you stayed?

(B) Negative commands and urgent requests

> **Não faça** isso.   **(fazer)**
> ⇒
> **Não faças** isso.
> *Don't do that.*
>
> **Não esteja** triste.   **(estar)**
> ⇒
> **Não estejas** triste.
> *Don't be sad.*

1 **Não atenda** a porta.   (**atender**)
   Don't answer the door.
2 **Não ocupe** essa cadeira.   (**ocupar**)
   Don't take that chair.
3 **Não pendure** o casaco aí.   (**pendurar**)
   Don't hang your coat there.
4 **Não desapareça mesmo**.   (**desaparecer**)
   Do keep in touch. (don't vanish)
5 (a) **Não vire** à direita, **vire** à esquerda.   (**virar**)
   (b) **Não virem** à direita, **virem** à esquerda.
      Don't turn right, turn left.
6 (a) **Por favor não vá** a essa festa, **venha** à nossa.   (**ir**; **vir**)
   (b) **Por favor não vão** a essa festa, **venham** à nossa.
      Please don't go to that party, do come to ours.

Passive Voice (Unit 16)

Você é respeitada por todos.   (**ser, respeitar**)
   $\Rightarrow$
(**Tu**) **és respeitada por** todos.
You are respected by everyone.

Você foi incluído no grupo.   (**ser, incluir**)
   $\Rightarrow$
(**Tu**) **foste incluído** no grupo.
You have been included in the group.

1 **Você é** muito **estimada por** nós.   (**ser, estimar**)
   We have a high regard for you. (you are highly regarded by us)
2 **Você é pretendido por** todas as jovens.   (**ser, pretender**)
   All the girls are after you. (you are highly sought after by the girls)
3 Quando é que **você foi roubado**?   (**ser, roubar**)
   When were you robbed?
4 (a) **Por** quem é que **você foi convidado**?   (**ser, convidar**)
   (b) **Por** quem é que **vocês foram convidados**?
      By whom were you invited?
5 (a) **Você foi instalada** no melhor hotel da vila.   (**ser, instalar**)
   (b) **Vocês foram instaladas** no melhor hotel da vila.
      You were lodged at the best hotel in town.

205

Reflexive Construction (Unit 17)

A que horas é que **você se deitou**?   (**deitar**)

⇒

A que horas é que (**tu**) **te deitaste**?

At what time did you go to bed?

Hoje **você levantou-se** muito cedo.   (**levantar**)
Hoje **você se levantou** muito cedo. (Am.)

⇒

Hoje (**tu**) **levantaste-te** muito cedo.
Hoje (**tu**) **te levantaste** muito cedo. (Am.)

Today you got up very early.

1 **Você demorou-se** muito.   (**demorar**)
   Você se demorou muito. (Am.)
   You took your time. (delayed yourself)
2 **Você ofereceu-se** para fazer isto?   (**oferecer**)
   Você se ofereceu para fazer isto? (Am.)
   Have you volunteered to do this? (offered yourself)
3 Não **se zangue**!   (**zangar**)
   Don't get cross!
4 **Afaste-se**! A árvore vai cair.   (**afastar**)
   Stand back! The tree is falling.
5 Cuidado! Não **se aproxime**.   (**aproximar**)
   Watch out! Don't come near.
6 (a) Como é que **você se chama**?   (**chamar**)
   (b) Como é que **vocês se chamam**?
       What is your name? (how do you call yourself / yourselves?)
7 (a) Não **se preocupe**.   (**preocupar**)
   (b) Não **se preocupem**.
       Don't worry.
8 (a) **Divirta-se**!   (**divertir**)
       Enjoy yourself!
   (b) **Divirtam-se**!
       Enjoy yourselves!

Pronominal Construction (Unit 18)

> Quando é que **você me viu**?   (**ver**)
>   ⇒
> Quando é que (**tu**) **me viste**?
> *When did you see me?*
>
> Muito prazer em **conhecê-lo**.   (**conhecer**)
>   ⇒
> Muito prazer em **conhecer-te**.
> *Delighted to meet you.*

1 **Você ama-me** ou não?   (**amar**)
   Você me ama ou não? (Am.)
   Do you love me or not?
2 Muito prazer em **conhecê-la**.   (**conhecer**)
   Delighted to meet you.
3 Com o alto-falante todos podem **ouvi-lo**.   (**ouvir**)
   With the loudspeaker everyone can hear you.
4 (a) **Você** não **me viu** lá.   (**ver**)
  (b) **Vocês** não **me viram** lá.
      You did not see me there.
5 (a) Onde é que **você nos vai encontrar**?   (**ir, encontrar**)
  (b) Onde é que **vocês nos vão encontrar**?
      Where are you going to meet us?
6 (a) Obrigada por **me proteger** da chuva.   (**proteger**)
  (b) Obrigada por **me protegerem** da chuva.
      Thank you for sheltering me from the rain.

Indirect Speech (Unit 19)

> Ela disse que no ano seguinte **você não ficaria** naquele hotel.   (**ficar**)
>   ⇒
> Ela disse que no ano seguinte (**tu**) **não ficarias** naquele hotel.
> *She said that the following year you would not stay at that hotel.*
>
> Ele perguntou se **você tinha declarado** isso na alfândega.   (**declarar**)
>   ⇒
> Ele perguntou se (**tu**) **tinhas declarado** isso na alfândega.
> *He asked whether you had declared that to Customs.*

1 Ele quer saber o que significa o que **você disse**. **(dizer)**
He wants to know the meaning of what you said.

2 Eu penso que **você apontou** para a causa do problema. **(apontar)**
I think that you have pointed to the cause of the problem.

3 Nós tínhamos notado que **você estava** preocupado. **(estar)**
We had noticed that you were worried.

4 Ele perguntou se **você possui** algumas casas nesta cidade. **(possuir)**
He has asked whether you own some houses in this city.

5 Ele disse que **você estava aguardando** resposta.   **(estar, aguardar)**
Ele disse que você **estava a aguardar** resposta. (Eur.)
He said that you were awaiting a reply.

6 Ele quer saber quando é que **você publicou** a notícia. **(publicar)**
He wants to know when you published the news.

7 Ele pede que **você** nos **comunique** a decisão assim que possível.
                                                (comunicar)
He asks for you to tell us the decision as soon as possible.

8 Eu penso que **você adquiriu** um hábito muito mau. **(adquirir)**
I think that you have acquired a very bad habit.

9 Eles disseram que **você tinha assinalado** no mapa o local do acidente.
                                              (ter, assinalar)
They said that you had marked on the map the location of the accident.

10 (a) Eu tinha pensado que **você teria** em mente um plano que
      consistisse em duas fases distintas.   **(ter)**
  (b) Eu tinha pensado que **vocês teriam** em mente um plano que
      consistisse em duas fases distintas.
      I had thought that you had in mind a plan that would consist
      of two distinct phases.

11 (a) Ele diz que **você vai conceder** benefícios especiais para os
      empregados assim que **puder**.
                                       (ir, conceder; poder)
  (b) Ele diz que **vocês vão conceder** benefícios especiais para os
      empregados assim que **puderem**.
      He says that you are going to grant special benefits for the
      employees as soon as you can.

208

Verb Tables

This section is a quick reference guide. It sums up key points that were explained throughout the units in this course, as follows:

* **tense endings for regular verbs**

* **irregular verb tenses**

* **irregular past participles**

* **radical-changing verbs**

* **orthography-changing verbs**

* **other changing verbs**

* **compound verbs conjugated like special verbs
      (irregular; radical-changing; orthography-changing;
      or displaying other anomalous changes)**

The two second person systems are covered. For *you* singular (talking to one person) you have the verb endings for both **você** and **tu**. For *you* plural (talking to more than one person) you have the verb endings for both **vocês** and **vós**. The latter is shown in brackets on the tables, as its use is very limited.

If you need more information on any of the points dealt with in this section, you have a choice of two different routes to the relevant pages in the course. You can either look up what you want on the contents pages, at the beginning of the book, or in the cross-reference index, at the very end of the book.

Regular Verbs (endings only) – Table 1 of 2

Infinitive	Subject / Person	Present	Preterite	Imperfect	Pluperfect (Simple)	Future	Command Forms
-ar	1. eu	-o	-ei	-ava	-ara	-arei	--
	2. tu	-as	-aste	-avas	-aras	-arás	-a
	2. você	-a	-ou	-ava	-ara	-ará	-e
	3. ele/ela	-a	-ou	-ava	-ara	-ará	-e
	1. nós	-amos	-amos/-ámos	-ávamos	-áramos	-aremos	-emos
	2. (vós)	(-ais)	(-astes)	(-áveis)	(-áreis)	(-areis)	(-ai)
	2. vocês	-am	-aram	-avam	-aram	-arão	-em
	3. eles/elas	-am	-aram	-avam	-aram	-arão	--
-er	1. eu	-o	-i	-ia	-era	-erei	--
	2. tu	-es	-este	-ias	-eras	-erás	-e
	2. você	-e	-eu	-ia	-era	-erá	-a
	3. ele/ela	-e	-eu	-ia	-era	-erá	-a
	1. nós	-emos	-emos	-íamos	-êramos	-eremos	-amos
	2. (vós)	(-eis)	(-estes)	(-íeis)	(-êreis)	(-ereis)	(-ei)
	2. vocês	-em	-eram	-iam	-eram	-erão	-am
	3. eles/elas	-em	-eram	-iam	-eram	-erão	--
-ir	1. eu	-o	-i	-ia	-ira	-irei	--
	2. tu	-es	-iste	-ias	-iras	-irás	-e
	2. você	-e	-iu	-ia	-ira	-irá	-a
	3. ele/ela	-e	-iu	-ia	-ira	-irá	-a
	1. nós	-imos	-imos	-íamos	-íramos	-iremos	-amos
	2. (vós)	(-is)	(-istes)	(-íeis)	(-íreis)	(-ireis)	(-i)
	2. vocês	-em	-iram	-iam	-iram	-irão	-am
	3. eles/elas	-em	-iram	-iam	-iram	-irão	--

For **-or** verbs follow the pattern for **pôr** in the tables for irregular verbs.

Regular Verbs (endings only) – Table 2 of 2

Subject / Person	Present Subjunctive	Imperfect Subjunctive	Future Subjunctive	Conditional	Personal Infinitive	Present Participle	Past Participle
1. eu	-e	-asse	-ar	-aria	-ar		
2. tu	-es	-asses	-ares	-arias	-ares		
2. você	-e	-asse	-ar	-aria	-ar		
3. ele/ela	-e	-asse	-ar	-aria	-ar	-ando	-ado
1. nós	-emos	-ássemos	-armos	-aríamos	-armos		
2. (vós)	(-eis)	(-ásseis)	(-ardes)	(-aríeis)	(-ardes)		
2. vocês	-em	-assem	-arem	-ariam	-arem		
3. eles/elas	-em	-assem	-arem	-ariam	-arem		
1. eu	-a	-esse	-er	-eria	-er		
2. tu	-as	-esses	-eres	-erias	-eres		
2. você	-a	-esse	-er	-eria	-er		
3. ele/ela	-a	-esse	-er	-eria	-er	-endo	-ido
1. nós	-amos	-êssemos	-ermos	-eríamos	-ermos		
2. (vós)	(-ais)	(-êsseis)	(-erdes)	(-eríeis)	(-erdes)		
2. vocês	-am	-essem	-erem	-eriam	-erem		
3. eles/elas	-am	-essem	-erem	-eriam	-erem		
1. eu	-a	-isse	-ir	-iria	-ir		
2. tu	-as	-isses	-ires	-irias	-ires		
2. você	-a	-isse	-ir	-iria	-ir		
3. ele/ela	-a	-isse	-ir	-iria	-ir	-indo	-ido
1. nós	-amos	-íssemos	-irmos	-iríamos	-irmos		
2. (vós)	(-ais)	(-ísseis)	(-irdes)	(-iríeis)	(-irdes)		
2. vocês	-am	-issem	-irem	-iriam	-irem		
3. eles/elas	-am	-issem	-irem	-iriam	-irem		

Note: Entries for 'vós' are in brackets in view of their very limited use.

211

Irregular verbs

Infinitive	Present	Preterite	Imperfect	Pluperfect (Simple)	Future
caber to fit	caibo cabes cabe cabe cabemos (cabeis) cabem cabem	coube coubeste coube coube coubemos (coubestes) couberam couberam	Regular	coubera couberas coubera coubera coubéramos (coubéreis) couberam couberam	Regular
crer to believe	creio crês crê crê cremos (credes) creem creem	Regular cri, etc.	Regular cria, etc.	Regular	Regular
dar to give	dou dás dá dá damos (dais) dão dão	dei deste deu deu demos (destes) deram deram	Regular dava, etc.	dera deras dera dera déramos (déreis) deram deram	Regular
dizer to say	digo dizes diz diz dizemos (dizeis) dizem dizem	disse disseste disse disse dissemos (dissestes) disseram disseram	Regular	dissera disseras dissera dissera disséramos (disséreis) disseram disseram	direi dirás dirá dirá diremos (direis) dirão dirão
estar to be	estou estás está está estamos (estais) estão estão	estive estiveste esteve esteve estivemos (estivestes) estiveram estiveram	Regular	estivera estiveras estivera estivera estivéramos (estivéreis) estiveram estiveram	Regular

Command forms	Present Subjunctive	Imperfect Subjunctive	Future Subjunctive	Conditional	Participles
(*)	caiba caibas caiba caiba caibamos (caibais) caibam caibam	coubesse coubesses coubesse coubesse coubéssemos (coubésseis) coubessem coubessem	couber couberes couber couber coubermos (couberdes) couberem couberem	Regular	Pres. cabendo Past cabido
--- crê creia --- creiamos (crede) creiam ---	creia creias creia creia creiamos (creiais) creiam creiam	Regular	Regular	Regular	Pres. crendo Past crido
--- dá dê --- demos/ dêmos (dai) deem ---	dê dês dê dê demos/ dêmos (deis) deem deem	desse desses desse desse déssemos (désseis) dessem dessem	der deres der der dermos (derdes) derem derem	Regular	Pres. dando Past dado
--- diz[e] diga --- digamos (dizei) digam ---	diga digas diga diga digamos (digais) digam digam	dissesse dissesses dissesse dissesse disséssemos (dissésseis) dissessem dissessem	disser disseres disser disser dissermos (disserdes) disserem disserem	diria dirias diria diria diríamos (diríeis) diriam diriam	Pres. dizendo Past dito
--- está esteja --- estejamos (estai) estejam ---	esteja estejas esteja esteja estejamos (estejais) estejam estejam	estivesse estivesses estivesse estivesse estivéssemos (estivésseis) estivessem estivessem	estiver estiveres estiver estiver estivermos (estiverdes) estiverem estiverem	Regular	Pres. estando Past estado

(*) Not applicable due to its meaning.

213

Infinitive	Present	Preterite	Imperfect	Pluperfect (Simple)	Future
fazer to do, make	faço fazes faz faz fazemos (fazeis) fazem fazem	fiz fizeste fez fez fizemos (fizestes) fizeram fizeram	Regular	fizera fizeras fizera fizera fizéramos (fizéreis) fizeram fizeram	farei farás fará fará faremos (fareis) farão farão
haver to exist, there to be, to have	hei hás há há havemos (haveis) hão hão	houve houveste houve houve houvemos (houvestes) houveram houveram	Regular	houvera houveras houvera houvera houvéramos (houvéreis) houveram houveram	Regular
ir to go	vou vais vai vai vamos (ides) vão vão	fui foste foi foi fomos (fostes) foram foram	Regular ia, etc.	fora foras fora fora fôramos (fôreis) foram foram	Regular
ler to read	leio lês lê lê lemos (ledes) leem leem	Regular li, etc.	Regular lia, etc.	Regular	Regular
medir to measure	meço medes mede mede medimos (medis) medem medem	Regular	Regular	Regular	Regular

Command forms	Present Subjunctive	Imperfect Subjunctive	Future Subjunctive	Conditional	Participles
---	faça	fizesse	fizer	faria	*Pres.*
faz[e]	faças	fizesses	fizeres	farias	fazendo
faça	faça	fizesse	fizer	faria	*Past*
---	faça	fizesse	fizer	faria	feito
façamos	façamos	fizéssemos	fizermos	faríamos	
(fazei)	(façais)	(fizésseis)	(fizerdes)	(faríeis)	
façam	façam	fizessem	fizerem	fariam	
---	façam	fizessem	fizerem	fariam	
---	haja	houvesse	houver		*Pres.*
há	hajas	houvesses	houveres		havendo
haja	haja	houvesse	houver		*Past*
---	haja	houvesse	houver	*Regular*	havido
hajamos	hajamos	houvéssemos	houvermos		
(havei)	(hajais)	(houvésseis)	(houverdes)		
hajam	hajam	houvessem	houverem		
---	hajam	houvessem	houverem		
---	vá	fosse	for		*Pres.*
vai	vás	fosses	fores		indo
vá	vá	fosse	for		*Past*
---	vá	fosse	for	*Regular*	ido
vamos	vamos	fôssemos	formos		
(ide)	(vades)	(fôsseis)	(fordes)		
vão	vão	fossem	forem		
---	vão	fossem	forem		
---	leia				*Pres.*
lê	leias				lendo
leia	leia				*Past*
---	leia	*Regular*	*Regular*	*Regular*	lido
leiamos	leiamos				
(lede)	(leiais)				
leiam	leiam				
---	leiam				
---	meça				*Pres.*
mede	meças				medindo
meça	meça				*Past*
---	meça	*Regular*	*Regular*	*Regular*	medido
meçamos	meçamos				
(medi)	(meçais)				
meçam	meçam				
---	meçam				

215

Infinitive	Present	Preterite	Imperfect	Pluperfect (Simple)	Future
ouvir *to hear*	ouço ouves ouve ouve ouvimos (ouvis) ouvem ouvem	*Regular*	*Regular*	*Regular*	*Regular*
pedir *to ask for*	peço pedes pede pede pedimos (pedis) pedem pedem	*Regular*	*Regular*	*Regular*	*Regular*
perder *to lose*	perco perdes perde perde perdemos (perdeis) perdem perdem	*Regular*	*Regular*	*Regular*	*Regular*
poder *can, may*	posso podes pode pode podemos (podeis) podem podem	pude pudeste pôde pôde pudemos (pudestes) puderam puderam	*Regular*	pudera puderas pudera pudera pudéramos (pudéreis) puderam puderam	*Regular*
pôr *to put*	ponho pões põe põe pomos (pondes) põem põem	pus puseste pôs pôs pusemos (pusestes) puseram puseram	punha punhas punha punha púnhamos (púnheis) punham punham	pusera puseras pusera pusera puséramos (puséreis) puseram puseram	porei porás porá porá poremos (poreis) porão porão

Command forms	Present Subjunctive	Imperfect Subjunctive	Future Subjunctive	Conditional	Participles
---	ouça				*Pres.*
ouve	ouças				ouvindo
ouça	ouça				*Past*
---	ouça	*Regular*	*Regular*	*Regular*	ouvido
ouçamos	ouçamos				
(ouvi)	(ouçais)				
ouçam	ouçam				
---	ouçam				
---	peça				*Pres.*
pede	peças				pedindo
peça	peça				*Past*
---	peça	*Regular*	*Regular*	*Regular*	pedido
peçamos	peçamos				
(pedi)	(peçais)				
peçam	peçam				
---	peçam				
---	perca				*Pres.*
perde	percas				perdendo
perca	perca				*Past*
---	perca	*Regular*	*Regular*	*Regular*	perdido
percamos	percamos				
(perdei)	(percais)				
percam	percam				
---	percam				
	possa	pudesse	puder		*Pres.*
	possas	pudesses	puderes		podendo
(*)	possa	pudesse	puder		*Past*
	possa	pudesse	puder	*Regular*	podido
	possamos	pudéssemos	pudermos		
	(possais)	(pudésseis)	(puderdes)		
	possam	pudessem	puderem		
	possam	pudessem	puderem		
---	ponha	pusesse	puser	poria	*Pres.*
põe	ponhas	pusesses	puseres	porias	pondo
ponha	ponha	pusesse	puser	poria	*Past*
---	ponha	pusesse	puser	poria	posto
ponhamos	ponhamos	puséssemos	pusermos	poríamos	
(ponde)	(ponhais)	(pusésseis)	(puserdes)	(poríeis)	
ponham	ponham	pusessem	puserem	poriam	
---	ponham	pusessem	puserem	poriam	

(*) Not applicable due to its meaning.

Infinitive	Present	Preterite	Imperfect	Pluperfect (Simple)	Future
querer to want	quero queres quer quer queremos (quereis) querem querem	quis quiseste quis quis quisemos (quisestes) quiseram quiseram	Regular	quisera quiseras quisera quisera quiséramos (quiséreis) quiseram quiseram	Regular
rir to laugh	rio ris ri ri rimos (rides) riem riem	Regular ri, etc.	Regular ria, etc.	Regular	Regular
saber to know	sei sabes sabe sabe sabemos (sabeis) sabem sabem	soube soubeste soube soube soubemos (soubestes) souberam souberam	Regular	soubera souberas soubera soubera soubéramos (soubéreis) souberam souberam	Regular
ser to be	sou és é é somos (sois) são são	fui foste foi foi fomos (fostes) foram foram	era eras era era éramos (éreis) eram eram	fora foras fora fora fôramos (fôreis) foram foram	Regular
ter to have	tenho tens tem tem temos (tendes) têm têm	tive tiveste teve teve tivemos (tivestes) tiveram tiveram	tinha tinhas tinha tinha tínhamos (tínheis) tinham tinham	tivera tiveras tivera tivera tivéramos (tivéreis) tiveram tiveram	Regular

Command forms	Present Subjunctive	Imperfect Subjunctive	Future Subjunctive	Conditional	Participles
(*)	queira queiras queira queira queiramos (queirais) queiram queiram	quisesse quisesses quisesse quisesse quiséssemos (quisésseis) quisessem quisessem	quiser quiseres quiser quiser quisermos (quiserdes) quiserem quiserem	Regular	Pres. querendo Past querido
--- ri ria --- riamos (ride) riam ---	ria rias ria ria riamos (riais) riam riam	Regular	Regular	Regular	Pres. rindo Past rido
--- sabe saiba --- saibamos (sabei) saibam ---	saiba saibas saiba saiba saibamos (saibais) saibam saibam	soubesse soubesses soubesse soubesse soubéssemos (soubésseis) soubessem soubessem	souber souberes souber souber soubermos (souberdes) souberem souberem	Regular	Pres. sabendo Past sabido
--- sê seja --- sejamos (sede) sejam ---	seja sejas seja seja sejamos (sejais) sejam sejam	fosse fosses fosse fosse fôssemos (fôsseis) fossem fossem	for fores for for formos (fordes) forem forem	Regular	Pres. sendo Past sido
--- tem tenha --- tenhamos (tende) tenham ---	tenha tenhas tenha tenha tenhamos (tenhais) tenham tenham	tivesse tivesses tivesse tivesse tivéssemos (tivésseis) tivessem tivessem	tiver tiveres tiver tiver tivermos (tiverdes) tiverem tiverem	Regular	Pres. tendo Past tido

(*) Not applicable due to its meaning.

Infinitive	Present	Preterite	Imperfect	Pluperfect (Simple)	Future
trazer	trago	trouxe		trouxera	trarei
to bring	trazes	trouxeste		trouxeras	trarás
	traz	trouxe		trouxera	trará
	traz	trouxe	*Regular*	trouxera	trará
	trazemos	trouxemos		trouxéramos	traremos
	(trazeis)	(trouxestes)		(trouxéreis)	(trareis)
	trazem	trouxeram		trouxeram	trarão
	trazem	trouxeram		trouxeram	trarão
valer	valho				
to be	vales				
worth	vale				
	vale	*Regular*	*Regular*	*Regular*	*Regular*
	valemos				
	(valeis)				
	valem				
	valem				
ver	vejo	vi		vira	
to see	vês	viste		viras	
	vê	viu		vira	
	vê	viu	*Regular*	vira	*Regular*
	vemos	vimos	via, etc.	víramos	
	(vedes)	(vistes)		(víreis)	
	veem	viram		viram	
	veem	viram		viram	
vir	venho	vim	vinha	viera	
to come	vens	vieste	vinhas	vieras	
	vem	veio	vinha	viera	
	vem	veio	vinha	viera	*Regular*
	vimos	viemos	vínhamos	viéramos	
	(vindes)	(viestes)	(vínheis)	(viéreis)	
	vêm	vieram	vinham	vieram	
	vêm	vieram	vinham	vieram	

Note:
Verb forms for 'vós' are shown in brackets in view of their very limited use.

220

Command forms	Present Subjunctive	Imperfect Subjunctive	Future Subjunctive	Conditional	Participles
---	traga	trouxesse	trouxer	traria	*Pres.*
traz[e]	tragas	trouxesses	trouxeres	trarias	trazendo
traga	traga	trouxesse	trouxer	traria	*Past*
---	traga	trouxesse	trouxer	traria	trazido
tragamos	tragamos	trouxéssemos	trouxermos	traríamos	
(trazei)	(tragais)	(trouxésseis)	(trouxerdes)	(traríeis)	
tragam	tragam	trouxessem	trouxerem	trariam	
---	tragam	trouxessem	trouxerem	trariam	
--- (**)	valha				*Pres.*
vale	valhas				valendo
valha	valha				*Past*
---	valha	*Regular*	*Regular*	*Regular*	valido
valhamos	valhamos				
(valei)	(valhais)				
valham	valham				
---	valham				
---	veja	visse	vir		*Pres.*
vê	vejas	visses	vires		vendo
veja	veja	visse	vir		*Past*
---	veja	visse	vir	*Regular*	visto
vejamos	vejamos	víssemos	virmos		
(vede)	(vejais)	(vísseis)	(virdes)		
vejam	vejam	vissem	virem		
---	vejam	vissem	virem		
---	venha	viesse	vier		*Pres.*
vem	venhas	viesses	vieres		vindo
venha	venha	viesse	vier		*Past*
---	venha	viesse	vier	*Regular*	vindo
venhamos	venhamos	viéssemos	viermos		
(vinde)	(venhais)	(viésseis)	(vierdes)		
venham	venham	viessem	vierem		
---	venham	viessem	vierem		

(**) Used only for special meanings, e.g., Valha-me Deus!, *Help me God!*

221

Irregular past participles

verb	irregular past participle
abrir	aberto *(open)*
aceitar	aceito, aceite *(accepted)*
acender	aceso *(lit)*
cobrir	coberto *(covered)*
dizer	dito *(said)*
eleger	eleito *(elected)*
entregar	entregue *(delivered)*
enxugar	enxuto *(dry)*
escrever	escrito *(written)*
expressar	expresso *(expressed)*
exprimir	expresso *(expressed)*
expulsar	expulso *(expelled)*
extinguir	extinto *(extinguished)*
fazer	feito *(done, made)*
frigir	frito *(fried)*
ganhar	ganho *(earned, won)*
gastar	gasto *(spent)*
imprimir	impresso *(printed)*
inserir	inserto *(inserted)*
limpar	limpo *(clean)*
matar	morto *(killed)*
morrer	morto *(dead)*
omitir	omisso *(omitted)*
pagar	pago *(paid)*
pegar	pego (Am.) *(caught)*
pôr	posto *(put)*
prender	preso *(fastened, arrested)*
romper	roto *(torn)*
salvar	salvo *(rescued, safe)*
secar	seco *(dry)*
soltar	solto *(free)*
suspender	suspenso *(suspended)*
tingir	tinto *(dyed)*
ver	visto *(seen)*
vir	vindo *(come)*

Root, spelling and other changes

Radical-changing verbs

-ir verbs like **repetir** e ↓	-ir verbs like **progredir** e ↓	-ir verbs o ↓	-ir verbs u ↓
i	**i**	**u**	**o**
Present, **eu**	Present, all persons except **nós** and old **vós**	Present, **eu**	Present, **tu**, **você(s)** and **ele(s)/ela(s)**
Present subjunctive, all persons	Present subjunctive, all persons	Present subjunctive, all persons	
Command forms from present subjunctive, i.e., for **você(s)** as well as *let's* (**nós**)	Command forms from present subjunctive, i.e., for **você(s)** as well as *let's* (**nós**)	Command forms from present subjunctive, i.e., for **você(s)** as well as *let's* (**nós**)	
	Command form for **tu** (affirmative)		Command form for **tu** (affirmative)

Examples:

repetir (*to repeat*) → eu repito

progredir (*to progress*) → você progride

dormir (*to sleep*) → durma!

cobrir (*to cover*) → que eles cubram

subir (*to climb*) → ele sobe

fugir (*to flee*) → foge!

223

Other cases

-ear verbs	-iar verbs like **odiar**	-oer verbs	-air verbs	-uir verbs like **construir** (see also Note below)	-uzir verbs
-e	**-i**	**-o**	**-a**	**-u**	**-z**
↓	↓	↓	↓	↓	↓
-ei	**-ei**	**-ó** (*)	**-ai** (**)	**-ó, -o** (*)	**-z** (***)
Present in all persons except **nós** and old **vós**	Present in all persons except **nós** and old **vós**	Present in **tu, você, ele/ela**	Present in **eu**	Present in **tu, você(s), ele(s)/ela(s)**	Present in **você, ele/ela**
Present subj. in all persons except **nós** and old **vós**	Present subj. in all persons except **nós** and old **vós**		Present subj. in all persons		
Command forms except for *let's* (**nós**) and old **vós**	Command forms except for *let's* (**nós**) and old **vós**	Command form for **tu** (affirmative)	Command forms for **você(s)** and *let's* (**nós**)	Command form for **tu** (affirmative)	Command form for **tu** (affirmative)

(*) in the Present, ending in **-óis** for **tu** and **-ói** for **você, ele / ela**; ending in **-ói** for the **tu** command form.

(**) in the Present, ending in **-ais** for **tu** and **-ai** for **você, ele / ela**; ending in **-ai** for the **tu** command form.

(***) no ending for **você**, **ele/ela** in the Present and optional in the Imperative for **tu**.

Examples:

rec**ear** (*to fear*) → eu rec**ei**o
remed**iar** (*to put right*) → remed**ei**a!
m**oer** (*to grind*) → tu m**ói**s; ele m**ói**
s**air** (*to go / come out*) → eu s**ai**o, tu s**ai**s; você s**ai**; s**ai**!; que eu s**ai**a
constr**uir** (*to build*) → tu constr**ói**s, ela constr**ói**, eles constr**oe**m; constr**ói**!
prod**uzir** (*to produce*) → ele prod**uz**; prod**uz**! *or* prod**uze**!

Note:

Most verbs in **-uir** – e.g., incl**uir** (*to include*), fl**uir** (*to flow*) – are regular but end in **-i** for **você**, **ele / ela** in the Present – você, ele / ela incl**ui** –, in **-is** for **tu** in the Present – (tu) incl**uis** –, and in **-i** for **tu** in the Imperative affirmative – incl**ui**.

Orthography-changing verbs

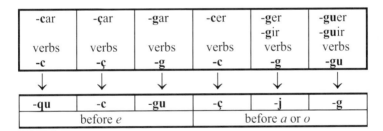

-**c**ar verbs **-c**	-**ç**ar verbs **-ç**	-**g**ar verbs **-g**	-**c**er verbs **-c**	-**g**er -**g**ir verbs **-g**	-**gu**er -**gu**ir verbs **-gu**
↓	↓	↓	↓	↓	↓
-**qu**	-**c**	-**gu**	-**ç**	-**j**	-**g**
before *e*			before *a* or *o*		

Examples:

fi**car** (*to stay*) → eu fi**quei**
come**çar** (*to start*) → come**ce**!
pa**gar** (*to pay*) → que ele pa**gue**
li**gar** (*to switch on*) → li**gue**!
conhe**cer** (*to know*) → eu conhe**ço**
fu**gir** (*to flee*) → fu**jam**!
er**guer** (*to lift*) → que eles er**gam**

Graphic accents

Some tenses and past participles where there is a sequence of two or more vowels (**a**, **e**, **i**, **o**, **u**) take a graphic accent over the particular vowel to be stressed in speech.

Tense	-oer verbs e.g., **moer**, *to grind*	-air verbs e.g., **sair**, *to go / come out*	-uir verbs e.g., **influir**, *to have an influence*
Present	**tu** and **você**, **ele** / **ela** forms (móis, mói)	**nós** and old **vós** forms (saímos, (saís))	**nós** and old **vós** forms(influímos, (influís))
Preterite	for **eu** (moí)	for all persons except **você**, **ele** / **ela** (saí, saíste, saímos, (saístes), saíram)	for all persons except **você**, **ele** / **ela** (influí, influíste, influímos, (influístes), influíram)
Imperfect	all persons (moía, moías, moía, moíamos, (moíeis), moíam)	all persons (saía, saías, saía, saíamos, (saíeis), saíam)	all persons (influía, influías, influía, influíamos, (influíeis), influíam)
Pluperfect (simple)	----------------	all persons (saíra, saíras, saíra, saíramos, (saíreis), saíram)	all persons (influíra, influíras, influíra, influíramos, (influíreis), influíram)
Commands	for **tu** (mói)	for old **vós** ((saí))	for old **vós** ((influí))
Imperfect subjunctive	----------------	all persons (saísse, saísses, saísse, saíssemos, (saísseis), saíssem)	all persons (influísse, influísses, influísse, influíssemos, (influísseis), influíssem)

226

		for **tu** and **vocês, eles / elas** (saíres, saírem)	for **tu** and **vocês, eles / elas** (influíres, influírem)
Future subjunctive	---------------	for **tu** and **vocês, eles / elas** (saíres, saírem)	for **tu** and **vocês, eles / elas** (influíres, influírem)
Personal Infinitive	---------------	for **tu** and **vocês, eles / elas** (saíres, saírem)	for **tu** and **vocês, eles / elas** (influíres, influírem)

	-oer verbs	**-air** verbs	**-uir** verbs
Past participle	e.g., moído	e.g., saído	e.g., influído

Examples:

m**oer** (*to grind*) → eu moí

d**oer** (*to hurt*) → doía

s**air** (*to go / come out*) → eu saí

s**air** (*to go / come out*) → ao saírem

atr**air** → (*to attract*) → eles atraíram

infl**uir** (*to have an influence*) → vocês influíram

constr**uir** (*to build*) → se nós construíssemos

concl**uir** (*to conclude*) → eles tinham concluído

Compound verbs

Please always remember that compounds of special verbs normally exhibit the same features as the single verbs with which they are formed. This is a list of frequently used compounds with special features.

compound verb	like
afluir *(to congregate)*	fluir *-uir verb*
atrair *(to attract)*	trair *-air verb*
compor *(to compose)*	pôr *irregular*
condizer *(to match)*	dizer *irregular*
conseguir *(to achieve)*	seguir *radical-changing +* *orthography-changing*
consentir *(to allow)*	sentir *radical-changing*
conter *(to contain)*	ter *irregular*
contradizer *(to contradict)*	dizer *irregular*
convir *(to suit)*	vir *irregular*
descobrir *(to discover)*	cobrir *radical-changing*
desfazer *(to undo)*	fazer *irregular*
influir *(to have an influence)*	fluir *-uir verb*
manter *(to maintain)*	ter *irregular*
obter *(to obtain)*	ter *irregular*
perseguir *(to chase)*	seguir *radical-changing +* *orthography-changing*
preferir *(to prefer)*	ferir *radical-changing*
pressentir *(to sense)*	sentir *radical-changing*
reabrir *(to reopen)*	abrir *irregular past participle*
recomeçar *(to restart)*	começar *orthography-changing*
reconhecer *(to recognize)*	conhecer *orthography-changing*
reconstruir *(to rebuild)*	construir *-uir verb*
referir *(to mention)*	ferir *radical-changing*
reimprimir *(to reprint)*	imprimir *irregular past participle*
repor *(to put back)*	pôr *irregular*
reproduzir *(to reproduce)*	produzir *-uzir verb*
satisfazer *(to satisfy)*	fazer *irregular*
sorrir *(to smile)*	rir *irregular*
sugerir *(to suggest)*	gerir *radical-changing*
supor *(to suppose)*	pôr *irregular*
transferir *(to transfer)*	ferir *radical-changing*

Key to the Exercises

This section contains the answers to all the exercises in the book. This is so that you can check your results and monitor your progress.

Unit 1

1.1 I would like to eat. I would like to sleep. I would like to swim. I would like to travel. **1.2** -ar: falar, nadar, fechar, viajar; -er: comer, beber;- ir: dormir, permitir; odd one out: repor.

Unit 2

2.1 (A) 2 Nós trabalhamos numa escola perto daqui. *We work in a school nearby.* **3** Nós aprendemos Português há dois meses. *We have been learning Portuguese for two months.* **4** Nós abrimos uma conta bancária amanhã. *We are opening a bank account tomorrow.* **(B) 2** trabalha **3** aprende **4** abre **5** moram **6** trabalham **7** aprendem **8** abrem.
2.2. 2 Eu estou de férias. **3** Nós somos americanos. **4** Eles conhecem esse país. **5** Ele vem amanhã. **6** Ele vai para o hotel agora. **7** Nós estamos com fome. **8** Ela tem dez anos. **9** Eu posso ir lá este fim de semana. **10** Eu prefiro chá mas ele prefere café.

The other second person (see pages 17-18)

1 (tu) vendes. **2** (tu) sais. **3** (tu) passeias. **4** (tu) segues. **5** (tu) sobes. **6** (Tu) viras à direita na próxima esquina. **7** (Tu) falas Português muito bem. **8** (Tu) és o meu melhor amigo. **9** (Tu) introduzes as moedas e pressionas a tecla. **10** Vocês podem vir também; cabem no carro.

Unit 3

3.1 Across: **2** Elas querem ir a pé. **3** As senhoras podem tomar um táxi. **4** Ele é um homem simpático. **5** Nós estamos perdidos. **6** "Tu" é uma alternativa familiar de "você". **7** Você dança muito bem. **8** O senhor está hospedado no melhor hotel da cidade.
    Down: **1** Os senhores podem estacionar aqui. **2** Ele parece estar contente. **3** "Vós" é uma forma de tratamento antiga. **4** Eu quero este. **5** Eu gosto do hotel. **6** A senhora fala Português muito bem. **7** Nós

estamos cansados. **8** Vocês têm duas praias perto do hotel.
3.2 **(A) 2** É fácil. **3** É uma hora. **4** Está quente hoje. **5** Dói aqui. **(B) 1** Vendem muito caro naquela loja. **2** Servem um prato de peixe delicioso naquele restaurante. **3** Dizem que essa fruta é muito boa para a saúde.

Unit 4

4.1 **(A) 1** Eu estou gostando disto. **2** Você está trabalhando muito. **3** Ela está pondo em ordem o apartamento. **4** Silêncio! O menino está dormindo. **5** Nós estamos escrevendo cartas. **6** Vocês estão preparando um bom jantar. **7** Eles estão fazendo isso há muito tempo. **(B) 1** Eu estou a gostar disto. **2** Você está a trabalhar muito. **3** Ela está a pôr em ordem o apartamento. **4** Silêncio! O menino está a dormir. **5** Nós estamos a escrever cartas. **6** Vocês estão a preparar um bom jantar. **7** Eles estão a fazer isso há muito tempo.
4.2 **Across: 1** Este inverno tem sido muito frio. **2** Vocês têm trabalhado demais. **3** O céu tem estado muito escuro. **4** Eu tenho comido mais fruta ultimamente. **5** Nós temos comprado menos pão esta semana.

Down: 1 Tem chovido muito nas últimas semanas. **2** Eu tenho trabalhado nesta firma desde o ano passado. **3** Eles têm estado doentes desde o verão passado. **4** Nós temos vindo à praia todos os dias desde o princípio das férias. **5** Essa menina tem crescido muito nos últimos meses.

The other second person

(A) 1 (Tu) estás fingindo. (Tu) estás a fingir. (Eur.) **2** (Tu) estás sofrendo desnecessariamente. (Tu) estás a sofrer desnecessariamente. (Eur.) **3** Vocês estão preparando um bom jantar. Vocês estão a preparar um bom jantar. (Eur.) **(B) 1** (Tu) tens dito isso muitas vezes. **2** (Tu) tens feito muita coisa ultimamente. **3** Vocês têm emagrecido muito nos últimos meses.

Unit 5

5.1 **1** O relógio parou. **2** Eles foram passear a pé. **3** Choveu durante a noite toda. **4** A porta estava aberta quando eu cheguei. **5** Enquanto eu cuidava das crianças, ele lavava a louça. **6** Ele leu esse livro do começo ao fim.
7 Ontem eu fui para a praia e fiquei lá o dia inteiro. **8** No sábado, de manhã, eles fizeram compras, à tarde, foram ao clube e, à noite, jantaram fora com amigos. **9** Quando era criança, eu vivia nos Estados Unidos. Vivi lá dez anos. **10** Naquela época nós morávamos numa casa perto da estação. A casa era muito grande.

5.2 (A) Quando vocês chegaram, **2** ela estava telefonando. **3** eles estavam dormindo. **4** nós estávamos lendo o jornal. *When you arrived,* **2** *she was phoning.* **3** *they were sleeping.* **4** *we were reading the paper.* **Letter ladder**: ESTAVA (sentences 1 and 2); ESTAVAM (sentence 3); ESTÁVAMOS (sentence 4). **(B)** Neste momento, **1** eu estou a almoçar. **2** ela está a telefonar. **3** eles estão a dormir. **4** nós estamos a ler o jornal. Quando vocês chegaram, **1** eu estava a almoçar. **2** ela estava a telefonar. **3** eles estavam a dormir. **4** nós estávamos a ler o jornal. (English translation as for **5.2 (A)**)

The other second person

(A) 1 (Tu) aprendeste Português rapidamente. **2** (Tu) tiveste sorte! **3** (Tu) disseste isso na reunião de ontem. **(B) 1** (Tu) parecias feliz na festa. **2** Naquela época (tu) trabalhavas no centro da cidade. **3** (Tu) costumavas telefonar para mim todos os dias. **(C) 1** (Tu) estavas pensando que ela não vinha quando a campainha da porta tocou. (Tu) estavas a pensar que ela não vinha quando a campainha da porta tocou. (Eur.) **2** (Vocês) estavam descalçando os sapatos quando eu entrei. (Vocês) estavam a descalçar os sapatos quando eu entrei. (Eur.)

Unit 6

6.1 Across: **2** Nós vamos ficar em casa. **3** Nós estaremos aqui. **4** O presidente irá ao norte do país. **5** Eles hão de saber que eu estive aqui.
    Down: 1 Ela vai ver o que pode fazer. **2** Ninguém estará acordado a estas horas. **3** Na próxima vez nós compraremos um carro novo. **4** Eu hei de descansar o dia todo. **5** Vocês sairão da sala no fim da prova.
6.2 1 (a) você fará (*you will do*). **(b)** nós traremos (*we shall bring*). **2 (a)** eu farei (*I shall do*). **(b)** nós diremos (*we shall say*). **3 (a)** eles trarão (*they will bring*). **(b)** eu trarei (*I shall bring*). **4 (a)** nós faremos (*we shall do*). **(b)** vocês dirão (*you will say*). **5 (b)** ele dirá (*he will say*).

The other second person

(A) (Tu) comprarás um carro novo, penso eu. **2** (Tu) saberás tudo em breve. **3** De acordo com o horário, vocês chegarão às 9 horas. **(B) 1** Cuidado! (Tu) vais cortar o dedo. **2** (Tu) vais fazer quarenta anos dois meses antes dela. **3** Então vocês vão ficar aqui até amanhã. **(C) 1** (Tu) hás de pertencer ao clube; vou recomendar. **2** (Tu) hás de receber o dinheiro, eu prometo. **3** Vocês hão de participar na reunião de amanhã.

231

Unit 7

7.1 (A) 1 Tome a primeira rua à direita, no cruzamento vire à esquerda e depois siga em frente. O supermercado fica a uns vinte metros à esquerda. *Take the first road on your right, at the crossroads turn left and then carry on straight ahead. The supermarket is about twenty metres on your left.* **2** Tomem a primeira rua à direita, no cruzamento virem à esquerda e depois sigam em frente. O supermercado fica a uns vinte metros à esquerda. **(B) 2** Virem à esquerda (*turn left*). **3** Sigam em frente (*go straight on*).

7.2. (A) 2 Faça o favor de repetir. **(B) 1** Pare! **2** Corra! **3** Saia daqui depressa! **(C) 1** Leve a bagagem para cima, por favor. **2** Traga o prato do dia, por favor.

The other second person

1 Abre a porta! **2** Fecha a janela, por favor. **3** Por favor, repete. **4** Sai daí! **5** Traz o livro amanhã. *or* Traze o livro amanhã. (the latter hardly heard nowadays) **6 (a)** Ah, desculpa! **(b)** Ah, desculpem! **7 (a)** Sobe! **(b)** Subam! **8 (a)** Fica aqui! **(b)** Fiquem aqui! **9 (a)** Boa noite, dorme bem. **(b)** Boa noite, durmam bem.

Unit 8

8.1 (A) 2 Convém que eles compreendam a situação. **3** É importante que você veja essa exposição. **4** Receio que ele ralhe com você. **5** É pena que o leite azede tão depressa. **6** Espero que o jantar agrade a todos. **7** Desejo que você encontre a carteira. **8** Talvez caiba tudo na mala. **9** Tomara que eles telefonem. **10** É possível que eles permitam a construção da piscina. **11** É necessário que ele viaje esta semana. **12** Oxalá que chova amanhã. **13** É provável que eu possa ir lá mais cedo. **14** Quero que você receba a carta sem mais demora. **(B)** AMAZONAS; ALGARVE.

8.2 1 Faça boa viagem! (*Have a good journey!*) **2** Durmam bem! (*Sleep well!*) **3** Tenham um bom fim de semana! (*Have a good weekend!*) **4** Esteja à vontade! (*Make yourself at home!*) **5** Venham já! (*Come straight away!*) **6** Faça esse trabalho! (*Get on with that work!*) **7** Esperem mais um pouco! (*Wait a bit longer!*)

The other second person

1 Eu espero que (tu) sejas muito feliz. 2 Eu desejo que (tu) faças boa viagem. 3 É possível que (tu) obtenhas um bom resultado. 4 **(a)** Eu duvido que (tu) saibas isso. **(b)** Eu duvido que vocês saibam isso. 5 **(a)** Ela pede que (tu) venhas já. **(b)** Ela pede que vocês venham já.

Unit 9

9.1 2 Eu gostaria de conhecer a cidade. 3 Nós adoraríamos conhecer a sua família. 4 Os senhores poderiam indicar-me o caminho para a estação? 5 Com dois meses de férias, eu visitaria três ou quatro países. 6 Eu levaria esse rapaz para o colégio, mas agora não tenho tempo. 7 Nós traríamos mais presentes para todos, mas não temos dinheiro.
9.2 1 Eu queria falar com o Sr. Gama. *I would like to talk to Mr. Gama.* 2 Eu queria marcar uma consulta para amanhã. *I would like to see the doctor tomorrow.* 3 Nós queríamos ficar num hotel perto da estação. *We would like to stay at a hotel near the station.* 4 Nós queríamos ter um apartamento de casal. *We would like to have an apartment for two.*

The other second person

1 Quem sabe se (tu) ficarias ou não milionário... 2 Eu sabia que (tu) farias isso. 3 **(a)** (Tu) poderias mostrar-me no mapa onde eu estou? **(b)** Vocês poderiam mostrar-me no mapa onde eu estou?

Unit 10

10.1 2 Ele esperava que nós estivéssemos lá hoje. 3 Faremos tudo quanto pudermos. 5 Seria melhor que vocês comprassem o carro. 6 Eu gostaria que eles viessem amanhã. **Word across**: FÉRIAS.
10.2 2 **(b)** Eu queria que você me fizesse um favor. *I would like you to do me a favour if possible.* 3 **(b)** Seria melhor que você saísse agora. *It would be better if you could please leave now.* 4 **(b)** Ele pediu que vocês viessem já. *He has asked whether you could please come straight away.*

The other second person

(A) 1 Eu pensava que (tu) apreciasses essa música. 2 Eu gostaria que (tu) considerasses esse assunto. 3 **(a)** Tomara que (tu) sorrisses. **(b)** Tomara que vocês sorrissem. 4 **(a)** Ele pediu que (tu) falasses mais baixo. **(b)** Ele pediu

233

que vocês falassem mais baixo. **(B)** **1** Será melhor se (tu) verificares que o carro tem combustível para a viagem. **2 (a)** Se (tu) vieres, podemos ir jantar juntos. **(b)** Se vocês vierem, podemos ir jantar juntos. **3 (a)** Vamos dar uma festa quando (tu) chegares. **(b)** Vamos dar uma festa quando vocês chegarem.

Unit 11

11.1 **1 (g)** Quando eu vou a Brasília, geralmente fico hospedada nesse hotel. **2 (d)** Quando eu fui ao Rio de Janeiro, fiquei num hotel em Copacabana. **3 (f)** Quando eu morava em Lisboa, ia à praia todos os fins de semana. **4 (h)** Quando eu cheguei, você ainda estava dormindo / a dormir. (Eur.) **5 (a)** Nós vamos acampar com vocês quando pudermos. **6 (e)** Se eles vierem, a festa ficará mais animada. **7 (c)** Se eu tivesse muito dinheiro, iria dar a volta ao mundo. **8 (b)** Embora o trabalho seja difícil, eles vão continuar.
11.2 **1** Quem quer que seja. **2** O patrão quer uma pessoa que saiba Inglês. **3** Eu farei tudo o que puder. **4** Eu queria alguém que fosse capaz de fazer isso. **5, 6** Venha o que vier.

The other second person

1 Fico sempre muito contente quando (tu) vens. **2** Se (tu) depositasses esse cheque, o saldo ficaria positivo. **3** Vou preparar o jantar antes que (tu) tenhas fome. **4 (a)** Paga quando puderes. **(b)** Paguem quando puderem. **5 (a)** Vem se puderes. **(b)** Venham se puderem. **6 (a)** (Tu) és o aluno que fala Português melhor. **(b)** Vocês são os alunos que falam Português melhor.

Unit 12

12.1 **(A)** **1** Há meses que tenho falado Português todos os dias. **2** Nós já tínhamos saído quando vocês telefonaram. **3** Amanhã, a estas horas, eles já terão partido na viagem de férias. **4** Espero que vocês tenham gostado da festa. **5** Se ele tivesse estudado mais, saberia esta matéria muito melhor. **6** Podemos sair, quando eu tiver terminado este trabalho. **(B)** **1** Já ia anoitecendo. **2** Essa máquina vai funcionando cada vez pior. **3** Eu venho conseguindo melhores resultados cada dia que passa. **4** Ele anda aproveitando as férias ao máximo. Ele anda a aproveitar as férias ao máximo. (Eur.) **5** Amanhã, às oito horas, estarei trabalhando no escritório. Amanhã, às oito horas, estarei a trabalhar no escritório. (Eur.)

12.2 Across: **2** Eu acabei por aceitar o convite para a festa. **3** Você devia embrulhar o presente num papel bonito. **4** Nós viemos a detestar isso. **5** Ele voltou a tocar a campainha da porta.

Down: **1** Geralmente eles começavam por tratar dos casos mais difíceis. **2** Nós podemos ir buscar o pacote amanhã. **3** Nós sabemos falar só uma língua estrangeira. **4** Eles continuam achando que tudo está bem.

The other second person

1 Amanhã, a esta hora, (tu) já terás embarcado no cruzeiro. **2** Neste momento (tu) estarias tomando banho de sol na praia se o avião não estivesse atrasado. Neste momento (tu) estarias a tomar banho de sol na praia se o avião não estivesse atrasado. (Eur.) **3** Parabéns! (Tu) vais falando Português cada vez melhor. **4** Por favor volta a telefonar em breve. **5 (a)** Discutimos o assunto quando (tu) tiveres reunido todos os dados. **(b)** Discutimos o assunto quando vocês tiverem reunido todos os dados. **6 (a)** Enquanto (tu) vais fazer compras, eu vou arrumar a casa. **(b)** Enquanto vocês vão fazer compras, eu vou arrumar a casa.

Unit 13

13.1 1 Eu comprei uma máquina de filmar. **2** Nós gostamos do modo de ser dele. **3** É melhor apagar a luz antes de sair. **4** Ter aprendido Português sem dúvida que tem sido muito útil. **5** Cantar e dançar é bom para a saúde. **6** Eu prefiro ficar em casa e ler um livro. **7** Comprar ou não comprar um carro novo, isso é uma decisão difícil.

13.2 (A) 1 Ela entrou na sala rindo. (*verb* rir) **2** Ele ganha a vida ensinando Português. (ensinar) **3** Amanhecendo, nós partiremos. (amanhecer) **4** Caminhando pela praia, tropecei num seixo. (caminhar) **5** Ele trouxe um presente, expressando assim a sua gratidão. (expressar) **6** Tendo terminado os exames, pude gozar as férias. (ter, ter terminado) **(B) 1** A luz está acesa. (*verb* acender) **2** A luz está apagada. (apagar) **3** Nem toda a gente gosta de peixe frito. (frigir / fritar) **4** Temos que preencher os impressos. (imprimir) **5** Talvez ele tenha trocado. (trocar) **6** Terminados os exames, eu fui viajar. (terminar)

Unit 14

14.1 2 Será difícil eles acordarem tão cedo. **3** É impossível eu acreditar nisso. **4** É melhor nós estacionarmos aqui. **5** Os pais compraram um computador para o filho usar. **6** Antes de falarmos com eles, temos que combinar o que vamos dizer. **7** Ela comprou os selos para nós enviarmos a

carta. **8** Receberemos o pacote depois de eles cobrarem o cheque. **9** Seria perigoso eles ultrapassarem nessa estrada. **Words down**: FADO (Portuguese song); SAMBA (Brazilian dance).
14.2 **(A)** **1** entrar. **2** clicar. **3** voltar. **4** navegar. **5** digitar. **6** buscar *or* pesquisar. **(B)** Façam o favor de manter o cinto apertado. *or* Façam o favor de manterem o cinto apertado.

The other second person

1 É necessário (tu) fazeres isso sem mais demora. **2** Já está na hora de (tu) voltares para casa. **3** Eu cortei uma fatia do bolo para (tu) experimentares. **4** É melhor (tu) cozeres esta carne agora. **5** Eu trouxe o caderno para (tu) corrigires os erros. **6 (a)** Isto é um questionário para (tu) responderes. **(b)** Isto é um questionário para vocês responderem. **7 (a)** É favor (tu) saíres pela porta da direita. **(b)** É favor vocês saírem pela porta da direita.

Unit 15

15.1 **(A)** **1** Ele é americano? **2** Esta loja fica aberta à noite? **3** Você conhece bem esta cidade? **4** Eles gostaram da festa ontem? **(B)** **1** O que é que aconteceu? **2** Quem é que chegou ontem? **3** Onde é que você trabalha? **4** Para onde é que você vai amanhã? **(C)** não é?
15.2 **(A)** **1** Eu não quero mesmo sair. *I really do not want to go out.* **2** Nós não vamos fazer isso. *We are not going to do that.* **3** Ele não foi ao trabalho na semana passada. *He did not go to work last week.* **4** Até agora o carro não funcionava. *Until now, the car was not working.* **5** Claro que isso não ajuda. *Of course, that will not help.* **6** Isso não seria uma boa solução. *That would not be a good solution.* **7** Não vire à direita. *Do not turn right.* **8** Não abram as janelas. *Do not open the windows.* **9** Por favor não esperem por mim. *Please do not wait for me.* **(B)** **1** - Provou. **2** - Vamos! **3** - Ainda não. **4** - Eu não sei, não sou daqui.

The other second person

(A) **1** (Tu) não sabes mesmo falar essa língua. **2** (Tu) tencionas fazer isso? **3** O que é que (tu) disseste? **4 (a)** Eu sei que (tu) não frequentaste essa escola. **(b)** Eu sei que vocês não frequentaram essa escola. **5 (a)** (Tu) gostaste do hotel onde ficaste? **(b)** Vocês gostaram do hotel onde ficaram? **(B)** **1** Não atendas a porta. **2** Não ocupes essa cadeira. **3** Não pendures o casaco aí. **4** Não desapareças mesmo. **5 (a)** Não vires à direita, vira à esquerda. **(b)** Não virem à direita, virem à esquerda. **6 (a)** Por favor não vás a essa festa, vem à nossa. **(b)** Por favor não vão a essa festa, venham à nossa.

Unit 16

16.1 Across: **1** O hotel foi avisado ontem. **2** Os recibos serão emitidos assim que possível. **3** A notícia estava sendo lida por todos. **4** A notícia estava a ser lida por todos. (Eur.) **5** Eu pensava que o carro seria alugado mais tarde. **6** Espero que as malas sejam transportadas por via aérea.

    Down: **1** Nós fomos todos convidados. **2** As passagens já tinham sido reservadas. **3** Penso que serei levada de táxi para o hotel. **4** Aqueles pontos turísticos são muito visitados por estrangeiros.

16.2 1 Está combinado! **2** A luz está acesa. **3** Eu estou hospedado num bom hotel. **4** Vocês estão convidados! **5** O quadro estava pintado a óleo. **6** O teatro tem estado encerrado para obras de renovação. **7** Espero que estejam todos sentados. **8** Estas bebidas são para aqueles que estejam com sede.

The other second person

1 (Tu) és muito estimada por nós. **2** (Tu) és pretendido por todas as jovens. **3** Quando é que (tu) foste roubado? **4 (a)** Por quem é que (tu) foste convidado? **(b)** Por quem é que vocês foram convidados? **5 (a)** (Tu) foste instalada no melhor hotel da vila. **(b)** Vocês foram instaladas no melhor hotel da vila.

Unit 17

17.1 (A) 1 Como é que a senhora se chama? **2** Como é que se escreve o seu nome? **3** Onde é que nós nos encontramos hoje à noite? **(B) 1** Por onde se vai para a praia? **2** Onde se vende água mineral? **3** Onde se alugam carros? **(C) 1** Eles já se levantaram? **2** Então você ainda não se barbeou? **3** Eu já me vesti mas ainda não me penteei. **(D) 1** Nós divertimo-nos na festa ontem à noite. Nós nos divertimos na festa ontem à noite. (Am.) **2** As crianças comportaram-se bem. As crianças se comportaram bem. (Am.) **3** Claro que as crianças se deitaram tarde.

17.2 2 As toalhas são mudadas todos os dias. **3** O jantar é servido a partir das 19 horas. **4** Os carros são guardados na garagem do hotel. **5** Um médico é chamado em caso de doença.

The other second person

1 (Tu) demoraste-te muito. (Tu) te demoraste muito. (Am.) **2** (Tu) ofereceste-te para fazer isto? (Tu) te ofereceste para fazer isto? (Am.) **3** Não te zangues! **4** Afasta-te! A árvore vai cair. **5** Cuidado! Não te aproximes. **6 (a)** Como é que (tu) te chamas? **(b)** Como é que vocês se chamam? **7 (a)** Não te preocupes. **(b)** Não se preocupem. **8 (a)** Diverte-te! **(b)** Divirtam-se!

Unit 18

18.1 Down: **1** Pedimos que nos ajude, se puder. **2** Sei o endereço deles mais ou menos; não o sei bem. **3** Estou com o cabelo molhado. Preciso enxugá-lo. **4** Eles querem que eu os acompanhe.

Across: **1** Falem mais alto para que todos possam ouvi-los. **2** Elas gostariam de ir ao clube. Levem-nas com vocês. **3** Eles trouxeram as malas e deixaram-nas na receção. **4** Esse preguiçoso ainda não apareceu! Vou acordá-lo.

18.2 (A) É verdade que Marta **1(b)** comprou um presente para mim. *bought a gift for me.* **2(a)** comprou um presente para você. *bought a gift for you.* **3(g)** comprou um presente para ele. *bought a gift for him.* **4(e)** comprou um presente para ela. *bought a gift for her.* **5(c)** comprou um presente para nós. *bought a gift for us.* **6(h)** comprou um presente para vocês. *bought a gift for you* (plural). **7(d)** comprou um presente para eles. *bought a gift for them* (male). **8(f)** comprou um presente para elas. *bought a gift for them* (female). **(B)** Muito prazer em **(a)** conhecê-los. **(b)** conhecer vocês. **(c)** conhecer os senhores.

The other second person

1 (Tu) amas-me ou não? (Tu) me amas ou não? (Am.) **2** Muito prazer em conhecer-te. **3** Com o alto-falante todos podem ouvir-te. **4 (a)** (Tu) não me viste lá. **(b)** Vocês não me viram lá. **5 (a)** Onde é que (tu) nos vais encontrar? **(b)** Onde é que vocês nos vão encontrar? **6 (a)** Obrigada por me protegeres da chuva. **(b)** Obrigada por me protegerem da chuva.

Unit 19

19.1 2 Ela pede que vocês ajudem. **3** Ele diz que eles entrem agora. **4** Eles pediram que nós cantássemos. **5** Eles disseram que você escolhesse um presente.

19.2 1 Ela diz que aquele músico compunha melodias lindas. **2** Eu penso que eles gostam de ler romances. **3** Ele explicou que geralmente traduz três páginas por hora. **4** Ele diz que vocês não se metam onde não são chamados. **5** Ela pede que vocês não bebam esse vinho. **6** Dizem que a última moda é saia comprida. **7** Ela pede que você anuncie que a reunião vai começar. **8** Eu calculo que ele possa ter tudo pronto amanhã. **Word down**: PARABÉNS.

The other second person

1 Ele quer saber o que significa o que (tu) disseste. **2** Eu penso que (tu) apontaste para a causa do problema. **3** Nós tínhamos notado que (tu) estavas preocupado. **4** Ele perguntou se (tu) possuis algumas casas nesta cidade. **5** Ele disse que (tu) estavas aguardando resposta. Ele disse que (tu) estavas a aguardar resposta. (Eur.) **6** Ele quer saber quando é que (tu) publicaste a notícia. **7** Ele pede que (tu) nos comuniques a decisão assim que possível. **8** Eu penso que (tu) adquiriste um hábito muito mau. **9** Eles disseram que (tu) tinhas assinalado no mapa o local do acidente. **10 (a)** Eu tinha pensado que (tu) terias em mente um plano que consistisse em duas fases distintas. **(b)** Eu tinha pensado que vocês teriam em mente um plano que consistisse em duas fases distintas. **11 (a)** Ele diz que (tu) vais conceder benefícios especiais para os empregados assim que puderes. **(b)** Ele diz que vocês vão conceder benefícios especiais para os empregados assim que puderem.

Verbs Vocabulary List

This is a list of verbs used throughout the book and their respective English translation. It will give you extra support when you read the examples in the units and do the exercises.

abolir *to abolish*
abrir *to open*
acabar *to finish, complete, end*;
   acabar de *to have just (done)*
acampar *to camp*
aceitar *to accept*
acender *to light, switch on*
achar *to find; to think*
acompanhar *to accompany*
acontecer *to happen*
acordar *to wake up*
acreditar *to believe*
acudir *to go to help*
adoecer *to fall ill*
adorar *to adore, love*
adormecer *to fall asleep*
adquirir *to acquire*
afastar *to remove*; afastar-se
   to move away
afluir (*like* fluir) *to congregate*
agradar *to please*
agradecer *to thank*
aguardar *to wait for, await*
ajudar *to help*
alegrar *to cheer up*; alegrar-se
   to rejoice
almoçar *to have lunch*
alugar *to rent, hire; to let, rent
   out*
amanhecer *to grow light* (dawn)
amar *to love*
andar *to walk, go; to be (doing)*
anoitecer *to grow dark*
   (nightfall)

ansiar *to long to, yearn for*
anular *to cancel, abolish*
anunciar *to announce*
apagar (*like* pagar) *to put out,
   switch off*
apanhar *to catch, pick up*
aparecer *to appear, turn up*
apertar *to hold tight, tighten,
   fasten* (belt)
apetecer *to fancy, feel like
   (doing)*
apontar *to aim at, point to*
apreciar *to appreciate, enjoy*
aprender *to learn*
apresentar *to present, produce,
   submit; to introduce* (someone)
aproveitar *to take advantage of,
   make the most of*
aproximar *to bring / take near*;
   aproximar-se *to come / go
   near*
arrendar *to lease*
arrombar *to break open*
arrumar *to tidy up, put in
   order*
assaltar *to break into; to rob,
   mug*
assinalar *to mark, point out*
assinar *to sign*
assustar *to frighten, startle*;
   assustar-se *to be, become
   frightened*
atender *to attend to; to answer*
   (phone, door)

---

atrair (*like* trair) *to attract*
atravessar *to cross, cross over*
avisar *to warn, tell*
avistar *to catch sight of*
azedar *to turn sour, go off*

baixar *to lower*
barbear *to shave*; barbear-se
  to have a shave
bastar *to be enough*
beber *to drink*
buscar *to fetch, search for*
buzinar *to toot the horn*

caber *to fit*
cacarejar *to cluck*
cair *to fall*
calçar *to put on* (shoes, gloves)
calcular *to calculate, reckon*
caminhar *to walk*
cansar *to tire*; cansar-se *to get
  tired*
cantar *to sing*
casar(-se) *to get married*
chamar *to call*; chamar-se *to
  be called*
chatear *to upset, pester*;
  chatear-se *to get upset, bored*
chegar *to arrive*; *to be enough*
chorar *to cry*
chover *to rain*
clicar *to click* (computer)
cobrar *to collect*
cobrir *to cover*
colocar *to put, place*
combinar *to combine*;
  to arrange, plan
começar *to begin, start*
comer *to eat*
comparecer *to appear*;
  to attend (meeting)

compor (*like* pôr) *to compose,
  organize*
comportar *to hold, bear*;
  comportar-se *to behave*
comprar *to buy*
compreender *to understand*;
  to comprise
comunicar *to communicate, tell*
conceder *to allow*; *to grant*
concluir *to end, conclude*
concordar *to agree*
condizer (*like* dizer) *to match*
conduzir *to lead, drive*
confiar *to trust*
conhecer *to know*; *to meet,
  make acquaintance*
conseguir (*like* seguir) *to get,
  obtain*; *to achieve, manage
  (to do)*
consentir (*like* sentir) *to allow,
  permit*
consertar *to mend, repair*
considerar *to consider*
consistir *to consist (of)*
construir *to build*
contar *to count*; *to tell*
conter (*like* ter) *to contain*
continuar *to continue, go on*
contradizer (*like* dizer)
  to contradict
contrair (*like* trair) *to contract*
conversar *to talk, discuss*
convidar *to invite*
convir (*like* vir) *to suit, be
  convenient*; convém que
  must
correr *to run*
corrigir *to correct*
cortar *to cut*
costumar *to accustom*; *to use
  (to do)*

241

cozer *to cook, boil*
crer *to believe, have faith; to think*
crescer *to grow*
cuidar *to look after*
custar *to cost; to be difficult*

dançar *to dance*
dar *to give*
declarar *to declare*
deitar *to lay down;* deitar-se *to lie down, go to bed*
deixar *to leave; to abandon; to let*
demorar *to delay; to take time*
deparar *to reveal; to come across*
depositar *to deposit*
desaparecer *to disappear*
descalçar (*like* calçar) *to take off* (shoes, gloves)
descansar *to rest*
descer *to climb down, come / go down*
descobrir (*like* cobrir) *to discover, uncover*
desculpar *to excuse, forgive;* desculpe! *sorry!*
desejar *to wish, want, desire;* deseja ...? *would you like ...?*
desesperar *to despair*
desfazer (*like* fazer) *to undo*
desligar (*like* ligar) *to disconnect; to switch off; to turn off*
despir *to undress;* despir-se *to get undressed*
destruir *to destroy*
detestar *to detest, hate*
dever *to owe;* devia *should, ought to*
devolver *to return, give back*

digitar *to key in* (computer)
dirigir *to direct, manage, drive*
dispor (*like* pôr) *to arrange*
distinguir *to distinguish, differentiate*
distrair (*like* trair) *to distract;* distrair-se *to amuse oneself*
distribuir *to distribute, share out; to deliver* (letters)
divertir *to amuse;* divertir-se *to enjoy oneself, have a good time*
dizer *to say; to tell*
doer *to hurt*
dormir *to sleep*
duvidar *to doubt*

eleger *to elect*
emagrecer *to slim, lose weight*
embarcar *to embark, go on board*
embrulhar *to wrap*
emitir *to give out; to issue*
empurrar *to push*
encerrar *to shut, close*
encher *to fill*
encontrar *to find; to meet*
engordar *to get fat, put on weight*
enlutar *to bereave*
ensinar *to teach*
entender *to understand*
entrar *to come / go in*
entregar *to deliver*
entreter (*like* ter) *to entertain, amuse, occupy*
enviar *to send*
enxugar *to dry, wipe dry*
erguer *to lift, raise*
errar *to be wrong, make a mistake; to err*

242

escolher *to choose, select*
escrever *to write*
escutar *to listen*
esperar *to wait for, expect, hope*
esquecer(-se) *to forget*
estacionar *to park*
estar *to be* (transitory)
estimar *to value*; *to have a high regard for*
estudar *to study*
esvaziar *to empty*
exigir *to demand*
experimentar *to try out, test*; *to taste*
explicar *to explain*
explodir *to explode*
expressar *to express*
exprimir *to express* (*the same as* expressar)
expulsar *to expel*
extinguir *to extinguish*

falar *to speak, talk*
faltar *to be lacking*; *to be absent*
fazer *to do; to make*; fazer ... anos *to be, become ... years old*; fazer compras *to shop, do the shopping*; fazer uma pergunta *to ask a question;* fazer boa viagem *to have a good journey*
fechar *to close, shut*
ferir *to injure, wound*; *to offend*
ficar *to stay*; *to become*; ficar hospedado *to stay (lodged)*
filmar *to film*
fingir *to pretend*
fluir *to flow*

frequentar *to attend* (school, college)
frigir *to fry*
fritar *to fry* (*the same as* frigir)
fugir *to flee, run away*
fumar *to smoke*
funcionar *to function, work*

ganhar *to earn, win*
garantir *to guarantee*
gastar *to spend*
gerir *to manage, run*
girar *to turn, rotate*
gostar *to like*; *to enjoy*; gostaria *I would / should like*
gozar *to enjoy*
guardar *to put away, keep*; *to watch over*

haver *to exist*; *there to be*; *to have*; *will*; *to be (supposed) to (do / be)*
hospedar *to put up, lodge*

imaginar *to imagine*; *to suppose*
impor (*like* pôr) *to impose*
imprimir *to print*
incendiar *to set on fire*
incluir *to include*
incomodar *to bother, trouble, annoy*
indicar *to indicate, show* (road directions)
influir (*like* fluir) *to have an influence; to matter*
informar *to inform, tell*
inserir *to insert, put in*
instalar *to install*; *to put up, accommodate*

introduzir *to introduce, insert*
ir *to go*; como vai? *how are you?*

jantar *to have dinner*
jogar *to play* (game)

lamber *to lick*
lavar *to wash*
lembrar(-se) *to remember*
ler *to read*
levantar *to lift*; levantar-se *to stand up, get up*
levar *to take*
ligar *to connect*; *to switch on*; *to turn on*
limpar *to clean, wipe clean*

mandar *to order, be in charge*; *to send*
manter (*like* ter) *to maintain, keep*
marcar *to mark*; *to book* (appointment)
matar *to kill*
mediar *to mediate*
medir *to measure*
melhorar *to improve*; *to get better*
mentir *to lie, tell a lie*
meter *to put in*
miar *to miaow*
moer *to grind*; *to tire out*
molhar *to wet*
morar *to live, reside*
morrer *to die*
mostrar *to show*
mudar *to change*; *to move*; mudar-se *to move* (house)

nadar *to swim*
nascer *to be born*
navegar *to navigate, sail*

notar *to notice, note*

obter (*like* ter) *to obtain*
ocupar *to occupy*
odiar *to hate*
ofender *to offend*; ofender-se *to take offence*
oferecer *to offer, give*
olhar *to look*
omitir *to omit*
ouvir *to hear*

pagar *to pay*
parar *to stop*
parecer *to look, seem, appear to*
participar *to notify*; *to take part*
partir *to leave, depart*
passar *to pass*; *to spend* (time)
passear *to stroll, take a walk*
pedir *to ask (for), request*
pegar *to catch, take hold of*
pendurar *to hang*
pensar *to think*; *to ponder*
pentear *to comb*; pentear-se *to do one's hair*
perceber *to understand, realize*
perder *to lose*
perguntar *to ask, enquire*
permitir *to allow, permit, authorize*
perseguir (*like* seguir) *to chase*
pertencer *to belong*
pesquisar *to investigate, research*
pintar *to paint*
piorar *to make worse, get worse*
poder *can*; *may*; *to be able*
pôr *to put*; pôr em ordem *tidy up*
possuir *to own, possess*

praticar *to practise*
precisar *to need*
preencher *to complete, fill in*
preferir (*like* ferir) *to prefer*
prender *to fasten; to arrest*
preocupar(-se) *to worry*
preparar *to prepare*; preparar-se *to get ready*
pressentir (*like* sentir) *to sense; to foresee*
pressionar *to press, put on pressure*
pretender *to intend (to do / be); to go for*
prevenir *to prevent; to warn*
procurar *to look for, seek; to try*
produzir *to produce*
progredir *to progress*
proibir *to prohibit, forbid*
prometer *to promise*
proteger *to protect*
provar *to prove; to try* (food, clothes)
publicar *to publish*
puxar *to pull*

quebrar *to break*
querer *to want; will; to wish, like*; eu queria *I would like*

ralhar *to scold*
reabrir (*like* abrir) *to reopen*
realizar *to achieve; to hold* (event)
recear *to fear*
receber *to receive, have*
recomeçar (*like* começar) *to restart*
recomendar *to recommend*
reconhecer (*like* conhecer) *to recognize; to admit*

reconstruir (*like* construir) *to rebuild*
recordar *to remember, recall*
reduzir *to reduce*
referir (*like* ferir) *to mention, refer*
reimprimir (*like* imprimir) *to reprint*
reinar *to reign*
relaxar *to relax*
remediar *to remedy, put right*
repetir *to repeat; to say / do again*
repor (*like* pôr) *to put back, replace*
reproduzir (*like* produzir) *to reproduce*
reservar *to reserve*
resolver *to solve, sort out; to decide*
respeitar *to respect*
responder *to answer*
retrair (*like* trair) *to withdraw*
reunir *to bring together*
rir *to laugh*
roer *to gnaw; to erode*
romper *to tear*
roubar *to steal; to rob*

saber *to know, get to know, know how to*
sair *to come / go out; to leave*
salvar *to rescue; to save*
satisfazer (*like* fazer) *to satisfy*
secar *to dry*
seduzir *to seduce; to fascinate*
seguir *to follow; to carry on; to go*
sentar *to sit*; sentar-se *to sit down*
sentir(-se) *to feel; to be sorry*

ser *to be* (inherent, permanent);
   ser capaz de *to be able to*
servir *to serve; to be useful;*
   to fit
significar (*like* ficar) *to mean,*
   signify
sofrer *to suffer*
solicitar *to ask, apply for*
soltar *to set free*
sorrir (*like* rir) *to smile*
subir *to climb, come / go up*
sugerir (*like* gerir) *to suggest*
supor (*like* pôr) *to suppose,*
   assume
suspender *to suspend; to lift*

telefonar *to phone*
tencionar *to intend, plan*
ter *to have;* ter ... anos
   to be ... years old;
   ter fome *to be hungry;*
   ter de / que *to have to*
terminar *to finish, end*
tingir *to dye*
tirar *to take away / out / off*
tocar *to touch; to ring* (bell);
   to play (instrument)
tomar *to take; to have* (drink,
   bath); tomar conta *to look*
   after; tomara *I hope, I wish*
tornar *to return; to do / be*
   again, anew
trabalhar *to work*
traduzir *to translate*
trair *to betray*
transferir (*like* ferir) *to transfer*
transportar *to transport, carry*
tratar *to treat; to deal with*
trazer *to bring*
trocar *to change*
tropeçar *to trip over*

ultrapassar *to go beyond;*
   to overtake, pass (car)
usar *to use; to wear*
utilizar *to use, make use of*

valer *to be worth, worthwhile*
vencer *to win; to defeat* (enemy)
vender *to sell*
ver *to see*
verificar (*like* ficar) *to check,*
   verify
vestir *to dress;* vestir-se
   to get dressed
viajar *to travel*
vir *to come*
virar *to turn*
visitar *to visit*
viver *to live*
voltar *to return, come*
   / go back

zangar *to annoy, irritate;*
   zangar-se *to get angry, cross*

246

Glossary of Grammatical Terms

This section provides you with extra support on grammatical terminology in addition to the explanations given throughout the units. Grammatical terms are usually explained the first time they appear in the book. In the definitions below you can check them when they come around again.

(The cross-reference index at the very end of the book will direct you to specific points about the verbs and grammatical meanings)

ADJECTIVE – a word that adds information about a noun by describing or qualifying it. **O carro é *novo*.** The car is *new*.

ADJUNCT – a word or phrase used to explain or amplify meaning. ***Cansado*, ele adormeceu.** *Tired*, he fell asleep.

ADVERB – a word or phrase that adds information about a verb, an adjective, or another adverb and makes its meaning clearer, fuller, or more exact. **Por favor fale *mais devagar*.** Please speak *more slowly*. **Eu fui lá *ontem*.** I went there *yesterday*.

AFFIRMATIVE – it is said of a verb or sentence with which we make a positive statement or state agreement to something, as opposed to a negative verb or sentence. **Eu *gosto* de bolos.** I *like* cakes.

AGENT – the doer of the action in the passive voice – **A galinha foi perseguida *pela raposa*.** The hen was chased *by the fox*. **Os carros foram vendidos *por eles*.** The cars were sold *by them*. See also VOICE.

AGREEMENT – a correspondence or mutual dependency between two or more forms which have to take on (agree with) the same grammatical features – ***os* carros *novos*,** the new cars (masculine, plural). Verbs in tenses agree in number and person with their subject, i.e., first, second or third person singular or plural. ***Nós moramos* aqui.** *We live* here (first person plural).

ANTECEDENT – the word (noun), phrase, or clause (acting in a nounlike way) to which a relative pronoun refers. **Aquele é *o aluno* que fala Português**. That one is *the student* who speaks Portuguese.

247

AUXILIARY – it is said of a verb which 'helps' the main verb to make up a tense. In the continuous tenses, "estar" is an auxiliary, and in the compound tenses, "ter" is an auxiliary. **Como eu *estava* dizendo**. As I *was* saying. **Você *tem* trabalhado muito**. You *have* been working hard.

CLAUSE – a group of words forming a coherent unit around a verb. *Eu fui lá ontem*. *I went there yesterday*. A sentence may consist of one or more clauses. See also SENTENCE.

COMMAND – term used for an order. Traditionally orders and instructions are conveyed in the imperative mood, but in modern Portuguese the present subjunctive is generally used for a polite approach – *Entre*. *Come* in. The infinitive is also used for a more impersonal approach, for example, in public instructions – *Puxar* **para abrir**. *Pull* to open. See also MOOD.

COMPOUND TENSE – generally speaking, a compound tense is one made up of a main verb and one or more auxiliaries. In a more precise sense, a Portuguese compound tense is what we in English usually refer to as a perfect or pluperfect tense. **Parecia que nada *tinha acontecido***. It looked like nothing *had happened*.

COMPOUND VERB – Portuguese compound verbs are usually made up of an initial element plus a verb. They normally exhibit the same features as the single verbs with which they are formed. **Ela *sorriu***, she *smiled* (**sorrir**, to smile), like **riu**, she *laughed* (**rir**, to laugh).

CONJUGATE – to inflect a verb, i.e., give it different endings and forms so as to apply it to a particular subject (**eu**, I, **você**, you, etc.) and change it into different tenses. *Eu gosto* **de viajar**. *I like* travelling. **No ano passado *eles compraram* um carro novo**. Last year *they bought* a new car. See also TENSE.

CONJUGATION – is the different endings and forms given to a verb. The term "conjugation" also means a grouping of verbs that display the same set of endings for the different tenses. There are three such groupings in the Portuguese language which are distinguished by their infinitive endings: **-ar**, **-er**, and **-ir**. There is also an additional group of verbs in **-ôr** and **-or**.

CONJUNCTION – a word or word-group which links together words, phrases and clauses – e.g., **quando**, when, **se**, if, **para que**, so that, **a não ser que**, unless. **Passo o dia inteiro na praia *quando* o tempo está bom**. I spend the whole day on the beach *when* the weather is fine.[1]

CONNECTIVE or CONNECTOR – a general term for a link word, or group of words, that joins other elements together, as is the case with conjunctions and relative pronouns. **Aquele é o aluno *que* fala Português**. That one is the student *who* speaks Portuguese.

CONSONANT – a speech sound such as that represented by the letters **t**, **s**, **c**, **b**, **z**, **g**, **m**, in which the breath is at least in part obstructed at some point in your mouth or lips. See also VOWEL.

CONTINUOUS TENSE – continuous tenses indicate that the action of the verb has not yet concluded and is progressing or merely continuing. **Já *vai* amanhecendo**. Daylight *is breaking*.

DEFINITE ARTICLE – the word for 'the', which in Portuguese can be masculine (**o**), feminine (**a**), singular (**o**, **a**) and plural (**os**, **as**) – *o* **senhor**, *the* gentleman, *a* **senhora**, *the* lady, *os* **carros**, *the* cars, *as* **casas** *the* houses.

DIRECT OBJECT – see OBJECT.

FEMININE – see GENDER.

FINITE – verb form that exhibits person, tense and mood, as opposed to non-finite. **Eu *iria* à festa, mas hoje não *posso***. I *would go* to the party, but today I *can* not. See also TENSE and MOOD.

GENDER – a grammatical convention which defines a Portuguese word as masculine or feminine – *o* **senhor**, the gentleman, (masculine), *a* **senhora**, the lady, (feminine); but also *o* **carro**, the car, (masculine), *a* **cadeira**, the chair (feminine).

IMPERATIVE – is the traditional tense and mood for an order or instruction but, in modern Portuguese, these are generally expressed in the subjunctive mood. ***Entre***. *Come* in. See also MOOD and COMMAND.

INDEFINITE ARTICLE – is the the word for 'a / an', which in Portuguese can be masculine (**um**) or feminine (**uma**) – *um* **senhor**, *a* gentleman, *uma* **senhora**, *a* lady, *um* **carro**, *a* car, *uma* **casa**, *a* house.

INDICATIVE – is the mood or frame of mind of the speaker who expresses what is being said as reality, as a matter of fact. **Hoje *é* domingo**. Today *is* Sunday. See also MOOD.

249

INDIRECT OBJECT – see OBJECT.

INFINITIVE – is the basic form of the verb, before the verb is manipulated so as to apply to a particular subject (**eu**, I, **você**, you, etc.) and changed into different tenses for present, past and future. When in the infinitive, a Portuguese verb ends in **-ar** (**comprar**, to buy), **-er** (**vender**, to sell), **-ir** (**partir**, to leave), **-ôr** / **-or** (**pôr**, to put, **impor**, to impose). It is in the infinitive that a verb normally appears in a dictionary.

INFLECT – to change the form of a word in order to indicate differences of number, gender, tense, etc. – *o* **carro novo**, the new car; *os* **carros novos**, the new cars. *Eu gosto* de viajar. *I like* travelling. *Nós gostamos* de viajar. *We like* travelling. See also AGREEMENT and CONJUGATE.

INTENSIFIER – word or phrase used for emphasis. **Isso ajuda *mesmo*.** or *Claro que* **isso ajuda**. That *does* help.

INTERROGATIVE – it is said of a word, word-group, or sentence for asking a question. *Como vai? How are you?*

INTRANSITIVE – see TRANSITIVE.

IRREGULAR VERB – a verb that does not always conform to the predictable models for its conjugation (**-ar**, **-er**, and **-ir**), like **pôr**, to put. Some verbs are irregular in fewer tenses than others.

MAIN CLAUSE – is the clause governing one or more subordinate clauses in a multi-clause sentence. *Vamos para casa antes que chova. Let's go home* before it rains.

MASCULINE – see GENDER.

MOOD – the term refers to the "mood" or frame of mind with which the speaker expresses what is being said, i.e., as a reality, probability, necessity, etc. See INDICATIVE, SUBJUNCTIVE and IMPERATIVE.

NEGATIVE – it is said of a verb or sentence with which we refuse, deny, contradict, or say "no", as opposed to an affirmative verb or sentence. **Eu *não gosto* de bolos**. I *don't like* cakes.

NOMINAL – a word or group of words behaving like a noun. *Caminhar* é **bom para a saúde**. *Walking* is good for your health.

NON-FINITE – a verb form that cannot combine with a subject to make a clause or sentence, as is the case with the infinitive in English, e.g., to read. Unlike English, in Portuguese the infinitive can be used as a personal infinitive, i.e., can be finite. **Esta revista é para _eles lerem_**. This magazine is for _them to read._

NOUN – a word that names a person, animal, place, thing, or idea. – **o senhor**, the _gentleman_, **a senhora**, the _lady_, **o gato**, the _cat_, **a praia**, the _beach_, **o carro**, the _car_, **o pensamento**, the _thought._

NUMBER – the indication of whether a word refers to "just one" (singular) or "more than one" (plural) of what it represents – **os carros novos**, the new car**s**, **eles moram aqui**, _they live_ here.

OBJECT – a direct object is whoever or whatever receives the action of the verb directly; an indirect object is whoever or whatever receives the action of the verb indirectly. **Ele não comprou _flores_** (direct object), He has not bought _flowers_. **Ele não me** (indirect object) **comprou _flores_** (direct object), He has not bought _me flowers._

PERFECT TENSE – except for the present perfect, Portuguese perfect and pluperfect tenses express action that was completed, or will be completed, before some point in time. **Às nove horas eles já _terão chegado_.** By nine o'clock they _will have arrived._

PERSON, FIRST – the individual who speaks or writes (singular) or the individuals who speak or write (plural). **Eu falo Português.** _I speak_ Portuguese. **Nós falamos Português.** _We speak_ Portuguese.

PERSON, SECOND – the individual (singular) or individuals (plural) spoken or written to. **Você gosta de café?** Do _you like_ coffee? (talking to one person) **Vocês gostam de café?** Do _you like_ coffee? (talking to more than one person).

PERSON, THIRD – people, animals, places, things, ideas (singular and plural) that may be spoken or written about. **Ela comprou um ramo de flores**. _She has bought_ a bunch of flowers. **As flores são lindas**. _The flowers are_ beautiful.

PERSONAL PRONOUN – a pronoun that varies in form depending on its grammatical person – **eu**, I (first person singular), **eles**, they (third person plural) – and its role in the sentence where it can be subject – **Eu telefonei**

ontem. *I* phoned yesterday. – or object – **Ele não *me* viu**. He didn't see *me*.
– or reflexive – **O gato não *se* lambeu**. The cat did not lick *itself*.

PHRASE – is a group of words which is part of a clause or sentence but does
not make sense on its own – ***por mim***, *by me*.

PLURAL – see NUMBER.

PREPOSITION – a word, or group of words, which links words or phrases
together in order to indicate a relationship for example of time, space, possession,
or personal attitude – ***por* eles**, *by* them, ***até* amanhã**, *until* / *by* tomorrow.

PROGRESSIVE TENSE – see CONTINUOUS TENSE.

PRONOUN – a word which takes the place of a noun, such as personal
pronoun **ele**, he (instead of e.g., **João**, John), or relative pronoun **que**
referring back to someone or something in the previous clause – **Estas são
as flores *que* ele comprou**. These are the flowers *that* he has bought.

RADICAL CHANGE – change that affects the root of the verb. **-Você prefere
chá ou café? - Prefiro café.** – Do you prefer tea or coffee? –I prefer coffee.

REFLEXIVE – where subject and object are the same. **O gato não *se*
lambeu**. The cat did not *lick itself*. The verb is used reflexively (lick itself)
with the assistance of a reflexive personal pronoun (itself).

REGULAR VERB – a verb that conforms to the predictable models for its
conjugation (**-ar, -er**, or **-ir**). See CONJUGATION.

RELATIVE CLAUSE – a type of subordinate clause which takes the place of
an adjective and therefore qualifies a noun or a nominal phrase or clause.
Aquele é o aluno *que fala Português*. That one is the student *who speaks
Portuguese* (the portuguese-speaking student).

RELATIVE PRONOUN – a pronoun that both stands for a noun, nominal
phrase or clause (the antecedent) and joins two clauses together. **Aquele é o
aluno *que* fala Português**. That one is the student *who* speaks Portuguese.
Estas são as flores *que* você comprou. These are the flowers *that* you have
bought.[2]

ROOT – the indivisible core of a word. You are left with the root of the
verb when you remove the infinitive final **-ar, -er**, or **-ir**.

SENTENCE – is a group of words complete in itself. It may consist of one or more clauses. *Vamos para casa*. *Let's go home.* (one clause) *Vamos para casa antes que chova*. *Let's go home before it rains.* (two clauses). See also MAIN CLAUSE and SUBORDINATE CLAUSE.

SIMPLE TENSE – a tense consisting of one single word, with changed endings, as opposed to a compound tense, i.e., consisting of more than one word. **Isso** *aconteceu* **ontem.** That *happened* yesterday.

SINGULAR – see NUMBER.

SPEECH – what someone else has said can be quoted directly in the person's exact words, i.e., as direct speech, or reported without using the person's exact words, i.e., as indirect, or reported, speech. **Ela disse:** *"Vou lá amanhã."* She said: *"I am going there tomorrow."* (direct speech) **Ela disse** *que ia lá amanhã*. She said *that she was going there tomorrow.* (indirect speech).

SPELLING CHANGE – some spelling changes are needed in a number of Portuguese verbs to reflect consistency in pronunciation – **Eu conheço essa praia**. I know that beach. **Ele conhece essa praia**. He knows that beach. (verb **conhecer**, to know). Other spelling changes are the result of radical changes – **Prefiro café**. I prefer coffee (verb **preferir**, to prefer).

SUBJECT – the subject is the doer of the action or the bearer of the state of being expressed by the verb – *Eu* **vendi o carro.** *I* have sold the car. *Ele* **está doente.** *He* is ill.

SUBJUNCTIVE – is the mood or frame of mind of the speaker who expresses what is being said as wish, hope, regret, concession, doubt, possibility, supposition, hypothesis, or a condition contrary to fact, rather than a matter of fact. **Espero que** *você venha* **à festa**. I hope *you'll come* to the party. See also MOOD.

SUBORDINATE CLAUSE – is a clause which cannot stand on its own because it does not express a complete meaning. It must be part of a larger unit in which it is dependent on a main clause and adds meaning to it. **Vamos para casa** *antes que chova*. Let's go home *before it rains.*

TENSE – the different sets of verb changes to express the time at which the action or state is viewed as occurring (present, past, or future). A tense also incorporates mood (see MOOD). **Eles *moram* no centro da cidade**. They *live* in the town centre. **Eu *farei* tudo o que *puder***. I *will do* all I *can*.

TRANSITIVE – a verb which takes a direct object because its meaning implies that the action influences someone or something – **Eu *comprei flores***, I have *bought flowers* – in contrast with intransitive verb, i.e., a verb with no direct object, as often is the case with verbs of motion – **Eles *dançaram* toda a noite**. They *danced* all night long.

VERB – a word conveying action, like **caminhar**, to walk, or a state of being, like **ser**, to be.

VOICE – is the relationship between the verb and the subject. It is said to be "active" when the subject does the action, and "passive" when the subject has the action done to it. **A raposa *perseguiu* a galinha**. The fox *chased* the hen. (active voice). **A galinha *foi perseguida* pela raposa**. The hen *was chased* by the fox. (passive voice).

VOWEL – a speech sound such as that represented by the letters **a, e, i, o, u**, in which the vibration of the vocal cords is the main characteristic. It is more open than a consonant. See also CONSONANT.

Note

[1] The word **quando** (when) can play different roles such as that of a conjunction and that of an adverb.

[2] The word **que** (what / which / who / that) can play different roles such as that of a pronoun and that of a conjunction.

Cross-reference Index

This index gives you a quick access to different points about the Portuguese verbs as explained throughout the book. You have a choice of grammatical entries, function entries and word-clue entries.

If you are unsure of the grammatical term you need, you can look up a verb form according to what you want to say. These usage-led entries – e.g., **past (talking about)** and **like (I would/should)** – are in bold type for easier identification.

261

... demais
    demais da conta.